Pagan Saints in Middle-earth

Claudio Antonio Testi

Pagan Saints in Middle-earth

2018

Cormarë Series No. 38

Series Editors: Peter Buchs • Thomas Honegger • Andrew Moglestue • Johanna Schön

Series Editor responsible for this volume: Thomas Honegger

Library of Congress Cataloging-in-Publication Data

Claudio Antonio Testi:
Pagan Saints in Middle-earth
ISBN 978-3-905703-38-2

Subject headings:
Tolkien, J.R.R. (John Ronald Reuel), 1892-1973
theology
philosophy
The Lord of the Rings
The Hobbit
The Silmarillion

Cormarë Series No. 38

First published 2018

© Walking Tree Publishers, Zurich and Jena, 2018

All rights reserved. No portion of this book may be reproduced, by any process or technique, without the express written consent of the publisher.

Translation: Chiara and Giampaolo Canzonieri

Italian original *Santi pagani nella Terra di Mezzo di Tolkien* published 2014 by Edizioni Studio Domenicano, Bologna.

Cover illustration 'Rohan' by Ivan Cavini

Set in Adobe Garamond Pro and Shannon by Walking Tree Publishers
Printed by Lightning Source in the United Kingdom and United States

Board of Advisors

Academic Advisors

Douglas A. Anderson (independent scholar)

Patrick Curry (independent scholar)

Michael D.C. Drout (Wheaton College)

Vincent Ferré (Université de Paris-Est Créteil UPEC)

Dimitra Fimi (Cardiff Metropolitan University)

Verlyn Flieger (University of Maryland)

Thomas Fornet-Ponse (Rheinische Friedrich-Wilhelms-Universität Bonn)

Christopher Garbowski (University of Lublin, Poland)

Andrew James Johnston (Freie Universität Berlin)

Rainer Nagel (Johannes Gutenberg-Universität Mainz)

Helmut W. Pesch (independent scholar)

Tom A. Shippey (University of Winchester)

Allan G. Turner (Friedrich-Schiller-Universität Jena)

Frank Weinreich (independent scholar)

General Readers

Johan Boots

Jean Chausse

Friedhelm Schneidewind

Isaac Juan Tomas

Patrick Van den hole

Johan Vanhecke (Letterenhuis, Antwerp)

To Giovanna, Tommaso, and Matilde
who are more precious to me
than the three Silmarils

Series Editors' Preface

This translation of the original volume *Santi pagani nella Terra di Mezzo* (2014) by Claudio A. Testi is part of Walking Tree Publishers' endeavour to make available original research in languages other than English to a wider audience for whom English functions as the scholarly *lingua franca*. The text does not want to deny its origin as an Italian (as well as theological and Catholic) piece of scholarship – it is part of the 'cultural experience' we want our readers to share – yet we hope to have made it as accessible as possible and wish our readers much joy whilst exploring the theological dimension of Tolkien's work in the footsteps of Thomas Aquinas.

Lastly, I would like to thank all those who contributed to the realisation of this publication: Chiara and Giampaolo Canzonieri (translation), Maryna Tymoshchuk (layouting and proofreading), Larissa Zoller (layouting and proofreading), Sophia Mehlhausen (proofreading), and Alexander Lariviere (language proofreading).

Jena, March 2018
Thomas Honegger

Table of Contents

Acknowledgements   i
Foreword by Verlyn Flieger   iii
Foreword to the English Edition   vii
Foreword to the Italian Edition   ix

Introduction   3

Part I: Analysis of the Different Perspectives

1 Tolkien's Work is Christian   13
    1.1 It Contradicts "Tolkien's Razor"   14
    1.2 It Confuses Allegory and Application with Exemplification and Interpretation   15
    1.3 It Confuses a Source with a Representation   21
    1.4 It Derives a Total Correspondence from a Partial Similarity by Ignoring the Differences   24
    1.5 It Diminishes the Vastness of the Tolkienian Perspective   25

2 Tolkien's Work is Pagan   27
    2.1 It Diminshes the Importance of those Texts where the Connection between the *Legendarium* and Christianity is More Evident   27
    2.2 It Erroneously Considers Some Elements of the *Legendarium* to Be in Opposition to Christianity   30
    2.3 It Confuses Historical Paganism with "Tolkienian" Paganism   36
    2.4 It Applies a Symbolic Reading to Tolkien's Work to the Detriment of its Comprehension   38
    2.5 It Diminishes the Scope of Tolkien's Perspective   41

3 Tolkien's Work is Pagan and Christian   43
    3.1 Points of View and Contradictions   43
    3.2 Dialectics and the *Legendarium*   57

Part II: The Synthetic Approach

4	Synthesis: Tolkien's Work is Pagan and in Harmony with Christianity	67
	4.1 Principles	67
	4.2 Definition and Use of the Term "Pagan"	68
	4.3 Enunciation of the Proposed Synthesis	71
5	Paganism in Tolkien's World and Its Harmony with Christianity	75
	5.1 Poetic and Hermeneutic Principles	75
	5.2 Paganism in Harmony with Christianity in Tolkien's Universe	98
6	Catholicism and the Works of Tolkien	127
	6.1 Clarification of the Term "Catholic"	127
	6.2 Why Tolkien's Work is "Fundamentally Catholic"	133

Conclusion	139
Afterword by Tom Shippey: On Coincidence, and Harmony	141
List of Abbreviations and References	147
Bibliography	155
Analytical Index	181
General Index and Index of Names	185

Acknowledgements

This is perhaps the most difficult part to write since there are so many people I would like to thank for their contributions towards this book; by no means consider the order in which I mention you as a measure of merit, because it is not.

Starting from far away, my deepest thanks to Verlyn Flieger and Tom Shippey, extraordinary people and scholars of unique insight, who have continuously answered my (too many) questions, urging me so many times to take my research in Tolkien's work more and more seriously.

Even more numerous were my discussions and debates with Italian "Tolkienians", who have endlessly enriched my knowledge. Roberto Arduini (president of AIST, *Associazione Italiana Studi Tolkieniani*) and Federico Guglielmi (who writes under the pseudonym of Wu Ming 4) are no doubt the ones with whom I had the most intense and enriching conversations about the matters dealt with in this book (amongst many others), but my thanks go also to the members of the Tolkien Study Group promoted by AIST, with whom I still meet to discuss the inexhaustible *Legendarium*. Among those are Alberto Ladavas (who helped me in proof-reading the original drafts), Giampaolo Canzonieri (unequalled resource as far as translation is concerned and "Tolkienian supervisor" of the English version of this book translated by his sister Chiara), Franco Manni (who like no one else knows how to combine rare scholarship and an endless will to help), Lorenzo Gammarelli (among the first I seriously collaborated with), Norbert Spina (inexhaustible source of Tolkienian details), Andrea Monda (who needs no presentation), Cecilia Barella (always greatly appreciated for her competence), and many others I cannot list here.

My thanks go also to all who have enriched with their questions the conferences, seminars and lectures I gave or organized, *in primis* the most "faithful" who attended the Tolkien-Lab in Modena, but also those who have written to me asking questions about this or that aspect of Middle-earth, without knowing that, by doing so, they helped me in understanding it better and better myself.

And how not to mention my friends at the *Istituto Filosofico di Studi Tomistici*, who have patiently supported (and suffered!) this interest of mine for Tolkien: Mario Enrico Cerrigone (with whom I had the most precious philosophical dialogues also on Tolkienian themes), Carlo Marchi (who was always there in time of need), Emmanuele Morandi (our late lamented president), Marco Prati and, last but not least, Adalberto Arrigoni.

Thanks also to Lubomir Zak, Sergio Parenti O.P., Alberto Strumia and Luciano Benassi, who always gave helpful and precious advice concerning the most complicated theological and religious questions, to Giorgio Carbone O.P. and the *Edizioni Studio Dominicano* for accepting this book for publication in Italy, and to Thomas Honegger, editor of the *Cormarë Series* by Walking Tree Publishers, for accepting its translation into English.

As last, even at the cost of looking pathetic or *démodé*, I'd like to thank J.R.R. Tolkien and Thomas Aquinas for letting me discover the beauty of intellectual research, a wondrous gift that only a few men have the priceless fortune to receive and experience in their life.

Foreword by Verlyn Flieger

Claudio Testi's *Pagan Saints* is an important work, and its appearance in this English translation is timely in its publication and valuable in its contribution to Tolkien scholarship. Over a span of years I have watched the progress of Claudio's argument as it developed from an idea to a thesis to a conference paper to a scholarly article and now, deservedly, to a book whose value to the current state of Tolkien studies cannot be overstated. The entire sequence has been an education in the life of the mind and the proper practice of scholarship.

What *Pagan Saints* intends to accomplish, which it succeeds admirably in doing, is nothing less than reconciling what have for many years existed in the world of Tolkien scholarship as opposing religio-philosophical readings of his fiction, readings that have developed into contending camps of Tolkien scholarship. Almost since its first publication scholars have argued, on the one hand, that *The Lord of the Rings* (and later its parent mythology the Silmarillion) was intentionally and explicitly Christian in content and message, and, on the other hand, that there are clear elements of, and obvious parallels to pre-Christian European mythologies that would seem to be in conflict with the perceived Christianity. The temptation has been to confuse what we know about Tolkien with what we see in his work. He was an emphatic Christian and a devout Catholic who wrote a fictive mythology that was intentionally pre-Christian. So was Tolkien pagan or Christian? And how were we supposed to know?

For too long these camps have faced one another across what appeared to be a fence labelled "either-or". In the present work Claudio Testi, whose earlier iteration of the ideas expressed herein was explicitly titled "Tolkien's Work: Is it Christian or Pagan," answers his own question, arguing persuasively that the "either-or" fence is not just unnecessary, it is non-existent, as is the face-off that makes Tolkien's work the object of contention rather than mutually beneficial understanding. He does this by substituting for the polarizing "either-or" position – if it's this it cannot be that – the more egalitarian and inclusive "both-and" approach in which the apparently conflicting readings can be seen not as contradictory but as complimentary, not mutually exclusive but mutually supportive.

The effect of this is two-fold. First, it renders contention unnecessary and indeed unproductive. Second, it disarms the combatants and invites them to the table, there to join one another in a conversation directed toward exploring and appreciating the harmonic counterpoint of Tolkien's work. In addition, it opens the door to the broader view that the sacred can exist in more than one context, and that Tolkien's so-called "mythology for England" was meant to support but not to replicate the Christianity it was intended to precede.

Circumstantial evidence for this can be found in Tolkien's essay on "*Beowulf*: the Monsters and the Critics" where in two separate references Tolkien lamented the fact that so little was known about pre-Christian English mythology. Discussing what he called the "creed of unyielding will" that informed the concept of northern courage, he had to acknowledge that of "English pre-Christian mythology we know practically nothing" (*MC* 21). A few pages later, now launching his defense of the monsters as essential to *Beowulf*, he returned to the subject, expressing "regret that we do not know more about pre-Christian mythology" (*MC* 24). While in neither statement did Tolkien make reference to his own mythology, it is difficult to imagine that he did not have it in mind as he wrote, since at that time, 1936, it was well on its way to completion if not yet polish. Moreover, both statements in the essay, coupled with his avowed intention of dedicating his mythology "to England," do make it clear that he was aware of a gap that his legendarium could fill, that would, albeit as fiction, take the place of that "pre-Christian mythology."

It was for this reason that Tolkien's letter to Milton Waldman, in which he described his ambition to write a mythology he could dedicate "to England", made a careful point to disqualify "the Arthurian world" as England's mythology on the grounds that it was involved in and explicitly contained "the Christian religion" (*Letters* 144). "Myth and fairy-story," he wrote, "must, as all art, reflect and contain in solution elements of moral and religious truth […] but not explicit, not in the known form of the primary 'real' world" (*Letters* 144). Typology to the contrary, you cannot simultaneously be pre-Christian and Christian. You can foreshadow Christianity, but if you present it as explicit in something that was meant to come before it, you have defeated your own purpose.

There is as well more concrete evidence than stories, evidence which, in the context of his stated purpose to create a lost English mythology, can not only suggest but can actually provide a real-world parallel to Testi's "both-and" approach. Here I will call upon history and archaeology to support literary criticism. Hard evidence exists in Europe and the British Isles for continuous worship in sites now identified as Christian but once pagan, sites ranging from France's Chartres and Notre Dame to Italy's Santa Maria del Fiore (otherwise known as the Duomo) to England's Westminster Abbey and to a host of less famous, small (often very small) local village churches across England and Europe. Found buried beneath the standing structures of these sites are the ruins of pagan fanes, the Christian churches apparently erected on top of them in the service of continuity. While this is not quite "both-and", neither is it the arbitrary "this or that" of the academic debate, closer perhaps to something like, "first this and then that". The gods may "go or come", as Tolkien observes in his essay (*MC* 22), but the impulse to worship remains and builds on itself.

It is in the spirit of this continuity that Mr. Testi sets out to propose (and I think achieves) a synthesis of two prominent and influential schools of Tolkien criticism. With ill will toward none and acceptance of all, he has brought his readers the best of both schools. He has shown how they work, and best of all, shown how they can work together.

Foreword to the English Edition

Tolkien's world is not Christian but Pagan; therefore his work is fundamentally Catholic.

This is the thesis I maintain in this book, which, in spite of its apparent paradoxical nature, I hope English-speaking readers will also in the end find sound and consistent with all of Tolkien's texts, both narrative and philological.

I won't describe here the origins of the book, about which interested readers may refer to the 'Foreword of the Italian Edition'; however, I want to specify that, although the subject matter is classic as far as Tolkien studies are concerned, the book had originally been written with a special eye on Italy, thus including passages, quotes and explanations that may sound redundant to more expert scholars but are nonetheless still needed for an Italian audience. Save for a few minor changes especially in the bibliography, I decided not to alter the structure of the book, not only because its thesis transcends the Italian scene but also because it will let English-speaking readers grasp something of the debate going on in Italy.

Foreword to the Italian Edition

This book takes its origins from a very simple question: Is Tolkien's work pagan or Christian?

I first posed this question to myself in earnest when, in 2011, I chose this theme as the subject matter for a paper I gave at the international conference *The Return of the Ring* at the University of Loughborough (England), organized by the Tolkien Society. The following summer, in the presence of some of the foremost Tolkien experts (Tom Shippey, Verlyn Flieger, Thomas Honegger, Peter Gilliver, Nils Agøy and many others), I opened my presentation with the prophetic words that a whole book would have been necessary in order to adequately develop the subject. And here it is!

Since then I have in fact unrelentingly kept elaborating the question: I've read most of the extremely vast bibliography on the theme, I've analysed the unpublished manuscripts at the Bodleian Library in Oxford and, most of all, I discussed the matter with numerous Tolkien scholars from both Italy and other countries.

A first result of this activity was the article 'Tolkien's Work: Is it Pagan or Christian: a Synthetic Approach' published as the opening feature in the 2012 issue of the prestigious *Tolkien Studies*. This article was followed by another paper more focused on the critical debate that was taking place in Italy ('Quale Teologia per la Terra di Mezzo di J.R.R. Tolkien') and was published in *Lateranum*; and at last, here is the book I had "prophetically" announced years ago.

As far as I am concerned, I consider this book "complete", inasmuch as I include here, widened and developed in the tiniest details, all possible themes I deem "essential" in order to fully identify the aspects of this complex subject.

While writing this book I often asked myself whether it was really necessary to publish yet another study on the subject. My answer was always "yes", because – and I say it in all modesty – I think that the thesis I have here developed presents some genuinely new aspects and has some originality of its own in the noblest sense of the word; I really strove to trace the question back to its very origin and I hope I succeeded to some extent in this endeavour.

It was certainly hard work and I fear it's going to be the same for the reader of this book, even if I tried to simplify the task by giving a very schematic structure to my work and as many bibliographic references as possible, and by adding an 'Analytical Index' and a more comprehensive combined 'General Index and Index of Names'.

Introduction

Introduction

For a Fair Critical Review of a Classic

Tolkien and His Critics

Tolkien is truly like an iceberg whose visible tip does not allow you to immediately apprehend the greatness underneath.[1] I realised this when I started to study Tolkien "professionally" and little by little discovered the philological, linguistic and philosophical structure at the foundations of his imposing edifice, a fact which I'll try to adequately expound – even if only in part – in this book. Tolkien's work is in fact of that kind which "has never finished to say what it has to say", which corresponds to one of the most famous definitions of a "classic" as given to us by Italo Calvino.[2]

Since it was first published, however, *The Lord of the Rings* has always been the target of fierce criticism and mistaken predictions of impending oblivion, the most conspicuous example of which being the review by Edmund Wilson of *The Fellowship of the Ring* where he defines the work as "juvenile trash".[3] The majority of "professional" critics have to this day failed to give Tolkien the adequate recognition he deserves among the masters of literature, which paradoxically may be a consequence of his continued success with readers. Moreover, the fact that he is appreciated by readers of all ages and nationalities may have led dismissive, uninformed critics to perceive his success as a cultural phenomenon bound to be ephemeral.

Despite this ostracism, Tolkien criticism has reached over the decades an increasingly higher level of competence and fairness; in this respect credit should be given to Tom Shippey's *The Road to Middle-earth*, published in 1982 and

---

1 This image was first coined by Clyde Kilby who was closely acquainted with Tolkien in the last years of his life and who also collaborated with him (Kilby 1977, 6); Divo Barsotti (with a fine and brilliant intuition, despite not being a "professional" Tolkien critic) gives us the same image when referring to *The Lord of the Rings* (Barsotti 1991, 221).
2 Calvino 1995, definition n. 6.
3 Wilson 1978, 55.

now, in its third, updated edition,[4] still considered the benchmark for whoever undertakes the study of Tolkien.

One year later Verlyn Flieger published *Splintered Light*,[5] and, apart from Shippey and Flieger, other scholars who must be mentioned for their competence and insight are John S. Ryan,[6] Paul Kocher,[7] Richard West,[8] John Garth,[9] Michael D.C. Drout,[10] Brian Rosebury,[11] Carl F. Hostetter,[12] and Janet Brennan Croft,[13] and such promising new critics as Dimitra Fimi,[14] Thomas Honegger,[15] Gergely Nagy,[16] and Renée Vink.[17] This interesting movement of critical studies has brought about the publication of several specialized magazines (*Mythlore, Mallorn, Hither Shore* and *Tolkien Studies*) and book series (above all Walking Tree Publishers' *Cormarë Series*), all of which are indispensable to a serious approach to the study of our author.[18]

Needless to say, the study of all of Tolkien's works is also essential, and this should include the twelve volumes of *The History of Middle-earth*,[19] the two

---

4 Shippey 2005; see the bibliography for other works by the same author.
5 Flieger 2002; also crucial is the study *A Question of Time* (Flieger 1997), where the author analyzes the value of time and dreams in the *Legendarium*. Her most relevant essays have recently been published in the collection *Green Suns and Faërie: Essays on J.R.R. Tolkien* (Flieger 2012).
6 See Ryan 2013.
7 Kocher 1977.
8 West 1967; West 2005. *Tolkien Studies* 2 contains a complete bibliography of West's works (Anderson 2005).
9 Garth 2003.
10 Drout 2004; Drout 2007.
11 Rosebury 2003; Rosebury 2008. The issue contains a complete bibliography of his works compiled by Anderson (Anderson 2008).
12 He is one of the foremost experts of Tolkienian languages and is the editor of the magazine *Vinyar Tengwar*, where you can often read essays by Tolkien himself (for a translation into Italian of some of these texts, see *LTP*). Together with Verlyn Flieger, he also edited the fundamental volume: Flieger and Hostetter 2000.
13 Croft 2004; Croft and Donovan 2015.
14 Fimi 2008.
15 Honegger 2005b; Honegger 2010, see the bibliography for other texts by the same author.
16 Nagy 2002; Nagy 2005.
17 Vink 2012; Vink 2015.
18 A theme that to this day has not yet been adequately studied by Tolkienian critics is the literary aspect and style of his works: "But the fact remains that a fully developed account of Tolkien's styles, and of their relation to styles in other 20th-century literature and to the styles of medieval and ancient literature, would greatly improve Tolkien studies" (Drout and Wynne 2000, 123). The best studies (trailblazing as they are) that have been published up to now on this subjects are: Walker 2009; Simonson 2008; Clark and Timmons 2000. Among the most interesting articles we suggest: Drout 2004b; Sullivan 2000; Bratman 2000; Christopher 2000; Jeffrey 2007; Rosebury 2003; Morini 1999.
19 Fundamental studies on the various stages of development of Tolkien's *Legendarium* are also: Kane 2009; Whittingham 2007; Flieger and Hostetter 2000; Turner 2007; issue n. 3 of *Hither Shore* (2006); and the pioneering Kilby 1977 (written even before the publication of *The Silmarillion*).

volumes of *The History of the Hobbit*, the collection of essays *The Monsters and the Critics* and *Tolkien On Fairy-stories* the critical edition of his essay 'On Fairy-stories'.

In my opinion, the knowledge of the texts I've just mentioned is the absolute minimum required in order to undertake a serious study of Tolkien. It is for this reason that I gladly quote Drout and Wynne's wishes and advice, which I myself try to conform to in this book:

> Good criticism will take note of what previous critics have said. Effective Tolkien criticism cannot be done using only the Ballantine paperback edition of *The Lord of the Rings*; critics must read what other critics have written (and they particularly must read both of Shippey's books). The body of Tolkien scholarship has received much unfair disparagement – there is, as we have tried to show, much excellent work in this corpus. No critic would think to publish an article on James Joyce without reading what other scholars have said. Tolkien deserves the same respect, particularly from those who would study him. (Drout and Wynne 2000, 125)[20]

And in Italy?

In Italy, although it was one of the first countries where *The Lord of the Rings* was translated, these developments – with a few commendable exceptions – have been for a long time completely ignored. At first, together with the introductory text by Emilia Lodigiani,[21] we should mention the laudable endeavour of Franco Manni, who since the early '90s with his magazine *Endorë* and his writings has given the opportunity to those interested to expand their horizons beyond their immediate scope. Among the most serious "exceptions" we must mention the critical study by Andrea Monda and Saverio Simonelli *Tolkien Il Signore della Fantasia*.[22]

Despite these commendable examples, the chance for a serious approach to the study of Tolkien's work has been extensively undermined by the particularly

---

20 On the same theme read also Drout 2005 and Honegger 2015. For an overall overview on the history of Tolkienian criticism see also Hammond and Scull 2006b, 191-98.
21 Lodigiani 1982.
22 Monda and Simonelli 2002. Vito Fascina too, although more recently, has followed the latest developments of foreign criticism (Fascina 2007).

narrow-minded debate over Tolkien's political views.[23] It will suffice for the reader to browse through the most popular Italian publications, consult the bibliographies or check how many international conferences the authors of these publications have attended in order to realize the limited scope of even the most respected Italian critics (see 2.4).

It is only in recent times, in the aftermath of Peter Jackson's film trilogy, that something has finally changed, also as a result of the publication of some fundamental texts on Tolkien (Italian translations of the two foremost works by Shippey and Flieger were published as late as in 2005 and 2007[24]) and of an increased awareness of what had been published abroad.

The Debate on Paganism and Christianity in Tolkien

Numerous debates have arisen within foreign Tolkien criticism,[25] including those on the mistaken allegorical interpretation of Tolkien's works,[26] a specific indication of Tolkien's sources,[27] the meaning of the *Legendarium*[28] conceived as a mythology for England[29] and the pagan or Christian content of his work.[30]

This central theme has been among the first to be discussed, if we just consider that already in 1954 Peter Hastings, who was manager of a Catholic bookshop,

---

23 See on this subject: De Turris 1992; del Corso and Pecere 2003; Mingardi and Stagnaro 2004; Wu Ming 4 2013, 103-30; Cilli 2016.
24 That is *The Road to Middle-earth* and *Splintered Light*, respectively, translated and published in the book series *Tolkien e Dintorni* ('Tolkien and his Surroundings') which I direct with other members of the *Associazione Italiana studi Tolkieniani* (Italian Association of Tolkien Studies). In the same series were also translated Garth 2003, Rosebury 2003, Pearce 1999, Green 1995, and other important books on and also by Tolkien.
25 Recommended bibliographies are: West 1981; Johnson 1986; see Drout and Wynne 2000.
26 Since the very beginning Tolkien himself has pointed out that those who attempted an allegorical reading of his works are mistaken (see 1.2). More recently a masterful debate on the allegoric value of *Smith of Wootton Major* has taken place with Tom Shippey and Verlyn Flieger as the leading scholars. The contents of the debate are reported in Flieger 2012d.
27 On this subject see Fisher 2011; Shippey 2000. An excellent text on the Welsh influence in Tolkien's works is Phelpstead 2011; on the influence of Celtic mythology see also Jones 2002; Flieger 2005; Burns 2005.
28 This was the definition Tolkien gave to the whole *corpus* of legends about his mythology, from the cosmogony of the Music of the Ainur to the Fourth Age that concludes *The Lord of the Rings*.
29 One of the first texts on this theme is Chance 2001 (first edition 1979). Chance's pioneering thesis has been the object of further critical debate resulting in a drastic reassessment of the idea that the *Legendarium* had been conceived of by Tolkien as a mythology for England; see for example: Flieger 2012f; Flieger 2012c; Hostetter and Smith 1996; Drout 2004; Honegger 2006; Birzer 2011; Stenström 1996; Fimi 2008, 50 ff.
30 See the list of abbreviations of Tolkien's works.

wrote to Tolkien expressing his outrage for having "over-stepped the mark in metaphysical matters"[31] on the problem of evil and elven reincarnation.[32] The debate went on up to the present day and to those who wish to have an exhaustive overview of the history of this *querelle* I suggest Kerry's foreword to *The Ring and the Cross* (where more than 200 contributions are quoted) and the article by Thomas Fornet-Ponse "'*The Lord of the Rings* is of course a Fundamentally Religious and Catholic Work': Tolkien zwischen christlicher Instrumentalisierung und theologischer Rezeption".[33] In Italy we also had some interesting controversies on similar questions,[34] the most recent being a debate between Andrea Monda and Wu Ming 4,[35] whom I consider to be among the foremost experts of Tolkienian studies in Italy.

The Roots of the Debate: "Tolkien's Problem"

What can the reason be that so much has been written (and so much more will be written) about the religious aspect of the Tolkienian universe? I think that the cause is found in the existence of a sort of "Tolkien's problem", comparable to the "Smith's problem" which for centuries has defied economists trying to figure out why in some of his works Adam Smith maintains two apparently contradictory statements (the invisible "amoral" hand vs. the necessity for the virtue of prudence in economic decisions).[36] In fact, we find in Tolkien some passages, which I will analyse later in detail (see 1.1), where he asserts that explicit references to religion are fatal to the very existence of myth. In doing so he becomes an advocate for what we could call "Tolkien's razor", if we consider that he tends to systematically eliminate all reference to faiths or religious cults:

> For one thing its [the Arthurian world's] 'faerie' is too lavish, and fantastical, incoherent and repetitive. For another and more important thing: it is involved in, and explicitly contains the Christian religion. (*Letters* n. 131)

---

31 *Letters* n. 153.
32 See *Letters* n. 153.
33 Fornet-Ponse 2004.
34 Passaro and Respinti 2004; see Barbiano 2003.
35 Monda and Wu Ming 4 2014.
36 See as an example Sen 1990.

On the other side he affirms, antithetical as it may seem, that the religious question is very important for the comprehension of his writings (see 2.1):

> *The Lord of the Rings* is of course a fundamentally religious and Catholic work. (*Letters* n. 142)

It is not by chance that Verlyn Flieger has recently pointed out that the presence of more or less intentional references to Christianity is one of the three major ambiguities in J.R.R. Tolkien's work.[37] In my opinion, we will be able to appreciate in full the greatness of the Oxonian Professor only if we keep these two opposites in mind, and only if we find a synthetic approach which will not limit itself by eliminating any reference to paganism (as the supporters of the Christian Tolkien wish for) or its opposite (to the advantage of the pagan Tolkien), or which will simply accept the contemporary presence of contradictory perspectives (Christian *and* pagan).

The Book: Object, Method and Structure

First of all we have to point out that the object of this research is not Tolkien as an individual: that he was a devout and authentic Catholic will not require any further analysis since his biography unequivocally testifies his faith.[38]

What really interests us are exclusively his works, both critical and narrative (although limited to the *Legendarium*[39]) and I'll try my best in order to analyse the texts and their structure with the utmost possible care.

As for the content of this volume, in the first part I'll focus my attention on the above mentioned three thesis (Christian [1], pagan [2], Christian *and* pagan [3]). I'll mention the foremost Italian and international scholars for each of the

---

37 Flieger 2014b.
38 He openly declares himself a professing "Roman Catholic" (*Letters* n. 195 and 213), particularly devout to Mary (*Letters* n. 142); he considered his mother a martyr of faith (*Letters* n. 142 and n. 267), recommended daily Communion (*Letters* n. 250) and believed in Guardian Angels (*Letters* n. 54 and n. 89). He considered that the freedom in sexual mores of the time was the sign of a widespread concupiscence, he saw marriage as a constraint on sexual instincts (*Letters* n. 43), he was against divorce (*Letters* n. 49), he went on pilgrimage to various cult sites such as Lourdes (*Letters* n. 89), and he loved to attend Latin Mass to the extent that he continued to pray in Latin even after the Vatican II Council reform (S. Tolkien 2010, 42-45). On Tolkien and Catholicism see also Edwards 2014, 291-299.
39 I will not examine the so called "minor" stories of his literary production.

three theories and, although I will point out what are, in my opinion, their main limits and mistakes, I will do it with the utmost respect and without any polemic intent.

In the second part I will develop my "synthetic" approach, which differentiates itself from the other interpretations inasmuch as it does not consider the terms "pagan" and "Christian" as mutually exclusive. In the first place [4] I will enunciate the principles of this approach based on the two-fold distinction between perspectives (internal and external) and levels (natural and supernatural). I will then proceed to demonstrate how these distinctions are to be found in Tolkien's critical and mythological writings [5] in which the underlying structure suggests that the culture of the "lay" Man *naturaliter sumptum* and the Christian revelation can be in great harmony with each other.

It is in this harmonic vision that, in my opinion, we can trace Tolkien's truly Catholic roots [6].

Part One

Analysis of the Different Perspectives

Chapter One

Tolkien's Work is Christian

According to this perspective, the *Legendarium* is seen as a world that intentionally *contains in itself explicit Christian values* (such as the reference to the incarnation of the Son of God, his sacrificial death, the Trinity *et similia* [see 5.1]), so that its stories and characters must therefore be interpreted in light of these values which they are intended to represent and spread. The most "radical" author in supporting this interpretation is certainly Joseph Pearce,[1] who has become the leading figure for many Catholic scholars (Stratford Caldecott,[2] Peter Kreeft,[3] John West Jr.[4]) or scholars from other Christian denominations (Ralph Wood,[5] Nils Agøy[6]), but he has also been the target of sharp criticism (we mention Drout and Wynne,[7] and Rateliff[8] among the most recent and authoritative ones). In Italy we have a group of authors who converge on similar views, from Guido Sommavilla[9] to the already mentioned Andrea Monda.[10]

Such an interpretation is liable of five main limitations which have to be analysed carefully.

---

1 See Pearce 1998.
2 See Caldecott 2003.
3 See Kreeft 2005.
4 See West Jr. 2002.
5 See Wood 2003; Wood 2011.
6 See Agøy 2011; Agøy 1998.
7 "But articles on religion and Tolkien have a tendency to rely upon Christian theology as a received truth, which is no doubt true for many Christians, but exceedingly unlikely to be persuasive to scholars, Christian or non-Christian, who would like to see arguments grounded in rigorous logic" Drout and Wynne 2000, 109.
8 See Rateliff 2016.
9 Sommavilla 1983.
10 Monda 2008, publication of the thesis for his degree in Religious Sciences. Along the same line of interpretation we find also Bertani 2011 and Maiettini 2011. We have obviously many other Italian Tolkienian scholars who are proponents of a "Catholic inspiration", but with a softer approach and therefore less suitable to be proposed as emblematic of an explicit Christian interpretation. Among those I would like to mention only Franco Manni and Marco Respinti.

1.1 It Contradicts "Tolkien's Razor"

As already pointed out in the Introduction, Tolkien judges the most evident flaw of the Arthurian Cycle to be that

> all the Arthurian world, but powerful as it is, it is imperfectly naturalized, associated with the soil of Britain but not with English; and does not replace what I felt to be missing. For one thing its 'faerie' is too lavish, and fantastical, incoherent and repetitive. *For another and more important thing: it is involved in, and explicitly contains the Christian religion.* (*Letters* n. 131, dated 1951, italics added)

This is not a simple "abstract" enunciation but a precept that Tolkien tries scrupulously to follow throughout all his mythopoeia. As an example taken from *The Book of Lost Tales*, we can mention the way he portrays Fui Nienna (the spouse of Vefántur/Mandos) as the judge who assigns Men to different places in Arda, which are very similar to Hell, Purgatory and Heaven;[11] Tolkien abandons this imitation of Christendom after the first draft of *The Silmarillion* ("Sketch of the Mythology") written in 1926,[12] and applies the same "razor" when writing *The Lord of the Rings* as he himself tells us:

> I am in any case myself a Christian; but the 'Third Age' *was not a Christian world*. (*Letters* n. 165, dated 1955, italics added)

> I have deliberately written a tale, which is built on or out of certain 'religious' ideas, but is not an allegory of them (or anything else), and *does not mention them overtly, still less preach them*. (*Letters* n. 211, dated 1958, italics added)

> With regard to *The Lord of the Rings*, I cannot claim to be a sufficient theologian to say whether my notion of orcs is heretical or not. *I don't feel under any obligation to make my story fit with formalized Christian theology*, though I actually intended it to be consonant with Christian thought and belief. (*Letters* n. 269, dated 1965, italics added)

Despite these unequivocal statements, some authors still consider the *Legendarium* a mythology that becomes more and more Christian in its development:

> Among the chief accomplishments in our growing appreciation of Tolkien's *The Lord of the Rings* is the consensus view that it is *indubitably a Christian*

---

11 *BLT I* 91-93.
12 "What happened to their spirits was not known to the Eldalië. They did not go to the halls of Mandos, and many thought their fate was not in the hands of the Valar after death. Though many, associating with Eldar, believed that their spirits went to the western land, this was not true. Men were not born again" (*SME*, 21).

> *epic* [...] If Tolkien had enjoyed several more lives beyond his allotted 81 years, he might have extended his mythological project to include the *Incarnation, crucifixion and resurrection*. (Wood 2011, 117, italics added)
>
> With the *History of Middle earth* now complete, we are able to see the relationship between Christianity and the *Legendarium* more as a process [...] In Tolkien's *Legendarium*, "Athrabeth" is the work where *'overt' Christianity sticks out most clearly*.[13] As the focus shifted more and more from 'stories' to working out in detail the philosophical and metaphysical framework in which they existed, *explicit Christianity in Roman Catholic form simply could not be avoided*. (Agøy 1998, 17 and 26, italics added)[14]
>
> But at the end of our ten surveys on contemporary epic [within which Tolkien's work is included] we may now dare to circumscribe the term and further define it as a *Christological epic*. (Sommavilla 1983, 456, italics added)[15]

Were that so, however, Tolkien would include truths in his sub-creation that pertain to the level of the Christian revelation and this would *fatally* destroy the spell of the fantasy narration [see *supra*].

1.2 It Confuses Allegory and Application with Exemplification and Interpretation

In order to understand this second limitation of the explicitly Christian interpretation, we should mention those texts in which Tolkien rigorously distinguishes between these fundamental concepts: exemplification, symbolism (meant in a two-fold connotation), allegory, interpretation and application.

Exemplification and Symbolism

With the term *exemplification*, Tolkien alludes to the fact that some of his characters or elements of his stories embody some universal themes and "values":

> do not let Rayner suspect 'Allegory'. There is a 'moral', I suppose, in any tale worth telling. But that is not the same thing. Even the struggle between darkness and light (as he calls it, not me) is for me just a particular phase of history, one example of its pattern, perhaps, but not The Pattern; and the actors are *individuals* – they each, of course, *contain universals*, or they

---

13 For a different interpretation of this text see 3.1.3.
14 Cécile Cristofari sees the *Legendarium* as a transition from a pagan perspective to an explicitly Christian vision that will culminate in *The Lord of the Rings* (Cristofari 2011).
15 Alberto Mingardi and Carlo Stagnaro explicitly affirm to consider *The Lord of the Rings* a Christian epic (Mingardi and Stagnaro 2004).

> would not live at all, but they *never represent them as such.* (*Letters* n. 109, dated 1947, italics added)

> [T]hrough Hobbits [...] the last Tale [*LotR*] is to *exemplify* most clearly a recurrent theme: the place in 'world polities' of the unforeseen and unforeseeable acts of will, and deeds of virtue of the apparently small, ungreat, forgotten in the places of the Wise and Great. (*Letters* n. 131, dated 1951, italics added)

> I would claim, if I did not think it presumptuous in one so ill-instructed, to have as one object the elucidation of truth, and the encouragement of good morals in this real world, by the ancient device of *exemplifying them in unfamiliar embodiments.* (*Letters* n. 153, dated 1954, italics added)

> We all, in groups or as individuals, *exemplify* general principles; but we *do not represent* them. The Hobbits are no more an 'allegory' than are (say) the pygmies of the African forest. (*Letters* n. 181, dated 1956, italics added)[16]

Already in these texts (as well as from the radical refusal of allegory[17] [see below]) we can observe how Tolkien's conceptions revolve completely outside the sphere of esoteric "symbolism" [see 2.4] as "hidden meanings"[18] where some elements of the narration should correspond to other elements of the primary world:

> A marked difference here between these legends [*The Silmarillion*] and most others is that the Sun is not a divine symbol, but a second-best thing. (*Letters* n. 131, dated 1951)

> There is *no* 'symbolism' or conscious allegory in my story. Allegory of the sort 'five wizards = five senses' is wholly foreign to my way of thinking. There were five wizards and that is just a unique part of history. To ask if the Orcs 'are' Communists is to me as sensible as asking if Communists are Orcs. (*Letters* n. 203, dated 1957)

> The use of *éarendel* in A-S [Anglo Saxon] Christian symbolism as the herald of the rise of the true Sun in Christ is completely alien to my use. (*Letters* n. 297, dated 1967)

> [T]he 'land of Morīah' [...] has no connexion (even 'externally') whatsoever. Internally there is no conceivable connexion between the mining of Dwarves,

---

16 And "The Elves *represent*, as it were, the artistic, aesthetic, and purely scientific aspects of the Humane nature raised to a higher level than is actually seen in Men" (*Letters* n. 153, italics added).

17 However it should be noted that Tolkien distinguishes symbol from allegory but is not a supporter of either: "A clear distinction between 'allegory' and 'symbolism' may be difficult to maintain, but it is proper, or at least useful, to limit allegory to narrative, to an account, however short, of events; and symbolism to the use of visible signs or things to represent other things or ideas. Pearls were a symbol of purity that especially appealed to the imagination of the Middle Age (and notably of the fourteenth century); but this does not make a person who wears pearls, or even one who is called Pearl, or Margaret, into an allegorical figure" (*SGPO* 17: see note 42).

18 See *Letters* n. 297 below.

and the story of Abraham. *I utterly repudiate any such significances and symbolisms. My mind does not work that way.* (*Letters* n. 297, dated 1967, italics added)

The refusal of "symbol" as "hidden meaning" explains why when Tolkien uses – albeit seldom – the term "symbol"[19] connected to his works, this should be interpreted with reference to the idea of exemplification we have just mentioned above. In other words, it should be clearly understood that an individual element of the story "embodies-symbolizes" at the utmost level a "universal" entity that everybody should be able to perceive without ambiguity nor the help of a "hypothesis" not inherent in the text. Just think of the One Ring:

> The primary symbolism of the Ring, as the will to mere power, seeking to make itself objective by physical force and mechanism, and so also inevitably by lies. (*Letters* n. 131)

In fact, the idea of exemplification (or "symbol" intended by this second meaning) used by Tolkien is very similar to that of the medieval *exempla* which can be seen as "short tales, useful to elucidate a theological principle" or as "incarnation of a quality in a character", be they real (such as Dante's Cato portrayed as *imago virtutis*) or imaginary.[20]

Interpretation and Allegory

If we affirm that Hobbits exemplify the role of the small and forgotten of world politics, or that the Ring symbolizes power, we give a certain *interpretation* to the story, a totally different thing from *allegory* which instead implies the deliberate awareness of the author to integrate strict parallelisms between the characters and other elements of the primary world in the story:

> I remain puzzled, and indeed sometimes *irritated*, by many of the guesses at the 'sources' of the nomenclature, and theories or fancies concerning

---

19 "So I took to 'escapism': or really transforming experience into another form and symbol with Morgoth and Orcs and the Eldalië" (*Letters* n. 73); "By the making of gems the sub-creative function of the Elves is chiefly symbolized" (*Letters* n. 131); "The particular 'desire' of the Eregion Elves – an 'allegory' if you like of a love of machinery, and technical devices – is also symbolised by their special friendship with the Dwarves of Moria" (*Letters* n. 153); "I have purposely kept all allusions to the highest matters down to mere hints, perceptible only by the most attentive, or kept them under unexplained symbolic forms. So God and the 'angelic' gods, the Lords or Powers of the West, only peep through in such places as Gandalf's conversation with Frodo: 'behind that there was something else at work, beyond any design of the Ring-maker's'; or in Faramir's Númenórean grace at dinner" (*Letters* n. 156). See *Letters* n. 183 [quoted in 2.4] and n. 142 [analyzed in 6.2].
20 Curtius 2002, 69-71.

> *hidden meanings*. These seem to me no more than private amusements, and as such I have no right or power to object to them, though they are, I think, valueless for the elucidation or interpretation of my fiction. (*Letters* n. 297, italics added; see *Letters* n. 203 above)
>
> I utterly repudiate any such 'reading', which angers me. The situation was conceived long before the Russian revolution. Such allegory is entirely foreign to my thought. (*Letters* n. 229)

In such respect, *The Lord of the Rings* (as well as the rest of the *Legendarium*) is by no means an allegory, nor are its characters allegories of other characters. Yet many Christian interpretations often suggest a "hidden code"[21] or "correspondences" that link Tolkienian and biblical characters,[22] such as Gandalf/Christ,[23] Gandalf/Patriarchs,[24] Aragorn/Christ,[25] Lembas/Eucharist,[26] Lórien/Paradise,[27] Frodo/Christ,[28] and Galadriel/Mary[29] (see the following paragraph). In a similar way we "discover" explicit parallels between the date the Fellowship sets out on their journey and Christ's birth date (December 25th) or the destruction of the Ring and the date of the Annunciation (March 25th), whereas Tolkien himself explains in an interview of 1967:

> You don't have to be Christian to believe that somebody has to die to save something, As a matter of fact, December 25th occurred strictly by accident, and *I left it to show that this was not a Christian myth anyhow*. It was a purely unimportant date, and I thought, Well there it is, just an accident. (quoted in Flieger 2014b, 153, italics added)[30]

It is therefore surprising to see how some authors, although well aware of these differences, still propose such an interpretation:

---

21 See the text by Caldecott 2008.
22 "This is perhaps the core of this work [*L'Anello e la Croce*]: the *correspondence* between the hobbits and the Last, the poor, the *anawím* in the Bible" Monda 2008, 89, italics added; see also Cucci and Monda 2010, 144 ff.
23 Pearce 2002, 93; Monda 2008, 153 (Gandalf, Aragorn and Sam as Christ figures); Caldecott 1999, 17-33, where he also establishes a parallelism between Mary and Elbereth.
24 "In Gandalf we see the archetypal prefiguration of a powerful Prophet or Patriarch [...] At times he is almost a Christ-like figure" (Pearce 2002, 93).
25 "Jesus, of whom Aragorn is but a type or prefiguration" (Caldecott 2003, 40).
26 Coulombe 1999, 57; Lynch 1978, 13-14; Filmer-Davies 1987, 19-21; see Kerry 2011b, 43.
27 Spirito 2003, 130.
28 Kreeft 2005, 222, see *infra*.
29 Caldecott 2003, 55; Coulombe 1999, 57.
30 In this interview Tolkien seems to refer to the passage in the 'Guide' where he affirms, when mentioning the term Yule: "but December 25th (setting out) and March 25th (accomplishment of quest) were intentionally chosen by me", as if to say the two dates happened by accident and he chose to keep them in order to demonstrate *they were not* evidence of a Christian myth.

> So even though *The Lord of the Rings* is not an allegory of the Gospels, we can find numerous parallels to the Gospel in *The Lord of the Rings* [...] For instance, Frodo's journey up Mount Doom is strikingly similar to Christ's Way of the Cross. Sam is his Simon of Cyrene [...] He [Christ] is more clearly present in Gandalf, Frodo and Aragorn, the three Christ figures. (Kreeft 2005, 222)
>
> I on the one hand do not intend to exhaust all the *interpretive* possibilities of Tolkien with my reading, though on the other I cannot deny that above all else I find in this story a rich symbolic power that enriches me not only as a reader but also as a Catholic. Therefore, *I want to unravel and unfold rather than exhaust the Catholic symbolism I find in the pages* of Tolkien's stories (in the characters, the narrative twists, etc.). (Monda 2014, 92, italics added)

If we just limit ourselves to the most common parallelism of Frodo/Christ, we cannot find one single phrase in Tolkien that validates this hidden reference. Proposing this kind of symbolism is most assuredly legitimate if taken as a possible *application* [see next paragraph], but certainly *not* as an *interpretation* of the text which should instead always be based on the "logic" inherent in the text itself. Indeed, what Tolkien affirms is only that Frodo exemplifies a "sacrificial situation",[31] inspired by the "and-lead-us-not-into-temptation" of the *Pater noster* and therefore only *analogous* to Christ's predicament[32] and in no way implicitly connected to it. The halfling, unlike the Son of God, is not without sin, and he perceives his inability to throw the Ring into Mount Doom as a failure,[33] thus preventing him from returning as a hero.[34] This poisons his soul and his body (also because of the wound inflicted by the Morgul-blade) and prevents him from enjoying a "happy and contented" life in the Shire, which, he says, "has been saved but not for me".[35] He is a tragic figure[36] who never fully recovers (at the most he faints and recovers his senses, a totally different thing from what Kreeft says), and must instead leave his friends in order to reach Eressëa, a place that has nothing in common with

---

31 *Letters* n. 181. According to Verlyn Flieger, Frodo's sacrifice is to be intended as Tolkien's tribute to the TCBS friends who died in war (Gilson and Smith); see Flieger 2008, 85-98.
32 I analyzed Tolkien's use of analogy in Testi 2004; Testi 2007.
33 *Letters* n. 181, n. 191, n. 192.
34 *Letters* n. 246.
35 See *LotR*, RK, 'The Gray Havens'; the English text reads "The Shire, it has been saved, but not for me" that has been mistakenly translated in the Italian edition of *LotR* into "la Contea, ed è stata salvata, ma non per merito mio [the Shire has been saved, but not because of my doing]".
36 Among the first to consider Frodo as a tragic hero was Harvey (Harvey 1985, 77); Croft, in an important study, describes Frodo as suffering from a post-traumatic stress disorder typical of war veterans (Croft 2004, 133-38). Long maintains that Tolkien wrote the *Lord* as an answer to the trauma of World War I (Long 2005); on this theme in Tolkien see also Fornet-Ponse 2009.

Paradise (celestial or terrestrial).[37] On the contrary, this will be a purgatorial sojourn in an island facing Valinor,[38] where he may have the chance to recover from the shadow that afflicts him, but nobody knows if the chance the Valar have given him will lead to a positive outcome.

Applicability and Meaning

Of course this doesn't mean that – for catechistic purposes[39] – we shouldn't use Frodo's journey to Mount Doom to better understand the *Via Crucis*, or 'The Music of the Ainur' to explain the creation in *Genesis*, or Gandalf's first appearance in white[40] to exemplify Jesus' transfiguration.[41] In fact, if we look at things from this perspective, we must strictly separate the concept of "application" (which entails the reader's freedom to apply a story to his personal experience) from that of allegory:

> But I cordially dislike allegory in all its manifestations and always have done so since I grew old and wary enough to detect its presence. I much prefer history, true or feigned, with its varied applicability to thought and experience of readers. I think that many confuse 'applicability' with 'allegory'; but the one resides in the freedom of the reader, and the other in the purposed domination of the author. (*LotR*, 'Foreword')

> That there is no allegory does not, of course, say there is no applicability. There always is. And since I have not made the struggle wholly unequivocal: sloth and stupidity among hobbits, pride and [illegible] among Elves, grudge and greed in Dwarf-hearts, and folly and wickedness among the 'Kings of Men', and treachery and power-lust even among the 'Wizards', there is I suppose applicability in my story to present times. (*Letters* n. 203)

> I have no didactic purpose, and no allegorical intent. (I do not like allegory (properly so called: most readers appear to confuse it with significance or applicability) but that is a matter too long to deal with here). (*Letters* n. 215)[42]

---

37 *Letters* n. 246 and n. 325.
38 *Ibid.*
39 "Manifest" examples of this perspective are: Bruner & Ware 2001; John Rateliff in his review of an essay by Spirito (Spirito 2008) considers it a "homily rather than an essay" (Rateliff 2009, 304).
40 *LotR*, TT, 'The White Rider'.
41 Monda 2008, 162.
42 "An allegorical description of an event does not make that event itself allegorical. And this initial use [pearls that slips from the Poet's hand through the grass as allegory of child's death and burial] is only one of the many *applications* of the pearl symbol" (*SGPO* 8, italics added).

In other words, it is one thing to "apply" the *Legendarium* to the contents of one's own faith or life, as Tolkien sometimes does ("Such is modern life. Mordor in our midst" he writes in *Letters* n. 135), and another is to "confuse" such applications with interpretations that touch upon the very meaning of the text in its essence.

> My comments should not be taken as a veiled statement that the approach Pearce, Boffetti, and others advocate is completely wrong and should be dismissed entirely. But I think we would be wise to remember Tolkien's words about the difference between allegory (purposed direction under the control of the author) and applicability (a process entirely under the reader's control). (M. Fisher 2006, 220)

After all, as Tolkien himself says, "[*The Lord of the Rings*] is not 'about' anything but itself. Certainly it has *no* allegorical intentions, general, particular, or topical, moral, religious, or political"[43] and we must not drift away from the text in order to understand it and disclose the meanings and logics at its foundations.

1.3 It Confuses a Source with a Representation

A mistake, similar in the outcome but based on different motivations, is that of exchanging a source for a representation. Undoubtedly the sources of the *Legendarium* are Christian *as well as* pagan, but the characters Tolkien has sub-created are made of a "blend" that can no longer be analysed, therefore it is impossible to consider them a "representation" of one of their sources. As Tolkien himself explains in 'On Fairy-stories', mythopoeia is similar to a cauldron you throw the "bones" into (that is to say the more or less historical sources that gave rise to the myth) together with the new ingredients (a reflection of re-elaborated versions of myths[44]) thus obtaining a soup (a new story), which is not the sum of its ingredients because they are no longer identifiable or distinguishable, nor indeed needed to taste the new story. In conclusion:

---

43 *Letters* n. 165; see n. 211.
44 *TOFS* 44-45.

We must be satisfied with the soup that is set before us, and not desire to see the bones of the ox out of which it has been boiled.[45] (*TOFS* 39)

The most frequent example we can mention for this group of Tolkienian essayists is that they consider Galadriel (or other female characters) as a sort of representation of Mary:

> This is the Mary [as painted in the Wilton Diptych] who is ever present to Tolkien, at the centre of his imagination, mantled by all natural beauty, the most perfect of God's creatures, the treasury of all earthly and spiritual gifts. What Elbereth, Galadriel, and other characters such as Lúthien and Arwen, surely express is precisely what Tolkien says he had found in Mary: *beauty both in majesty and simplicity.* (Caldecott 2003, 61)

> For Tolkien, Elvishness and Catholicism were closely related. I think you can detect a 'hidden code' that refers to Catholic themes and ideas, such as the Eucharist and the Blessed Virgin Mary, in *The Lord of the Rings*. (Caldecott 2008, 226)[46]

The Virgin[47] (as well as Morrigan of the Welsh stories,[48] Circe, Medea,[49] the Eternal Woman by Haggard,[50] or the magic princesses of MacDonald[51]) is certainly one of the sources for Galadriel, but she cannot be considered a representation of Mary (nor can any of the other female figures mentioned above[52]). In support of this parallel we often find a quote from letter n. 142 where Tolkien writes to his Jesuit friend Robert Murray (who had compared Galadriel to Mary):

> I think I know exactly what you mean by the order of Grace; and of course by your references to Our Lady, upon which all my own small perception of beauty both in majesty and simplicity is founded. (*Letters* n. 142)

---

45 In more formal terms: if A, B, C are sources of P, it doesn't follow that P represents A (or B, or C). This undue interpretation is unfortunately very common in many studies of Tolkienian sources, and not only among the Christian interpretations of Tolkien's work, as underlined by Drout and Wynne: "The second major weakness of source study arises not so much from the identification of a false (or equivocal) source, but from the deeply embedded assumption that once a source is identified, the meaning of Tolkien's text has been discovered [...]. Finding a source merely defers the problem of interpretation, it cannot eliminate it" (Drout and Wynne 2000, 107).
46 For a harsh criticism on Caldecott see Seaman's review based on Tolkien's letter about the "fatal" error concerning the Arthurian cycle, quoted in 1.1. (Seaman, review of Caldecott and Honegger 2008, 298).
47 Burns 2011, 252.
48 Burns 2011, 253; Burns 2005, 106 ff.; Hutton 2011, 57-70; Carter 2007.
49 Hutton 2011b, 101.
50 Rateliff 2011.
51 Burns 2011, 252-53.
52 Among the possible sources for Beren and Lúthien, validated by a stronger adherence to the text, I would like to mention the following: Guinevere and Lancelot (Flieger 2000), Orpheus and Eurydice (Libran-Moreno 2007), Pyramus and Thisbe (Stevens 2004).

Please note that Tolkien does not claim in this letter that Galadriel is a representation of Mary. He only says that Mary is the main source for his idea of beauty. In another letter he affirms that his Catholic faith is one of the main "fundamental facts" that are somehow related to his work, and writes:

> And there are a few basic facts, which however drily expressed, are really significant. For instance I was born in 1892 and lived for my early years in 'the Shire' in a pre-mechanical age. Or more important, I am a Christian (which can be deduced from my stories), and in fact a Roman Catholic. The latter 'fact' perhaps cannot be deduced; though one critic (by letter) asserted that the invocations of Elbereth, and the character of Galadriel as directly described (or through the words of Gimli and Sam) were clearly related to Catholic devotion to Mary. Another saw in waybread (lembas) = viaticum and the reference to its feeding the *will* and being more potent when fasting, a derivation from the Eucharist. (*Letters* n. 213)

But if we read carefully the passage, we observe that Tolkien *never* affirms that Elbereth or Galadriel are representations of Mary (whereas the connection *lembas*/Eucharist is suggested by a reader without any endorsement of this "interpretation" by the author). Moreover, as Tolkien again admits in 1971,[53] Galadriel was living in Middle-earth as a penitent because she had first followed Fëanor in his rebellion against the Valar and in the massacre of the Teleri: she was anything but "immaculate" when *The Lord of the Rings* was published. She became so only in 1973,[54] on the base of a note written by Tolkien shortly before his death, in which he puts Galadriel in opposition to Fëanor.[55] This late "sanctification" further weakens the parallel Galadriel/Mary. The same applies for many other characters and elements; among the sources for Eärendel we can find the medieval poem *Crist*,[56] but the half-elf is not a representation of Christ; in a similar way the inspiration for the *lembas* may derive in part from the Eucharist, but this does not mean that it therefore represents the Eucharist (*supra*).[57]

---

53 *Letters* n. 320; see n. 299.
54 *Letters* n. 353.
55 *UT*, 'The Story of Galadriel and Celeborn'.
56 Tolkien explicitly denies this connection in *Letters* n. 297, quoted above in 1.2. *Exemplification and Symbolism*. On the influence of the poem *Crist* by Cynewulf on the character of Eärendel see: Hammond and Scull 2006b, 233-34.
57 Fornet-Ponse underlines well these differences when he says that the Eucharist "is instituted by Christ [...] it has to be received in a service; it is intended for all Men and not restricted to Elves and a few exceptions; and in some cases confession is necessary before receiving communion" (Fornet-Ponse 2007, 177).

1.4 It Derives a Total Correspondence from a Partial Similarity by Ignoring the Differences

Many of these authors rightly highlight some similarities between parts of the *Legendarium* and contents of the Scriptures and Revelations, but, starting from these mere similarities, they construct a monolithic Christian nature in Tolkien's work. For instance, they start from similarities in style and content between 'The Music of the Ainur' and *Genesis*, and they infer that 'The Music of the Ainur' is Christian:

> The theology of *The Silmarillion* is orthodox in nature, paralleling the teachings of traditional Christianity to a remarkable degree. [...] This Catholic Theology, explicitly present in *The Silmarillion* and implicitly in *The Lord of the Rings*, is omnipresent in both. (Pearce 1998, 94)

However, this approach to the *Legendarium* inevitably causes them to ignore the remarkable differences existing between the Tolkienian and the Christian mythologies to the point that they affirm that:

> In Christian faith, like in Tolkien's cosmogony, evil enters into the world because of the fall of the brightest of the angels. (Bertani 2011, 43)

Concerning the question of how evil came into the world, Tolkien himself explicitly points to the difference between his own mythology and Christian theology.[58] In the *Legendarium* evil has been present in the world since the beginning of creation (therefore it does not "enter" it), being a "concretization" of Eru's work in 'The Music of the Ainur' which also contains Melkor's "discord", whereas in the Christian revelation evil enters the world only after the Fall of Man:

> In the cosmogony there is a fall: a fall of Angels we should say. Though quite different in form, of course, to that of Christian myth. (*Letters* n. 131, dated 1951)
>
> I suppose a difference between this Myth and what may be perhaps called Christian mythology is this. In the latter the Fall of Man is subsequent to and a consequence (though not a necessary consequence) of the 'Fall of the Angels': a rebellion of created free-will at a higher level than Man; but it is not clearly held (and in many versions is not held at all) that this affected the 'World' in its nature: evil was brought in from outside, by Satan. In this Myth the

---

58 See Purtill 2003, 199 ff.: with great honesty and competence the author lists (and explains) the main differences between Tolkienian and Christian theologies.

rebellion of created free-will precedes creation of the World (Eä); *and Eä has in it, subcreatively introduced, evil, rebellions, discordant elements of its own nature already when the Let it Be was spoken.* (*Letters* n. 212, dated 1958, italics added)

Moreover, the Tolkienian mythology contains other considerable differences if compared to the biblical narrative: what can be said, for instance, about the angels who seem to have a gender in Tolkien (whereas this is not contemplated in the Gospel of Matthew 22:30[59]) and some of them even seem able to have children with the other Sons of Ilúvatar (Melian with Thingol)? This is certainly not orthodox,[60] neither are many other elements we will further analyse in 5.2.1.

1.5 It Diminishes the Vastness of the Tolkienian Perspective

The last limitation of those interpretations that use a Christian approach as the exclusive criterion is that of reducing the enormous scope of Tolkien's body of work to a single dimension. Pearce goes as far as stating that:

> It is not merely erroneous but patently perverse to see Tolkien's epic as anything other than a specifically Christian myth. (Pearce 2002, ix)

These words are very strong (indeed *too* strong!) and eventually they turn against the author. In fact, when he (intentionally?) ignores those passages where *Legendarium* and Christianity most evidently appear to be different, he distances himself from Tolkien. Proposing a specifically Christian interpretation as the *sole* possible reading corresponds to an outright perversion of Tolkien's vision. All the more so because this hermeneutic one-sidedness, as observed by

---

59 "In the resurrection they neither marry nor are given in marriage, but are like angels in heaven."
60 In Genesis (*Gen.* 6:1-4) we read that "When man began to multiply on the face of the land and daughters were born to them, the sons of God saw that the daughters of man were attractive. And they took as their wives any they chose […]. The Nephilim [or "giants"] were on the earth in those days, and also afterward, when the sons of God came in to the daughters of man and they bore children to them." But the Italian *Jerusalem Bible* (1991, 10th edition) comments: "Late Judaism and almost all early ecclesiastic writers saw fallen angels in those "sons of God". Since the 4th century, however, the Fathers, for a more spiritual notion of angels, have commonly interpreted the "sons of God" as Set's descendants and the "daughters of man" as Cain's descendants."

Rateliff[61] and Bratman,[62] does not account for the deeply philological inspiration of the *Legendarium*, his attention towards languages and their evolutions, nor his love of pagan sagas; if we want to fully understand Tolkien's work, we should be aware that all these elements carry an equal weight, to say the least, to that which he gives to his relationship with Christianity.

---

61 "A minority view, vigorously expressed by Joseph Pearce, seeks to stress Tolkien's Catholicity instead, going as far as to claim that only Catholics can truly understand Tolkien's work (see for example Pearce's foreword to Bradley J. Birzer, *J.R.R. Tolkien's Sanctifying Myth: Understanding Middle-earth* [Pearce 1999b])" (Rateliff 2006, 97 note 66). Also Edwards, who thinks that though "Religion took a central role in Tolkien's life; he is often seen now, too, a specifically Catholic writer," criticizes Pearce (Edwards 2014, 291, 294).

62 "Pearce's principal thesis is a presentation of an aggressively proselytizing Catholic view of Tolkien's work, claiming that 'Tolkien states unequivocally that the religious element is more important than the linguistic' as if one has to trump the other" (Bratman 2008, 292). On the relationship between Christian faith and Fantasy see also Hein 1998 and Sturch 2007.

Chapter Two

Tolkien's Work is Pagan

Another group of authors – even if they don't completely deny the importance of the Christian elements in the formation of the *Legendarium* – assert *the prevalence of an essentially pagan perspective* manifestly opposed to the "orthodox" Christian vision of life and history. The various perspectives within this group are less monolithic than those just mentioned above; we find interpretations ranging from the extremely "radical" (such as Madsen[1]) to the more "moderate" (from Hutton[2] to Morillo[3]) up to the environmentalist-polytheistic vision set forth by Curry.[4] Among the authors in Italy who share a similar approach, I would like to mention Gianfranco de Turris and Alberto Lombardo. However, this particular perspective encounters considerable critical limitations – some of them almost a mirror image of those already mentioned – which I will list systematically.

2.1 It Diminishes the Importance of those Texts where the Connection between the *Legendarium* and Christianity is More Evident

'On Fairy-stories': Creator and Sub-creator

This perspective tends to minimize (almost to the point of ignoring) those texts where the importance of the Christian revelation unequivocally emerges in the formation of the *Legendarium*. Madsen, for instance, considers the epilogue to 'On Fairy-stories' (which we will analyse in detail in 5.1.1) as only a simple "postscript" to the essay, similar to the story of Aragorn and Arwen in *The Lord of the Rings*. This is problematic since both the epilogue and the appendices are

---

1 Madsen 2004; Madsen 2011.
2 Hutton 2011; Hutton 2011b.
3 Morillo 2011.
4 Curry 1997 and Curry 2014.

essential parts of both works.⁵ The scholar herself affirms, with a disconcerting line of reasoning, that the

> epilogue [of 'OFS'] is itself useful evidence: the fact that Tolkien could make such an open statement of his Christian belief suggests that where he did not make it, he did not wish to make it. (Madsen 2011, 161-62)

It is almost as if to say that Tolkien, by not explicitly professing his faith, implicitly denies it. It would be pointless to linger on the weakness of this reasoning: it would suffice to observe in the same way (and just as erroneously) that, if Tolkien on some occasions explicitly denies the identity between his world and Christianity [1.1], he affirms it each and every time that he does not deny it.

Moreover, Madsen affirms that *The Silmarillion*, where the theological content present in the text cannot be ignored – one need only think of 'The Music of the Ainur' (see 5.2.1) – is a "collection of private legends",⁶ but she forgets that in the early '50s Tolkien was contemplating the publication of *The Silmarillion* together with *The Lord of the Rings*.⁷ Similarly, Madsen, with the aim of justifying the absence of Eru/God in *The Lord of the Rings*, affirms that he is never mentioned with the exception of "two fairly cryptical and untheological references in the appendices".⁸ One of the two above mentioned passages defines death as the "gift of the One to Men",⁹ whereas the second recalls how the flooding of Númenor was the One's doing.¹⁰ Now, we are simply unable to see any cryptic meaning in these two very clear theological references. Furthermore, the belief that the number of times a name is mentioned could be proof of its importance may result in an ideological criticism that can lead to misinterpretations of Tolkien's work. In fact Tolkien is an author who would *never* use such important words by mistake and he was perfectly aware of their religious significance as well as other fundamental "details".¹¹ Likewise, Hutton thinks that Tolkien's use of the term "heathen" within the story is not very clear,¹² whereas Tolkien was perfectly aware of the decisive function he assigned to this term [4.2, 5.2.2].

---

5 *Letters* n. 89 and n. 181.
6 Madsen 2011, 152.
7 *Letters* n. 131.
8 Madsen 2004, 35.
9 *LotR*, App A v.
10 *LotR*, A A.1 1116.
11 *Letters* n. 156.
12 Hutton 2006, 233.

Ainulindalë: Angelic powers and polytheism

Similarly, we often find that some authors, with the intention of validating "J.R.R. Tolkien's polytheistic sentiment",[13] ignore or do not take in due account those letters of Tolkien's in which he confirms the influence of his Catholic faith in the genesis of his work.[14] For instance, Lombardo and Passaro affirm that:

> The Ainur are pagan gods through and through […] they greatly differ from the "angels" of monotheism […] notwithstanding Humphrey Carpenter's opinion, it is not true that the universe created by Tolkien be ruled by God, the One, and that the Valar be under him [*sic*] in the hierarchy. (Lombardo 2007, 101)

> One of the aspects of the "secondary world" that is incompatible with orthodox Christian teaching is the existence of a Pantheon. (Passaro 2000, 37)

But Tolkien himself, although with some differences, affirms in some letters and in the *Legendarium* (especially in 'The Music of the Ainur': see 5.2.1.)[15] the "angelic" nature of these powers and how they differ from Eru, who alone can create things out of nothing:

> The cycles begin with a cosmogonical myth: the *Music of the Ainur*. God and the Valar (or powers: Englished as gods) are revealed. These latter are as we should say angelic powers, whose function is to exercise delegated authority in their spheres (of rule and government, *not* creation, making or re-making). (*Letters* n. 131)

Partiality in the Collected Letters

In order to diminish the importance of the *Letters* (where the role of Tolkien's Catholicism is undisputedly central), they draw attention to the fact that only selected letters were made available, implicitly speculating about possible neo-pagan contents in the unpublished letters, and argue that

> [t]he famous collection of letters, edited by Humphrey Carpenter […] are a very different class of document, with particular pitfalls and limitations. For one thing they are not evenly spread across his long adult life, but survive

---

13 Lombardo 2007.
14 *Letters* n. 213; see *ibid.* n. 142 analysed in 6.2.
15 The difference between Eru and the Valar is a constant in the development of the *Legendarium*: see the first two chapters of Whittingham 2007.

overwhelmingly from the last three decades of it. The 1910s and 1920s, in which he developed his mythology, are especially badly represented. (Hutton 2011, 58)

That the collection of the published letters is incomplete and cannot be taken as a source as authoritative as the works published when Tolkien was still alive is undoubtedly correct. However, one shouldn't diminish the value of Tolkien's letters as they contain essential information for the understanding of the depth of his work. Moreover, they are quoted by the most authoritative critics and even by the more "pagan" ones when their content helps to support their thesis (see 2.2.1 for the use made by Hutton of letter n. 250).[16]

2.2 It Erroneously Considers Some Elements of the *Legendarium* to Be in Opposition to Christianity

This specific kind of mistake can be subdivided into two classes according to the erroneous evaluations of parts of Tolkien's work or of the real content of Christian theology (Catholicism in particular).

2.2.1 Forced Pagan Readings of Parts of Tolkien's Work

Pantheism and the Legendarium

A common mistake of many pagan readings is that of considering some Tolkienian passages as antithetic to the authentic Christian message, thus paving the way for inevitably forced interpretations. An example of this case is given by Patrick Curry when he refers to a passage in 'On Fairy-stories'. In his *Defending Middle-earth*, he first quotes Russel Hoban[17] affirming the existence of a divine pantheistic force which projects itself onto our psyche and thus is responsible for our idea of divinity:

> gods do not replace one another. Let prophets and kings do what they will: gods are a cumulative projection of everything in us. I'm not trying to reduce this to psychiatry – I mean that we worship the gods projected by the god-force that projects us as well on the screen. (Curry 1997, 115-16)

---

16 For a similar critique see Holmes 2011.
17 Russel Hoban (1925-2011) was a well known writer of fantasy.

Furthermore, Curry argues in favour of a parallel with Tolkien and quotes one of his passages from *Mythopoeia* in 'On Fairy-stories':

> Or as he also says, 'We make fiction because we are fiction… We make stories because we are stories'. Now, Tolkien's almost identical statement – 'We make still by the law in which we're made'[18] – assumes a theistic Creator who made us. But the logic of what he is saying, it seems to me, can be accommodated by Hoban's 'god-force' without any significant loss. (Curry 1997, 116)

Curry's pantheistic reading emerges clearly from this passage, where he aims at denying the existence of one Creator superior to any other entity in order to allow instead a polytheistic interpretation of Tolkien's work that confines any Christian content exclusively to the moral level:

> The spiritual world of Middle-earth is a rich and complex one. It contains both a polytheist-cum-animist cosmology of 'natural magic' and a Christian (but non-sectarian) ethic of humility and compassion. (Curry 1997, 28)

> *The Lord of the Rings* transcends any strictly monotheistic reading.
> (Curry 1997, 117)

We will later examine in detail the thesis maintained in 'On Fairy-stories' [5.1.1] and the "structural" monotheism of the *Legendarium* [5.2.1]. At present I merely want to demonstrate the inconsistency of Curry's reading. Suffice it to say, the essay explicitly refers to a Creator God who bestows upon Man the analogous power of sub-creating myths and stories with happy endings, and redeems Man by means of the *Evangelium's* double eucatastrophe of Christ's incarnation and resurrection.[19] We must also not forget that Tolkienian ecology is interpreted by Dickerson and Evans, and Siewers[20] in a Christian mode and, in my opinion, with a much greater abundance of textual evidence.

If Curry's statement leaves us perplexed, it is all the more so with Madsen's thesis asserting that the "escapism" of fairy-stories in Tolkien's essay is in reality the attempt of a Christian to escape from Christianity, from Christian history and theology.[21]

---

18 *TOFS* 213.
19 *TOFS* 94-97.
20 Dickerson and Evans 2006; see Siewers 2009. For Curry's critique of Dickerson and Evans, see Curry 2007.
21 Madsen 2004, 47.

By contrast, Hutton appears to be much more cautious when he affirms that there are moments in Tolkien's life and passages in his works which may suggest that "Tolkien's religious faith was not a robust and untroubled one but subject to doubt and loss of confidence".[22] He refers to letter n. 250, where Tolkien confesses: "Out of wickedness and sloth I almost ceased to practise my religion – especially at Leeds, and at 22 Northmoor Road." Hutton maintains that in the '20s and '30s Tolkien was going through a "less Christian" phase,[23] during which a large part of *The Silmarillion* was conceived. Indeed, if compared to *The Lord of the Rings*, *The Silmarillion* shows much less "orthodox" contents which can be linked more easily to a pagan mode of religiosity. But how can we interpret this confession made by Tolkien on the alleged interruption of his religious practices? As fittingly pointed out by Nils Agøy, Hutton "forgets" to quote the lines that just precede the "self-incriminating" phrase, where Tolkien affirms "[b]ut I fell in love with the Blessed Sacrament from the beginning – and by the mercy of God *never* have fallen out again",[24] which can only mean that he never ceased receiving the Eucharist. In that letter he may probably mean that in those years he didn't attend mass nor did he confess with the same regularity and fervour as in other years [see Introduction, note 38]. This, however, didn't restrain him from writing poems for a Catholic review in 1923, being "classified" a Catholic and a "papist" by Lewis in 1926, and taking part in a congress of the Catholic association *Pax Romana*[25] in 1928.

2.2.2 Erroneous Interpretations of Christianity

Obscurity of Christianity

The most astonishing thing in Hutton's critique (and this reminds us of the second type of mistaken evaluation) is the poor understanding of the dramatic nature of the Christian message. He implicitly admits his conviction that the doubts and dark moments a believer can go through (or considering history

---

22 Hutton 2011, 59.
23 Hutton 2011, 60.
24 *Letters* n. 250, italics added.
25 See Agøy 2011.

as a "long defeat"[26]) may be signs of a faltering, uncertain faith. However, this is a common condition with a majority of Christians. Just think of the "dark night of the soul", those moments or even long periods of time when one may suffer the absence of God in one's life, which has been experienced by St John of the Cross, Saint Teresa of Avila (both Doctors of the Church) and more recently by Saint Mother Teresa of Calcutta, who affirms, in a much stronger and radical way than Tolkien:

> There is so much deep contradiction in my soul. Such deep longing for God – so deep that it is painful – a suffering continual – and yet not wanted by God – repulsed – empty – no faith – no love – no zeal. Souls hold no attraction – Heaven means nothing – to me it looks like an empty place – the thought of it means nothing to me and yet this torturing longing for God. (Mother Teresa & Kolediejchuk 2007, 169)
>
> They say *people in Hell suffer eternal pain* because of the loss of God – they would go through all that suffering if they had just a little hope of possessing *God. In my soul I felt just that terrible pain of loss, of God not wanting me, of God not being God, of God not really existing.*
> (Mother Teresa & Kolediejchuk 2007, 200, italics added)

However, these dark moments, instead of throwing suspicion upon these giants of the faith, reveal the real calibre of their spirituality, which in due proportion should also apply to J.R.R. Tolkien.

Neoplatonism and Christianity

Hutton,[27] once again quite rightly, reminds us that Tolkien and other Inklings show a strongly accentuated streak of Neoplatonism; think of the Ainur, Valar and Maiar and the extremely important role these divine beings play in the cosmogony and history of Arda.[28] However, conceiving these elements as antithetic to Christianity is certainly erroneous and a sign of an inadequate knowledge of Christian theology; consider St. Augustine's Platonism, the Neoplatonic texts by Pseudo-Dyonisius (which in the Middle Ages were thought to have been

---

[26] "Actually I am a Christian, and indeed a Roman Catholic, so that I do not expect 'history' to be anything but a 'long defeat' – though it contains (and in a legend may contain more clearly and movingly) some samples or glimpses of final victory" (*Letters* n. 195; see 5.2.3).
[27] Hutton 2006, 229; Hutton 2011, 62.
[28] Zimmer detects Neoplatonic influences in the philosophy of the Tolkienian language based on a unitary conception of words and things (Zimmer 2004).

written by St. Paul's disciple who was converted in the Areopagus) and the recently rediscovered Neoplatonism of St. Thomas Aquinas.[29]

The Church and the Elves

Another "classical" argument used in the pagan readings is that of pointing out that the Elvish people in the *Legendarium* do reincarnate and that the doctrine of reincarnation is categorically rejected by official theology.[30] To confute this thesis, we can observe the following:

1 The concept of the reincarnation of the Elves is never present in any of Tolkien's works published during his lifetime; the idea of their "rebirth in the children" appears only in The Silmarillion, published in 1977, and in Letters. If these texts are not considered as reliable sources [see 2.1], they should all the more not be so when referring to the Elves' reincarnation;
2 We should also take into consideration that the concept of reincarnation in the *Legendarium* has gone through a considerable process of development, so much so that starting in 1958-60 Tolkien abandons the theory of rebirth in the children and "explains" the return of the Elves after their death by the Valar's creation of a new body in which each soul can find a new dwelling.[31] This concept clearly distances itself from the classical

---

29 Fabro 1939; Geiger 1942.
30 See, as examples: Hutton 2011b, 96; Curry 1997, 112.
31 The refusal of rebirth in the children, a constant in the *Legendarium* for over forty years, is particularly meaningful if we also consider that this idea persists implicitly during and after the writing of *The Lord of the Rings* (where, however, the idea of rebirth in the children is never mentioned). In 1954, in fact, during a conversation with Mr Hastings [see Foreword] Tolkien hints at this possibility causing great perplexity in Mr Hastings, who will later write to him asking for an explanation on the matter. In a draft letter of 1954, Tolkien writes: "'Reincarnation' may be bad *theology* (that surely, rather than metaphysics) as applied to Humanity; and my *Legendarium*, especially the 'Downfall of Númenor' which lies immediately behind *The Lord of the Rings,* is based on my view: that Men are essentially mortal and must not try to become 'immortal' in the flesh. But I do not see how even in the Primary World any theologian or philosopher, unless very much better informed about the relation of spirit and body than I believe anyone to be, could deny the *possibility* of re-incarnation as a mode of existence, prescribed for certain kinds of rational incarnate creatures" (*Letters* n. 153). Despite these peremptory statements, Tolkien (most likely because of the letters received from several fans) begins at this moment to seriously question himself over the issue of rebirth. First, in Laws, he puts forth an extreme attempt to "fix" the theory of rebirth, inevitably meeting, in doing so, with the many "absurdities" implied by the theory itself.

idea of reincarnation and gets closer, even with its profound differences, to the Christian idea of the resurrection of the body.[32]

3   In addition, these authors fail to consider the most obvious fact that the Church has never denied the existence of the Elves for the simple reason that they don't exist in our world![33]

4   In fact, Tolkien never writes of the reincarnation of human beings. Even in *The Notion Club Papers*, an unfinished novel by Tolkien, where the main character travels backwards in time to relive the experiences of his remotest ancestors. But here Tolkien unequivocally affirms that this sort of time travel is not a reincarnation but only a *"transfer"* of memories from the ancestors, and rejects reincarnation without a shadow of a doubt:

> The theory is that the sight and memory goes on with descendants of Elendil and Voronwë (= Tréowine) but *not reincarnation*; they are different people even if they still resemble one another in some ways even after a lapse of many generations (*SD* 278, italics added).[34]

At the beginning we have a matter of aporias of a moral/social nature related to the *fëa* of married Elves, because of which, in order to avoid the possibility of a sort of "bigamy", he introduces Mandos' judgement that will allow freedom not to return to those who do not wish to reunite with the still living spouse (*MR* LawsA 227). Soon, however, other problems of "psychological" nature surface: in the case of rebirth, the elf will in fact gradually reacquire the memories of his past existence and find himself with the memory of four different parents (two for each life) (*MR* 221-22). In 'Converse', for the first time after fifty years, we witness a first breakthrough since *the Valar are conferred* with the power of allowing the Elves to return in an adult body created by them, whereas *rebirth becomes only "one" (no longer the only one) way* and, if chosen by the elf, will need *approval by Eru* in person (*MR*, Converse 362; Converse A-B-C). However, what will be conclusive and bring Tolkien to definitively *refuse* the thesis of rebirth is the *"discovery" of the metaphysical principle of harmony between hröa and fëa*. This is resolutely reaffirmed in the comment to 'Athrabeth' (*MR* 330) and will be a fundamental reason for the refusal of the rebirth of the children in 'Reincarnation' (where Tolkien affirms that it is in the *fëa's* own power to rebuild the body). This result (along with the refusal of the ideas from 1966 and the definitive acceptance of the solution of the body rebuilt by the Valar) will once again be confirmed more than ten years later in NotesR (1972) and 'Glorfindel' (1970-72, in *PME* 337-85) (see Testi 2012 and Devaux 2014).

32   The main difference is that from a Christian perspective it is the same body that is resurrected, while in Elvish reincarnation the soul comes back in an equivalent but different body.

33   On the theme of reincarnation in the history of the Catholic Church see in any case the brilliant volume by Cantoni 1997.

34   For the sake of completeness we should also mention an essay by Verlyn Flieger, even if the author cannot be included in the "multitude" of the "pagan" interpreters [see 3.1] "It seems safe to say that at some level and in its own particular fashion, Tolkien did at least not disbelieve in reincarnation" (Flieger 2007, 110).) Flieger bases her analysis in great part on the "strange" episode of Merry in the Barrow (at the moment when the hobbit appears to be "possessed" by the soul of a dead warrior [*LotR*, FR 'Fog on the Barrow-downs', 175]. For a critique of Flieger's article see Nagel 2007, 216. In my opinion, the idea of mnemonic *transfer* adequately explains Merry's experience in the Barrow-downs, which would otherwise be an episode of reincarnation lasting only a few seconds.

In any case the possible "non-orthodoxy" of parts is not sufficient to affirm the total incompatibility of a work with the contents of the Revelation. In fact we can find non-orthodox stances even among the greatest Doctors of the Church: for instance Thomas Aquinas affirms in *Summa Theologica* that the Virgin Mary is not Immaculate, in contrast to the dogma of the Immaculate Conception![35]

2.3 It Confuses Historical Paganism with "Tolkienian" Paganism

The pagan approach stresses the fundamental importance (and pre-eminence) of pagan sources in the genesis of the *Legendarium* (see Morillo,[36] Curry,[37] Hutton,[38] and, in Italy, de Turris[39]), but in most cases does not sufficiently take into account the important differences between Middle-earth and the pagan civilizations of history. In the publications by Ronald Hutton, one of the foremost contemporary experts on paganism, we can distinguish three periods, each one different from Tolkienian paganism.

1) Ancient paganism

Ancient paganism denotes those beliefs that took shape in the pre-Christian West or outside this context (Norse cultures included). In this kind of paganism we encounter customs that are totally absent from the pagans in the *Legendarium*, such as nudity in many religious rites of the ancient Greeks and Vikings.[40] As for human sacrifices, performed as we have evidence for by the Germanic tribes[41] and the Egyptians[42] (who were for Tolkien a source of inspiration for the Númenóreans[43]), they are mentioned in a completely negative way and only

---

35 Aquinas, *S. Th.* III q. 27 a. 2.
36 Morillo 2011, 115.
37 Curry points to the possible pagan sources for Galadriel, Gandalf, Radagast and other pagan elements in the *Legendarium* such as the midsummer festival in the Shire (Curry 1997, 111-15).
38 Hutton 2011b, 101.
39 de Turris 2012, 6-8.
40 Hutton 2006, 195-200.
41 Turville-Petre 1975, 251-61; du Chaillu 2005, Vol. 1, 364. Shippey (2000b, 198), too, mentions the human sacrifices perpetrated by the Germanic tribes, as described by Tacitus (*De Origine et situ Germanorum*, 131).
42 Najoivits 2003, Vol. 1, 41.
43 *Letters* n. 211.

with regard to those Númenóreans who chose to practice the cult of Melkor after they had fallen under Sauron's spell.[44]

2) Late ancient paganism

This form of paganism developed at the beginning of the second century AD and differs from the previous one (among other things) by its more marked monotheism and structured theological doctrine. In this kind of paganism we find a much more accentuated ritualism where religiosity and magic (intended as dominion over nature)[45] superimpose themselves. The ritual aspect is almost entirely absent in the religiosity of the Free Peoples, whereas it is typical of the Númenóreans corrupted by Sauron [see *supra* and 5.2.2]. As far as magic is concerned, Tolkien's stance is much more elaborate than commonly thought.[46] Without going into details, it will suffice to mention the emblematic episode in *The Lord of the Rings* when Gandalf reluctantly conjures up the salvific flame as a last resort (after attempting all non-magical means) in order to avoid the hobbits' freezing to death.[47] This is just to show how magic in Tolkien has in general a negative connotation, because its practice may lead to an ever growing lust for power. It is not by chance that the Elves' "innocent" wish to obtain the knowledge that would preserve the cosmos from corruption gives rise to the One Ring [see text quoted in 2.4].

3) Modern paganism

According to Hutton, the cultural matrices of this kind of paganism (Wiccan paganism in particular) derive mostly from certain nineteenth-century cultural trends (from Haggard up to Yeats and Lawrence).[48] The principles of paganism according to Hutton are as follows:

---

44 "The power of Sauron daily increased, and in that temple, with spilling of blood and torment and great wickedness, men made sacrifice to Melkor that he should release them from Death. And most often from among the Faithful they chose their victims" (S, Ak).
45 Hutton 2006, 106-107.
46 The bibliography on this subject is extremely vast. We want to mention only Shippey 2007g, and Bonechi 2003.
47 *LotR*, FR, 'The Ring Goes South'.
48 Hutton 2001, 151 ff.

1. "An acceptance of the inherent divinity of the natural world, and a rejection of any notion of the creation of that world by a power outside itself."[49] This pantheism [see Curry in 2.1] is remarkably distant from the Tolkienian cosmogony where Eru's power transcends that of the Valar and, by means of the Secret Fire, conceives the music of the Ainur that will create Eä [see 5.2.1].
2. "The second component is the rejection of any concept of a divinely prescribed law for human behaviour, and therefore the concept of sin and salvation."[50] Now it is true that we do not find divine laws that are directly prescribed by Eru in the Legendarium, but the concept of the Fall (and therefore of sin) is essential in the development of the story of Arda, which evolves towards a final salvific ending in the mysterious Arda Healed [see 5.2.3].
3. "[T]he third component is an acceptance that divinity can be both female and male. This formulation leaves room for a further range of conceptualisation, from a single bisexual Great Spirit to a genuine polytheism, although duotheism – by which a goddess and a god appear in various aspects – is the most commonly articulated."[51] None of these three hypotheses apply to Middle-earth, if we disregard the fact that the Valar are of male and female gender; they, however, are altogether different in degree and power from the One [see 5.2.1].

2.4 It Applies a Symbolic Reading to Tolkien's Work to the Detriment of its Comprehension

This approach is typically found in some Italian authors and repeats the mistake of the allegorical Catholic reading, especially with regards to the erroneous meaning assigned to the genuinely Tolkienian idea of symbolism (intended as exemplification: see 1.2). In fact, in the so called "symbolic-traditional" approach, they interpret Tolkien's texts by superposing a matrix on certain elements that changes their meaning into something not present in the text and that only a few may be able to detect. de Turris is particularly clear about this approach and he affirms his determination to read Tolkien in the light of Julius Evola's

---

49 Hutton 2001, 390.
50 Hutton 2001, 390.
51 Hutton 2001, 390.

and other authors' symbolism.⁵² There is no proof whatsoever that Tolkien had knowledge of these texts (as some of these critics quite honestly admit⁵³) but this obstacle can be easily bypassed because

> in 1928 Evola writes [...] "the authors can be the first to ignore the added meaning given by what they think is their own 'creation'. That meaning however exists, although it is detected and recognized *only by those who have eyes*". (de Turris 2013, 11, italics added)

The problem is that those who do not "have eyes" cannot see these meanings because they are not manifest in the sources, in the text or in the conscious intent of the author. To some extent this gives origin to an esoteric reading that "bends" the text towards this particular type of symbolic reading:

> as just said, interpretation should be symbolic or metaphorical. Based on these premises, it is just *as clear as day* that the Fellowship of the Ring exemplifies in its members values such as friendship, comradeship [...] It is also *evident* that their journey towards Mount Doom be in itself an initiatory journey [...] that The One Ring be the symbol of evil or dictatorial power in opposition to the Men's and Elves' rings and that Mordor is the *manifest* symbol of modernity. (de Turris 2007b, 136-37, italics added)

But these symbolic associations are "manifest" only to "those who have eyes". Just to limit ourselves to the text quoted above, it will suffice to mention that a traitor such as Boromir is part of the Fellowship and that the journey of the Fellowship and the changes he causes in them (especially in the hobbits) are neither symbolic nor initiatory:

> The calculable people reside in relatively fixed circumstances, and it is difficult to catch and observe them in situations that are (to them) strange. That is another good reason for sending 'hobbits' – a vision of a simple and calculable people in simple and long-settled circumstances – on a *journey* far from settled home into strange lands and dangers. Especially if they are provided with some strong motive for endurance and adaptation. Though *without any high motive people do change (or rather reveal the latent) on journeys: that is a fact of ordinary observation without any need of symbolical explanation.* (*Letters* n. 183, italics added)

---

52 Author of *Imperialismo Pagano* (Evola 2004, *Pagan Imperialism*).
53 For instance Stefano Giuliano in his well-documented study "makes use of" Dumézil's studies, but with his intellectual honesty reports that there is no certainty that Tolkien had read him (Giuliano 2013, 57).

Likewise, the rings of the Elves and Men cannot be considered "good" *per se*. In fact, it is out of their desire to know and preserve things from corruption that the Elves got in contact with Sauron (in a moment in history when he appears to be "redeemed") with the intent of learning those crafts which would make them capable of forging the Rings of Power:

> Then all listened while Elrond in his clear voice spoke of Sauron and the Rings of Power, and their forging in the Second Age of the world long ago. A part of his tale was known to some there, but the full tale to none, and many eyes were turned to Elrond in fear and wonder as he told of the Elven-smiths of Eregion and their friendship with Moria, *and their eagerness for knowledge, by which Sauron ensnared them*. (*LotR*, FR, 'The Council of Elrond', italics added)

> But the Elves are *not* wholly good or in the right. Not so much because they had flirted with Sauron; as because with or without his assistance they were 'embalmers'. (*Letters* n. 153)

> Mere *change* as such is not represented as 'evil': it is the unfolding of the story and to refuse this is of course against the design of God. But the Elvish weakness is in these terms naturally to regret the past, and to become unwilling to face change: as if a man were to hate a very long book still going on, and wished to settle down in a favourite chapter. Hence they fell in a measure to Sauron's deceits: they desired some 'power' over things as they are (which is quite distinct from art), to make their particular will to preservation effective: to arrest change, and keep things always fresh and fair. (*Letters* n. 181)

Neither can we find a single passage in Tolkien that acknowledges the parallel Mordor/Modernity. Tolkien understands "symbol" not as a hidden representation, but as a tangible "exemplification" of certain universal concepts: if anything, the Ring is therefore an exemplification of power and not only of the evil powers of Modernity [see 1.2]:

> You can make the Ring into an allegory[54] of our own time, if you like: an allegory of the inevitable fate that waits for all attempts to defeat evil power by power. But that is *only because all power magical or mechanical does always so work*. (*Letters* n. 109, italics added)

The use of extrinsic symbolic matrices – from Guenon to Evola – is in my opinion the most serious limitation of this approach and may mislead one into ignoring

---

54 Here Tolkien seems to grant them the use of the term "allegory", but seen in this context it seems to take on somehow the meaning of a *captatio benevolentiae* towards the Unwins more than a real *imprimatur*.

both the complexity of Tolkien's work and the most significant critical studies on the matter that would never endorse these associations so easily.

For example, you may see Frodo as a symbol of the superman who ends his life happy and content sailing away to dissolve into the "Wholeness",[55] a much less plausible interpretation than that of Frodo seen as *alter Christus* mentioned in 1.2. I'm afraid these are mostly "circular" readings, as can be easily demonstrated in the bibliographies that have long been proposed by these authors, where an average of 70% of the mentioned titles refer to volumes with the same symbolic approach.[56]

2.5 It Diminishes the Scope of Tolkien's Perspective

The exclusively pagan approach diminishes the scope of the Tolkienian perspective just like the Christian one does and, as it is now clear, misleads scholars into ignoring important aspects of the *Legendarium* [*supra*, 2.1 and 2.4]. It may also lead to an interpretation of the texts (or even Tolkien's life itself) which is keen on searching for (and finding) non-existent, neopagan elements [2.2, 2.3], and which tends to forget that for Tolkien "all this is 'mythical', and not any kind of new religion or vision".[57] Catherine Madsen, for instance, considers the "recovery" that fairy-stories may bring about (or in other words the power of "'seeing things as we are (or were) meant to see them' – as things apart from ourselves" (*TOFS* 67), as the

> most compelling thing about the book [i.e. *LotR*] – and also the least Christian: for this kind of attention is unmediated, available to anyone of any persuasion, and not contingent upon belief [...]. Nothing in the awakening of the senses points one inevitably toward Christ; if anything, it points one to the world. (Madsen 2004, 44)

---

55 Bonvecchio 2008b, 51 ff.; see Casseri 2007, 183-198.
56 To prove what has just been said, see: Polia 1980; de Turris 1992; Bologna 1992; de Turris 2007b; Fusco 2007; Casseri 2007; de Turris 2011; Bonvecchio 2008b; de Turris 2008. You will find 67 quotations of critical reviews (biographies excluded) out of which 48 (72%) refer to authors of this list (plus others who in some way or other are related to them), 14 (20%) are foreign works and 5 (8%) Italian essays with a different approach. Although with a different cultural basis, Poppi, too, proposes a symbolic interpretation of Tolkien's works (Poppi 1990).
57 *Letters* n. 211.

Now, while it is certainly true that this "recovery" does not point toward Christ directly, it is certainly false that this concept is "the least Christian" one only because it has the world as its object. It would be similar to claiming that an authentic experience of nature's beauty cannot lead to the awareness of the existence of a Creator. In fact, this is the "normal" path followed by rational theology, which starts from the created world in order to understand the existence and nature of its Creator. A prime example of such an approach is the famous Aristotelian demonstration of the Unmoved Mover[58] which merged into Thomas Aquinas' first way.[59]

To conclude, such pagan reductionism – as well as the Christian exclusiveness – cannot facilitate the complete and adequate comprehension of Tolkien's perspective which is not liable to be ascribed to either one or the other of these theological poles.

---

58 Aristotle, *Physics*, books VII-VIII.
59 Aquinas, *S. Th.* I q. 2 a. 3. We know that Tolkien was not a philosopher, but I would like to note that in *Letter* n. 310 he outlines a sort of "theological demonstration" of God's existence (see Thomas' fifth way), associating it with the themes of ethics and purpose in every man's life. For a comparison (and a complete bibliography) between Tolkien and Aquinas see Testi 2014; see also Testi 2016.

Chapter Three

Tolkien's Work is Pagan and Christian

Between these two opposites we find those authors (and after all they are the majority) who do not take a clear-cut stand but simply admit the presence of both Christian and pagan elements in the *Legendarium* with no pre-eminence of either element: "Christian, but not only!" is a popular characterisation of the *Legendarium*.[1] If that were so, it would be legitimate to think – as the most insightful critics do – that we are facing a "contradictory" universe just because it contains both the Christian thesis and the pagan antitheses.

Unlike the other readings examined in 1 and 2, it is not easy to identify this approach in a well-defined "school". Therefore, it is impossible for me to enumerate its most common "weaknesses", and I will limit the analysis to two authoritative figures of this approach: Verlyn Flieger and (for Italian Tolkien scholarship) Wu Ming 4.

3.1 Points of View and Contradictions

3.1.1 Traditions, Mediators and Translators: The Tolkienian Polyphony

Verlyn Flieger, one of the foremost experts on Tolkien, writes:

> No careful reader of Tolkien's fiction can fail to be aware of the polarities that give it form and tension. His work is built on contrasts – between hope and despair, between good and evil, between enlightenment and ignorance – and these contrasts are embodied in the polarities of light and dark that are the creative outgrowth of his contrary moods, the 'antithesis' of his nature. Carpenter describes him as a man of extreme contrasts. (Flieger 2002, 2)

---

1 Evans 2012.

"A man of antitheses" is both the title of the first chapter of *Splintered Light* and the characterisation of J.R.R. Tolkien given by Carpenter.[2] However, Flieger doesn't uncritically align herself with the pagan readings, as Carpenter later does,[3] but she stresses the fact that we find in the *Legendarium* a number of not entirely "orthodox" elements (rebirth,[4] Doom[5] and a Creation already marred by evil[6]) and also affirms the manifest importance of Tolkien's faith in the genesis of his works (just think of the notion of Eucatastrophe[7]). For Flieger, it "seems clear that Tolkien is deliberately mingling pagan and Christian elements so that neither will predominate" (Flieger 2012e, 226)[8].

In fact, according to Flieger, when reading Middle-earth tales we should never forget that they have been made available to us thanks to a long chain of "mediators", the last of them usually being J.R.R. Tolkien the "translator".[9] Indeed, a fundamental characteristic of Tolkien's works is that, according to his literary conceit, his *Legendarium* is supposedly written by different narrators (who are not to be confused with the real author)[10] who write from different points of view. This literary conceit varies considerably within the different contexts, but is a constant throughout the whole Tolkienian body of work, and Christopher Tolkien committed a serious mistake when, in the 1977 edition of *The Silmarillion*, he omitted the titles of the chapters that referred

---

2   Carpenter 1977.
3   After publishing fundamental biographical studies on Tolkien and the Inklings and editing the letters, Carpenter became increasingly critical of Tolkien and ironic about his works and their readers: in 1985 he went so far as to say that Tolkien had attempted the creation of a new religion as an alternative to traditional religions. For an overview on Carpenter's position see Anderson 2005b.
4   See Flieger 2007.
5   See Flieger 2009b.
6   Flieger 2012e.
7   See, for example, the third chapter of *Splintered Light* (Flieger 2002) for the connection between Gospels, eucatastrophe and narration.
8   The passage refers only to Eärendel's myth, but corresponds to Flieger's opinion on the rest of the *Legendarium*.
9   In 'The Footsteps of Ælfwine' (Flieger 2012f) Verlyn Flieger analyses the deep causes (inseparably connected with myth and narration) at the base of the necessity of a "fictional" mediator between the stories narrated in the *Legendarium* and our "real" world. See also Flieger 2005.
10 Technically they can be distinguished as follows: *real author* (the writer in "flesh and blood", e.g. J.R.R. Tolkien), *implicit author* (an ever present structural principle structuring the text), *narrator* (the source of the text transmission, who may not exist or be more or less evident: e.g. Rúmil or Pengolod), *narratee* (the character to whom the text is narrated and who, as the narrator, may exist or not or may be more or less evident: Ælfwine), *implicit reader* (counterpart of the *implicit author*, in other words the supposed audience of the narration) and as last the *real reader* (the reader in "flesh and blood" who actually reads the text). On these themes, also intertwined with the different points of view, see for instance Chatman 1981, 153-66. I'm grateful to Roberto Arduini for having suggested this clarification.

to the different traditions on which the texts had been based. For example, in version D (1951) of 'The Music of the Ainur'[11] (the version closest to the one Christopher decided to publish in 1977), the narration is introduced by the following title:

> *Ainulindalë*
> *The Music of the Ainur*
> *This was written by Rúmil of Tuna*
> *and was told to Ælfwine in Eressëa*
> *(as he records) by Pengolod the Sage*

We can recognize here a series of traditions and handed down versions thousands of years old (Rúmil, Pengolod, Ælfwine), but all this "depth" in time is lost in *The Silmarillion* of 1977 because Christopher omitted the titles. However, he acknowledged this mistake with admirable intellectual honesty and made up for it by publishing, from 1983 to 1996, the twelve volumes of *The History of Middle-earth*, which consist of a great part of the different versions and tales of the *Legendarium* recovered from the miscellaneous notes written by his father from 1917 to 1973. Tolkien used the conceit of the chain of transmission ever since *The Book of Lost Tales*. He would present the tales as having been handed down by narrators, compilers and scribes (in addition to those already mentioned we find Lindo, Daeron and Findegil), which may include characters of our own historical past (the Anglo-Saxon Eriol, who was later replaced by Ælfwine) or Middle-earth halflings (Bilbo, Frodo and Sam), all of them making their own versions which at the end of the chain were translated by Tolkien. At the beginning of the chain we have the remote oral tradition that starts with the whisperings of Manwë to the Elves[12] and ends with J.R.R. Tolkien "the translator" who, at a given moment, abandons the idea of finding a device that could explain their arrival in our primary world.[13] In the 'Prologue' to *The Lord of the Rings*, he narrates how Bilbo Baggins wrote *The Red Book of Westmarch* (that is the origin of *The Hobbit*), which Frodo (and in part Sam) completed with their accounts of the War of the

---

11 *MR* 30.
12 "Hear now things that have not been heard among Men, and the Elves speak seldom of them; yet did Manwë Súlimo, Lord of Elves and Men, whisper them to the fathers of my father in the deeps of time" (*BLT 1* 52); "I have conversed with the Valar who were present at the making of the music ere the being of the World began" (*MR* 318).
13 "in the latest writing there is no trace or suggestion of any 'device' or 'framework' in which it was to be set. I think that in the end he concluded that nothing would serve, and no more would be said beyond an explanation of how (within the imagined world) it came to be recorded" (*BLT 1*, 5).

Ring. Also attached was the *Translations from the Elvish by Bilbo Baggins*, three volumes of stories on the Elder Days (in essence *The Silmarillion*), which Bilbo collected and wrote down or translated during his long stay in Rivendell. However, there is no explanation of how this material was handed down to Tolkien,[14] who "translated" the volume from Westron (the "common language" of Middle-earth) into contemporary English. This long chain of compilations becomes more and more elaborate if we think that each different event is narrated from different points of view. *The Silmarillion*, for instance, is elf-centric,[15] one version of the myth of Númenor is written by men,[16] *The Hobbit* and *The Adventures of Tom Bombadil* by halflings,[17] and *The Lord of the Rings* also by halflings with a certain contribution of Elvish culture.[18]

Flieger's analysis is masterful as usual and her argumentation on the different points of view are undoubtedly essential for a full understanding of the *Legendarium*. Tolkien uses this idea to tell us that truth is never definitively attainable. Still, although only in part, we can "truly" grasp it with our limited intelligence and knowledge. This position has nothing of relativism and is perfectly in line with a thomistic philosophy that admits the plurality of partial truths in opposition to the One Truth. From this perspective, considering that "whatever is received is received in the manner of the receiver"[19] (or each subject innerly perceives reality and acknowledges it according to unique modalities influenced by culture and nature), there are *just as many modalities to acknowledge the same object* as the existing conscious subjects. Therefore, we can only envisage a plurality of truths (or points of view):

> Our knowledge does not measure things, but is measured by them. I say therefore that the first measure of truth is only one [God], but the second measure, or the things, are many, so that there are many truths. Moreover, even if there were only

---

14 This conceit of Tolkien's has been present since the 'Foreword' to the first edition of *The Fellowship of the Ring*.
15 *Letters*, n. 121 and n. 131.
16 See below.
17 *Letters*, n. 131; *ATB*, 'Foreword'.
18 *Letters* n. 131. However, in the *Legendarium* we find other points of view: 'Tal-Elmar', for instance, was written in 1968 and Tolkien describes it as: "a tale that sees the Númenóreans from the point of view of the wild men" (*PME* 422: here the Númenóreans are sketched in quite dark shades). And we must not forget the dialogues between orcs in *The Lord of the Rings* that present their point of view (see below).
19 "Omnis quod recipitur, recipitur ad modum recipientis." This principle is attested in many passages; we mention: in *II Sent.* d.3 q.3 a1; *ibid.* d. 15 q.1 a.2 ad 3; *Contra Gentiles* I, c. 73; *S. Th.* I q 75 a. 5; *S. Th.* I-II q. 67 a. 2; in *II De Anima I.xii* n. 377; *De Pot.* q.7 a 10 ad 10.

one measure of truth [i.e. only one thing], still there would not be only one truth: because truth is not the measure, but the commensuration or adequation: and *with respect to one measure there can be different commensurations in different* [knowers] (Aquinas, *I Sententiarum* ds. 19 q.5 a. 2 ad 2; italics added).

In this respect we can compare the *Legendarium* to the polyphonic novel that, according to Bakhtin,[20] was introduced by Dostoyevsky. The similarity is not surprising if we consider that the author of *The Brothers Karamazov* has (unexpectedly) more than one affinity with adventure tales: the evolution of the characters, the intertwining of events and consciences, the empathy for the humiliated, and the exceptionality of everyday reality are all elements that can be found in both literary worlds.[21] According to Bakhtin, a novel can be defined as polyphonic if you can find:

1. a plurality of characters with consciences (points of view) in opposition to one another;[22]
2. each point of view takes shape as a function of the other's point of view;[23]
3. the author's point of view becomes just one of the different points of view;[24]
4. all points of view are equivalent to one another.[25]

Note that this polyphony is not relativistic,[26] but is an expression of an authentic realism[27] used by Dostoyevsky as a means of exploring the abyss of the human soul as it had never been done before.[28]

---

20 Bakhtin 1984. For an application of Bakhtin's perspective to figurative arts see the masterful essay by Uspenskij 2001, where he shows how the divine and human points of view meet and differentiate themselves in the image of the Lamb painted on the altarpiece.
21 Uspenskij 2001, 133-38.
22 As Dostoyevsky himself says, "My characters are very diverse in the expressions their faces must assume […] Think of each what you will: each says for himself: "The full right is on my side" — you be the judge of these conflicting claims. I do not judge" (Bakhtin 1984, 66).
23 Bakhtin 2002, 99, 235 ff.
24 Bakhtin 2002, 77.
25 Bakhtin 2002, 12.
26 "We see no special need to point out that the polyphonic approach has nothing in common with relativism (or with dogmatism). But it should be noted that both relativism and dogmatism equally exclude all argumentation, all authentic dialogue, by making it either unnecessary (relativism) or impossible (dogmatism). Polyphony as an artistic method lies in an entirely different plane" (Bakhtin 1984, 69).
27 "They call me a *psychologist; this is not true*. I am merely a realist *in the higher sense*, that is, I portray all the *depths of the human soul*" (Bakhtin 1984, 60).
28 Bakhtin 2002, 353.

These insights provide a suitable framework for the understanding of the "polyphony" in Tolkien's work, as can be seen in some recent studies.[29] The subject is extremely vast and deserves further analysis. In this context, however, I would only like to point out some polyphonic moments undoubtedly present in the *Legendarium*, as well as the other, already mentioned points of view of the narration:

- 'The Debate between Finrod and Andreth' ('Athrabeth Finrod ah Andreth') is a perfect example. In this text, similar in structure to a Platonic dialogue, an elvish prince and a human woman (representing the different traditions that come into contact) engage in a debate on death and the destiny that awaits them. Polyphony becomes manifest when (as we will see later) Finrod, taking up (and going beyond) Andreth's point of view, foresees a much wider perspective than that which they had proposed at the beginning of the dialogue.
- Another example of a polyphonic moment in *The History of Middle-earth* is the discussion taking place amongst the Valar on whether it would be just to allow the Elf Finwë to remarry, because his wife Míriel's soul abandoned her body after having giving birth to Fëanor.[30] At the end of this carefully moderated discussion, the Valar grant Finwë permission to remarry even if they are well aware that, in a world affected by evil, what is right does not necessarily exclude pain.[31]
- In *The Lord of the Rings* polyphony is clearly present in 'The Council of Elrond', where more than ten characters speak in turn and, as long as they continue in the discussion, discard their proposals because they acknowledge the observations set forth by the others so that, in the end, the final decision to bring the Ring to Mount Doom and destroy it is taken just because they

---

29 Garbowski 2004, 83 and, 8 (he suggests a similarity between Tolkien and Bakhtin in connection with the unique and tangible value of the word as opposite to the archetypal one, and he quotes Bakhtin's concept of polyphony as suitable for the understanding of Tolkien's points of view); Saxton (2013) demonstrates that the polyphony in Tolkien may be defined as "collaborative" and is not intended as strongly and radically as in Dostoevsky; Simonson (2008, 141) refers to polyphony but fails to elaborate on how it differs from a simple dialogue); Glofcheskie (2008, 134) quotes Bakhtin on different types of dialogue and proposes for Tolkien the idea of "collaborative creativity".
30 *MR* 239-51.
31 On "Justice is not healing" see Rutledge 2012, where she highlights an analogy between the tormented judgment of the Valar and the inadequacy of the Law compared to the concept of Grace maintained by St Paul (see *Gal* 3, 19; *Heb* 7,9).

adopt the point of view of Sauron who would have never expected such an outcome.[32]

Again in *The Lord of the Rings* we find dialogues reporting the point of view of the Free Peoples' enemies. The most interesting among them are the dialogues between the orcs, and in particular:

- Uglúk, an Uruk-hai of Isengard, speaking to the Mordor orcs, reiterates the importance of blind obedience to his orders.[33] In this episode it is just Uglúk's blind obedience that saves Merry and Pippin's lives. However, I think we should evaluate this event against a more complex background and compare it with those episodes where the less strict application of rules is crucial to the positive outcome of the story: Éomer lets Aragon, Legolas and Gimli pass[34] even if this means violating Rohan's rules; the guard Beregond leaves his guard post in order to save Faramir.[35]
- Grishnákh, a Mordor orc from the above episode, describes kindness as vice.[36] The context of this episode is similar to the famous *The Screwtape Letters* by C.S. Lewis, where in the enemy's perspective vices are seen as virtues and vice versa.
- Gorbag, who finds Frodo just after he was stung by Shelob, criticizes the Elves for their habit of leaving their companions in enemy's hands,[37] a false and paradoxical assertion by orcs who, in the same dialogue, recall (while laughing) having left one of their fellows screaming for days in Shelob's den.

However, it is essential to underline that polyphony in Tolkien is always "limited", in the sense that he *never* describes Sauron's point of view (or, before him, Melkor's) as equivalent to the others' (see condition 4 in Bakhtin's analysis). In other words, we never find in the *Legendarium* a character similar to Ivan

---

32 At first Elrond was convinced that the proposal of concealing the Ring was too predictable and therefore proposed to destroy it. However, it is in great part Gandalf who most vigorously affirms that "he [Sauron] is very wise, and weighs all things to a nicety in the scales of his malice. But the only measure that he knows is desire, desire for power; and so he judges all hearts. Into his heart the thought will not enter that any will refuse it, that having the Ring we may seek to destroy it" (*LotR*, FR, 'The Council of Elrond').
33 *LotR*, TT, 'The Uruk-Hai'. Oddly enough, Uglúk is Tom Shippey's favourite character (2003, ix).
34 *LotR*, TT, 'The Uruk-Hai'. See also 3.2.
35 *LotR*, RK, 'The Pyre of Denethor'.
36 *LotR*, TT, 'The Uruk-Hai'.
37 *LotR*, RK, 'The Choices of Master Samwise'.

Karamazov whose nihilistic thoughts seem to get the upper hand over his brother Alexei's religious views. In fact, his deep and lucid argument presents the same atheistic justifications of destruction and dominion which Melkor and Sauron follow.[38] Tolkien, by contrast, always unmasks these tendencies as evil and false and never gives them plausibility.[39] This explains why recent studies are justified in talking about "cooperative polyphony" in Tolkien, meaning that they find a plurality of points of view (of the characters but also of the narrators seen as something apart from the author) that cooperate in the debate in order to widen the perspectives of their conclusions, notwithstanding the fact that Melkor/Sauron's points of view always remain an evil to be avoided.[40]

3.1.2 Diversity and Contradictions

Once it has been established that an absolute point of view is not possible, Flieger can identify the two different perspectives in two possible situations:

A) Different, non-contradicting points of view

In this case the "absolute" truth concerning the human condition is compared to a prism where the different facets are the partial points of view that cannot catch reality in full[41] and therefore "none [of these traditions] has preeminent authority".[42] In this case, an absolutely true point of view *doesn't exist*, but all of them *are partially true* because each one of them is part of a wider and more complex truth.

> Gandhi declared that absolute truth is a diamond which can never be seen whole, but whose facets all show a part. The stories of Beowulf and Oedipus are facets – different stories with culturally differing values – of a larger truth about the human condition. (Flieger 2014, 164)

---

38 Annihilation and dominion are respectively Melkor's and Sauron's desires.
39 On the falseness of the atheism spread by Sauron in Númenor see *MR* 397. In this sense, Russian scientist Kirill Yeskov's *The Last Ringbearer* (Yeskov 2010) is not, in my opinion, Tolkienian in spirit as it narrates the War of the Ring (and its follow-up) from the point of view of Mordor, which is described as the land of science and reason, in opposition to the "magic" fanaticism of Gandalf and the other Free Peoples who are led by a king (Aragorn) who takes possession of the throne in an almost illegal manner (see also Vink 2013).
40 See especially Saxton 2013, 173; Glofcheskie 2008.
41 Flieger 2005, 46-47; Flieger 2012b, 105.
42 Flieger 2014, 165.

This statement also applies to other aspects of biblical theology, which teaches that the sacred scriptures were inspired by God, but that the authors who actually wrote them were doing so from a historically determined point of view,[43] allowing us only glimpses of a partially unveiled greater truth. As a consequence, Flieger reminds us, it shouldn't be a surprise that we find two different narrations of the creation of Man in *Genesis*[44] or that we have four different Gospels reporting, often with differing details, the various events of Jesus' life.[45] The same applies to the *Legendarium*, where for example we find three different renderings of the myth of Númenor:

- 'The Fall of Númenor', expressing the Elvish point of view;
- 'The Drowning of Anadûnê', reporting, at least according to Christopher Tolkien, human legends;
- 'The Akallabêth', included in the published *Silmarillion*, which is a mixture of the first two perspectives[46].

This difference, however, is not problematic in its logic if we consider that the different points of view help to achieve an ever deeper understanding of the multifaceted truth.

B) Contradictory points of view

This is the most difficult category to fit properly. Certainly, if the contradiction refers to versions of a story conceived at different times, then the problem is easily solved by resorting to the simple fact that over time Tolkien modified his own concept of the story. Instances of this kind are quite frequent and numerous among the different versions of the *Legendarium*, including also some characters

---

43 For the Muslims the author of the *Quran* is God himself, and Muhammad only received it. See Campanini (2005, 14): "for the Muslims the Author of the Quran is God, that for sure didn't sit down to write it. For the Muslims it is absolutely unacceptable, a most grave blasphemy, to say that the author of the Quran is the Prophet Muhammad." This radical difference is also present in the idea that according to the *Quran* it is God who teaches Adam all the names (*Quran*, The Sura al-Baqarah, The Heifer, n. 31) whereas in *Genesis* it is Adam who has the power of naming the animals (*Gen.* 2, 20). Worth noting is the great internal debate in Muslim theology on whether the *Quran* was created or not (see Corbin 1989, 118 and 126; d'Ancona 2005, 291).
44 Flieger 2012b, 105.
45 On the synoptic problem see Poppi 1990, 22 ff.
46 Flieger 2014, 166-67.

in *The Lord of the Rings*.⁴⁷ But how can we categorize those contradictions when they recur in the same narration and, most of all, affect the very cornerstones of Tolkien's poetics? According to Flieger, this is exactly what happens in the version of the 'Athrabeth' known to us:⁴⁸ she proposes a reading for this text that differentiates itself from the explicitly Christian reading of Agøy quoted in 1.1.⁴⁹ Flieger stresses that according to Finrod, a scholar of Elvish traditions, death *is* a gift and *is* part of human nature; Andreth reminds the Elf that these ideas had been brought to the Elves by the People of Bëor (the very people she belongs to), but at the same time she tells him that she knows of a cultural tradition of the People of Marach (Men who will later come into contact with the Elves in the West) according to which death is *not* part of human nature and is *not* a gift. Moreover, we have yet another, even more "problematic" contradiction because they continue debating about:

- the fall of Man;
- the reunion of the soul (*fëa*) with the body (*hröa*);
- the future salvation of Arda;
- Eru's intervention in the world to save it.

These topics are reminiscent of the Christian idea of original sin, resurrection of the body, the Apocalypse, and the incarnation of the Son. But this explicit "interference" of the revealed religion, in accordance with Tolkien's razor, would be "fatal" for the myth [see 1.1] because

> if Andreth and Adanel are right, Tolkien's invented godhead, Eru, is wrong, the premise of his invented mythology is undermined and his whole structure is dismantled. (Flieger 2014, 174)

---

47 Concerning Galadriel and Celeborn, Christopher Tolkien affirms that "here are severe inconsistencies 'embedded in the traditions'" (*UT*, 'The History of Galadriel and Celeborn'). But the examples are countless: from Beren who was first conceived of as an Elf, to Strider who was a Hobbit.

48 I'm referring to note 9 (*MR* 343-44) of this work, where Tolkien, using the translator conceit, affirms that there are various versions of the debate of Númenórean tradition: Númenóreans considered themselves descendants of the people of Marach and this explains why Andreth answers reluctantly to the questions posed by Finrod on the death of Man. It is also said that 'The Tale of Adanel' belongs to a Númenórean tradition differring from the one that gave origin to the 'Athrabeth' and that "nothing is hereby asserted concerning its 'truth', historical or otherwise" (*MR* 344).

49 Agøy is explicitly mentioned and criticised in Flieger 2014 (see Flieger 2005, 45-55). The critics' attention towards this text has grown considerably over the last few years. Besides the already mentioned texts by Agøy, see Fornet-Ponse 2005; Wolf 2005; Vink 2008; Wood 2003, 156 ff; Vink 2004; Birzer 2009, 55 ff.

Verlyn Flieger solves this dilemma in a very simple and clear-cut manner: she affirms that Tolkien's second version of the opening of the 'Athrabeth' was a mistake:

> Tolkien was right the first time, in the statement to Walden which begins this essay [see *Letters* n. 131 quoted in 1.1]. His later insertion into the Legendarium of explicit Christianity was an error in judgment. (Flieger 2014, 176)

Although I have the utmost respect for the author, I believe there could still be another reading that would somehow "absolve" Tolkien from this serious mistake.

3.1.3 Critical Analysis of the 'Debate Between Finrod and Andreth'

My own "solution" consists of *denying the presence of explicitly Christian contents* in this text, thus eliminating the contradiction pointed out by Flieger. I have already analysed the theme in a more structured essay and I would like to present in the following the main principles I developed.[50]

First of all I'd like to point out that if we interpret "death" as the separation of body and soul, then Andreth's idea of death seen as not natural is considered erroneous Catholic Theology.[51] For the latter the idea of death as separation between body and soul is in fact so deeply rooted in Man's nature that – as we read in *Genesis* – in order not to die he must eat from the tree of life that temporarily "suspends" this separation which, by its own nature, would have taken place also in Eden.

Likewise, the idea of Man's Fall, where he loses his primary Edenic condition, is not exclusively Christian but, for example, can be found already in Hesiod and in the Egyptian tradition (see 5.2.3).

As for the last three eschatological assertions which we are going to examine (reunion of soul and body, reconstruction of Arda, Eru's intervention in Arda), we should bear in mind that this text had been conceived of as a treatise of

---

50 Testi 2012b.
51 Church *condemned* the propositions affirming that death is not a natural condition of man (Denzinger 1995, n. 2617) and that man's immortality was a natural conditions (ibid. n. 1978). For Saint Thomas Aquinas as well "death of Man is natural" (*S. Th.* II-II q. 164 a. 1 co). For a complete exam of this problem see Testi 2012b, 188.

rational theology (and not of "revealed" theology), very similar to Plato's dialogues, where two sharp intellects exchange their thoughts on the meaning of life and death using the rational instruments available to them. Each brings his own knowledge and traditions into the debate and, by following the thread of their reasoning, Finrod rationally conceives (or at least adumbrates) these truths by means of a series of elaborate *"reductiones ad absurdum"*[52] without resorting to any supernatural elements.

Indeed, Tolkien explains in his Commentary how this dialogue is based on two facts commonly accepted in Arda (1. existence of Elves; 2. existence of the Valar) and on seven "axioms" that Finrod recognizes as true because their acknowledgement derives from nature, experience, reasoning and the angelic revelations bestowed on the Elves:

A existence of Eru;

B existence of two "incarnated" peoples (Men and Elves) whose members are made through the union of *fëa* and *hröa* (soul and body);

C harmony between *fëa* and *hröa* intended as a reciprocal and perpetual union;[53]

D unnaturalness, both for Elves and Men, of the separation of the body from the soul due to the corruption of Arda caused by Melkor;[54]

E Elvish immortality intended as "serial longevity" but limited to the existence of Arda;

F possibility for the Elvish *fëa*, after it has been detached from its body, to go back to an incarnated life thanks to the power of the Valar;

G destiny of human *fëa* not dependent on the destiny of Arda.

In the continuation of the dialogue Andreth introduces new elements of Mannish origin, and these will allow Finrod to rationally argue and "prove" the three truths which, having being proved, are then *not* revealed.

---

52 *Reductiones ad absurdum* are those demonstrations where a thesis is hypothetically affirmed, demonstration is given that from such a hypothesis a contradiction follows, and therefore one is forced to reject the hypothesis that was initially affirmed.

53 "*Hröa* and *fëa* he would say are wholly distinct in kind, and not on the 'same plane of derivation from Eru [...] but were designed each for the other, to abide in perpetual harmony" (*MR*, Commentary 330).

54 "The separation of *fëa* and *hröa* is 'unnatural', and proceeds not from the original design, but from the Marring of Arda, which is due to the operations of Melkor" (*MR*, Commentary 330-31).

Andreth's first theorem: the abandonment of the body implies disharmony

First the wise-woman posits a necessary logical consequence: *if* the body were destined to be abandoned in Arda by *fëa* (hypothesis I) *and* if the human soul were not bound to the history of Arda (axiom G), *then* the consequence would be eternal separation and disharmony (the negation of axiom C):

> For were it "natural" for the body to be abandoned and die [hypothesis I], but "natural" for the *fëa* to live on [axiom G], then there would indeed be disharmony in Man [negation of axiom C]. (*MR* 317)

Therefore, in more formal terms, the negation of C derives from I and G.

Proof for a future reunion of body and soul

Finrod takes up and continues Andreth's conclusion and, in a polyphonic acceptance of her point of view (see 3.1.1), "adopts" her line of reasoning to demonstrate the necessary falseness of the definitive abandonment of the body in Arda (hypothesis I):

> [Finrod:] 'For if your claim is true, then lo! a *fëa* which is here but a traveller [axiom G] is wedded indissolubly to a *hröa* of Arda [axiom C]; to divide them is a grievous hurt [from I and G derives the negation of C], and yet each must fulfil its right nature without tyranny of the other. Then this must surely follow: *the fëa when it departs must take with it the hröa* [negation of hypothesis I]. (*MR* 317-18, italics added)

In other words: G and I imply the nullification of C, as said by Andreth from her point of view. But Finrod affirms that, since C is an axiom, it is *true*; therefore, in order to avoid this illogicality, hypothesis I must by necessity be false (G cannot be false since it is also an axiom): that is *the soul cannot abandon the body in eternity*. If things being so, this reunion of soul and body must somehow occur in a given future and cannot take place in the Arda that we know (hence *fëa* is not tied to *hröa*, axiom G):

And what can this mean unless it be that the *fëa* shall have the power to uplift the *hröa*, as its eternal spouse and companion, into an endurance everlasting beyond Eä, and beyond Time? (*MR* 317-18, italics added)[55]

Argument in favour of the future salvation of Arda

In order that this reunion may take place, it is necessary that the "matter" of Arda (of which the body is made) is saved in times to come and in eternity from the corruption that afflicts it:

> Thus would Arda, or part thereof, be healed not only of the taint of Melkor, but released even from the limits that were set for it in the "Vision of Eru" of which the Valar speak. (*MR* 318)[56]

Argument in favour of Eru's intervention

Such a salvation of the world can only be Eru's prerogative, as Finrod himself realizes when he understands that Ilúvatar's design has not been completely revealed to the Valar:

> For that Arda Healed shall not be Arda Unmarred, but a third thing and a greater, and yet the same. I have conversed with the Valar who were present at the making of the Music ere the being of the World began. And now I wonder: Did they hear the end of the Music? Was there not something in or beyond the final chords of Eru which, being overwhelmed thereby, they did not perceive? Or again, since Eru is for ever free, maybe he made no Music and showed no Vision beyond a certain point. Beyond that point we cannot see or know, until by our own roads we come there, Valar or Eldar or Men. (*MR* 318)

Andreth confirms[57] that there is a tradition that really speaks of this Old Hope, differing both from *amdir* (the expectation of an uncertain boon based

---

55 Finrod also gathers that, given the impossibility for *fëa* to abandon *hröa*, Man, still without sin according to Eru's original plan, should have been taken up into heaven before soul and body separated. In other words, "the 'assumption' was the natural end of each human life, though as far as we know it has been the end of only 'unfallen' member of Mankind" (*MR*, Commentary 333). Here Tolkien refers to the Virgin (*MR* 357, note 6). See his letter from 1958 where he affirms that the "Assumption of Mary, the only *unfallen* person, may be regarded as in some ways a simple regaining of unfallen grace and liberty" (*Letters* n. 212).
56 Note that in the draft of 'Athrabeth', Arda Reconstructed was conceived first of all as a legend of Men and not as a "deduction" of Finrod's (*MR*, Athrabeth 353).
57 *MR* 320.

on something certain) and *estel* (a faith not based on experience but from the inner nature of the subject).[58]

Conclusion: rational theology, but no explicit Christianity

To conclude, unlike Flieger, I think that 'The Debate between Finrod and Andreth' does not contain essentially Christian elements which would be fatal for the myth and would contradict Tolkien's razor. In my opinion, Tolkien pushes to the limit the cognitive power of fantasy sub-creation in order to demonstrate how some philosophical truths could be deduced, also within a secondary world, exclusively on the basis of the culture and knowledge of the sub-created world itself. The eschatological "truths" contained in the 'Debate' are not the result of revealed truths, but Finrod reaches his "conclusions" with the help of Andreth's contribution and through a demanding and complex reasoning, after which he succeeds in seeing beyond the Music of the Ainur.

3.2 Dialectics and the *Legendarium*

The view of the intrinsically contradictory nature of Tolkien's work is shared in Italy by the renowned Wu Ming 4, though his arguments differ from Flieger's. Wu Ming 4 emphasizes the differences between the Tolkienian world and the Christian universe and considers them to be veritable inconsistencies, with the aim of averting (not without reason) an "allegorizing" Catholic reading of Tolkien's works:

> On the contrary, the subtle *incoherence* of the big picture, the collision between Christian and other elements of inspiration, is what renders the applicability of Tolkien's work inexhaustible. Without this collision, his tales would otherwise risk being reduced to a mere translation of the message found in the Gospels – resembling the moral allegory which Tolkien so forcefully rejected. (Wu Ming 4 2014, 94-95, italics added)

---

58 *MR* 321-22.

In support of his thesis, Wu Ming 4 quotes Shippey's authoritative opinions on the problem of evil and the absence of a final eschatological salvation in Tolkien's universe:[59]

> Tom Shippey has reflected at length on these "*inconsistencies*" and on the subtle shifts made with regard to Christian narrative. For example, when he observes in the pages of *The Lord of the Rings* a relatively ambiguous conception of evil, oscillating between an orthodox Boethian and a heretical Manichaean point of view: "Tolkien sets up a running ambivalence throughout the whole of *The Lord of the Rings*, which acts as an answer at once orthodox and questioning to the whole problem of the existence and source of evil in a universe created [...] by a benevolent God."[60] Or, when he analyses the internal eschatology of Tolkien's sub-creation, coming to the conclusion that "*The Lord of the Rings*, then, contains within it hints of the Christian message, but refuses just to repeat it. The myths of Middle-earth furthermore determinedly reject any sense of ultimate salvation."[61] (Wu Ming 4, 93, italics added)

We can direct at least two objections to this passage: one of a critical nature, the other one philosophical.

1) *From a critical point of view* we can observe that Wu Ming 4 quotes Tom Shippey's authority but without analysing his thesis in detail. On the other side, Shippey has chosen an hermeneutic approach revolving around the idea of "virtuous pagans" that, as we will see, is closer to the synthesis I will propose later [4]. If we examine these two classical themes that highlight a certain ambivalence in the *Legendarium*, we observe (in disagreement with Shippey and indirectly with Wu Ming 4) that:

As for the problem of evil, it is affirmed that, against the Boethian thesis of evil as *privatio boni*,

> [t]here is an alternative tradition in Western thought, one which has never become 'official' but which nevertheless arises spontaneously from experience. This says that while it may be all very well to make philosophical statements about evil, *evil nevertheless is real*, and not merely an absence; and what's more it can be resisted, and what's more still, not resisting it (in the belief that one day Omnipotence will cure all ills) is a dereliction of duty. The danger of this opinion is that it tends towards Manichaeanism, the heresy which says that Good and Evil are equal and opposite and the universe is a battlefield. (Shippey 2005, 160, italics added)

---

59 *MR* 321-22.
60 Shippey 2000b, 130.
61 Shippey 2000b, 210.

Shippey, and Wu Ming 4 as a consequence, consider these two visions as incompatible but present in Tolkien;[62] however, what seems to escape them is that in reality even evil as *privatio boni* does not exclude the actual and concrete existence of evil things and (most of all) of evil persons which must be fought because of their nature. It will suffice to mention Satan, the "Prince of the World",[63] who is such a real entity that he even challenges Jesus Christ with various temptations and demonic possessions.[64]

As for the absence of an eternal salvation, in view of *The Lord of the Rings* there is nothing to object to, but this (and here lies in my opinion Wu Ming 4's mistake) does not imply being in contradiction to the Christian perspective. Undoubtedly, we do not have a salvific perspective similar to Paradise, but it is just as much true that, both in *The Lord of the Rings* and in other parts of the *Legendarium*, we find hints of an afterlife. In other words, an absence is not necessarily a contradiction, but it can be seen as a partial perspective that will be harmonically complemented by a broader vision.

---

62 Shippey 2000b, 167; Shippey 2005, 166 ff.
63 *John* 12:31.
64 The extremely profound analysis given by Shippey deserves a far more detailed discussion. Firstly, he disputes the classical concept of evil as *privatio boni* and proposes another, not well identified tradition that considers the suppression of evil a duty and affirms that this concept *tends* towards Manichaeism but is *not* Manichaean, which a superficial reading of Shippey's text may lead one to infer. In fact, as Shippey shows in the above quoted passage, he is well aware that Manichaeism conceives Good and Evil as dualistically originated co-principles, whereas Tolkien is absolutely clear in affirming that Evil appears only after the creation of the Ainur and Melkor by Eru. In his analysis, however, Shippey rigidly associates the Augustinian-Boethian conception with the theory of evil being innate in the subjects who make "evil" choices, and associates the other conception to an evil that resides in the object thus implying the "existence" of evil objects. So depending on the view one adopts, Shippey affirms that the Ring is in the first case an amplifier of the moral limitations of the subjects, in the other case it is itself a sentient entity with powers of its own (Shippey 2005, 160 ff.). Now, what he doesn't seem to fathom is that there could be other subjects who freely choose darkness instead of light and at the same time tend to corrupt other realities; evil subjects who are, moreover, truly "real" and "objective" (for example Satan or definitely wicked people such as Hitler or Stalin). Therefore, also the Boethian conception also explains the wickedness of the Ring (that reverberates Sauron's evil will). Sure, the Ring and his owner (and the same Satan) are ontologically "good" because of their very existence, but just because of that corrupting nature they lack moral virtues and, for this reason, must be fought and destroyed. In a private exchange of views with Shippey, I asked him if the "unorthodox" Christian tradition he refers to is somehow similar to the idea of *malicidium* theorized by Bernard of Clairvaux (Bernard of Clairvaux, *De Laude novae militiae ad milites Templi liber*, 90-91) to "justify" the actions of the Knights Templar: he answered that "this alternative tradition was one which arose from experience, and that seems to me to be exactly relevant to Bernard's concept of 'malicidium'. There is such a thing as evil; it is our duty to fight it; fighting it (under proper conditions) is not sinful *per se*" (e-mail of October 24th, 2013). For a critical review on Shippey, see Houghton and Keese 2005, 131-59; Wood 2007, 85-102.

2) If we examine now the *philosophical* objection, we observe that the whole structure of Wu Ming 4's thesis has a dialectic matrix that the author openly admits, as is well shown in his answer to an email I sent him:

> I'm convinced that my reading is equal and opposite to your own. Just as you do, I think that paganism and Christianity in Tolkien's work do coexist. You see them in harmony, unified by his Catholic theological vision. I, instead, perceive them as dialectic (because, as you point out, I have a marxist background). Where you see unity, I see multiplicity. But the truth is that our two visions are different from the long-standing *querelle* between "paganizing" and "professing" Tolkienian scholars, or, we can say, go beyond it and redirect the debate to another plane and, I dare say, to a higher level. (Wu Ming 4, email of July 6th 2013)

We also find the same dialectic structure in the excellent volume *Difendere la Terra di Mezzo*,[65] where the author gives us a very well documented study of J.R.R. Tolkien's work and, at the same time, succeeds in successfully "releasing" it from certain ideologically biased readings such as the symbolic-traditional one.[66] I will not spend any more time on this debate (which I, for that matter, endorse), but I will put forward some examples of that very same dialectic approach of Wu Ming 4 which lets contradictory elements in Tolkien's work come to the surface. Namely:

- In the chapter 'Nascita e destino di un fenomeno letterario' ('Birth and destiny of a literary phenomenon')[67] he gives an outline of how *The Lord of the Rings* has been received since its publication, with a special focus on the positive relationships Tolkien entertained with left-wing intellectuals both on a personal level (for example Naomi Mitchison) and in terms of literary sources (Simone de Beauvoir). The impression created by this account is almost as if Tolkien's conservative faith went along with elements of the opposite direction (see *infra*) and that his work should mainly be interpreted as "a *dialectic* reaction to the innovation and literary experimentalism of the historical avant-garde of the twentieth century."[68]
- The accurate analysis of the relationship between "Hobbits and habitat"[69] ends with the statement that "not even in the bucolic Shire is it possible to

---
65 Wu Ming 4 2013.
66 Wu Ming 4 2013, 103 ff. See 2.4.
67 Wu Ming 4 2013, 15 ff.
68 Wu Ming 4 2013, 42, italics added.
69 Wu Ming 4 2013, 131 ff.

escape the *contradiction* between civilization and culture [...] In other words, we could say that Hobbits are an interlude; a *contradiction* between progress and development."[70] Once again, it is one thing to highlight a tension between civilization and nature, and another to consider it contradictory or, in other words, impossible to be re-harmonized into a unitary and well-balanced framework, as is the way of life in the Shire even with all its limitations.

Before formulating my philosophical remark, it is important to define what "contradiction" exactly means:

A   a *contradiction* is a phrase that affirms and denies the same predicate for the same subject:

"A is B *and* A is not B"

These two situations can never occur simultaneously; if one is true, the other is false, and if one is false the other is true.

B   I will call *opposition* (and not *contradiction*[71]) a phrase that indicates opposite tendencies within the same subject, as for instance:

"A tends to B *and* A tends to non-B"

These two situations may also take place simultaneously in the same subject "A", with the result of internal tensions and contradictions. In this respect the character of Frodo is a very fitting example because he experiences opposing tendencies (for instance, it is true that "Frodo tends to put on the Ring *and* Frodo tends *not* to put on the Ring", and all this at the same time) but it is also true that it is not possible that "Frodo has the Ring on *and* Frodo doesn't have the Ring on" (this being a contradiction). Similarly, the relationship between civilization and nature is one of opposition, not contradiction, which is just to demonstrate that Wu Ming 4 does not adequately distinguish the two concepts.

---

70 Wu Ming 4 2013, 165, italics added.
71 This difference between contradiction and opposition (or "real-opposition") is masterfully examined by Immanuel Kant in his 'Attempt to Introduce the Concept of Negative Magnitudes into Philosophy'. For an analysis and a complete bibliography see also Berto 2005, 88 ff.

Finally, about the relationship between Tolkien's Catholic faith and the pagan culture he was so much engrossed in, Wu Ming 4 affirms:

> [Tolkien] nurtured an authentic faith, that he didn't live out of inertia or love for a quiet life, but at times problematically, putting it in relationship, or sometimes in *contradiction*, with the Norse paganism that had given origin to the myths and masterpieces he cherished so much, and bringing with himself the doubts and shadows of a soul more tormented than it showed on the outside.[72]

I don't intend to give a "definitive" critique of this dialectic reading. It is a well known fact that when we touch the ultimate foundation "of the essential thought, each confutation is senseless";[73] I can only recommend to those who advocate for a "contradictory" Tolkien to maintain a well defined distinction between contradiction and opposition (see *supra*). What in my opinion is a real limitation of such an approach is that although it wants to recognise contradictory elements in Tolkien's work (sometimes even when they just don't exist[74]), it is, as a rule, not able to enclose the whole body of Tolkien's work in a unitary framework, as Wu Ming 4 himself admits in the above mentioned email where

---

72 Wu Ming 4 2013, 77 italics added.
73 Heidegger 1987, 289.
74 We can see this, for example, in his notable analysis 'Un dialogo nel Riddermark' ('A dialogue in the Riddermark'). Here Éomer asks Aragorn a decisive question ("How shall a man judge what to do in such times?" *LotR*, TT, 'The Riders of Rohan') and gets the following answer: "Good and ill have not changed since yesteryear; nor are they one thing among Elves and Dwarves and another among Men. It is a man's part to discern them, as much in the Golden Wood as in his own house" (*ibid.*). In this chapter he underlines the opposition between ethical conscience and law intended as obedience to orders (Wu Ming 4 2013, 200), seeing in it a difference with the doctrine of natural law (Wu Ming 4 2013, 198). But if the natural law is intended as Thomas Aquinas conceived it, then it will never oppose itself to, but will actually presuppose the conscience of individuals in their choices; which means that it has the difficult task of adapting most general principles to individual situations (*Summa Theologica* I.79.13) so that, in a given circumstance, the right thing to do is sometimes a "violation" of a principle that could have so far seemed universally cogent. Thomas Aquinas affirms that it "is therefore evident that, as regards the general principles whether of speculative or of practical reason, truth or rectitude is the same for all, and is equally known by all [see Aragorn's words to Éomer about good and ill]. As to the proper conclusions of the speculative reason, the truth is the same for all, but is not equally known to all: thus it is true for all that the three angles of a triangle are together equal to two right angles, although it is not known to all. But as to the proper conclusions of the practical reason, neither is the truth or rectitude the same for all, nor, where it is the same, is it equally known by all. Thus it is right and true for all to act according to reason: and from this principle it follows as a proper conclusion, that goods entrusted to another should be restored to their owner. Now this is true for the majority of cases [as in most of cases obedience is indispensable, as Éomer well knows]: but it may happen in a particular case that it would be injurious, and therefore unreasonable, to restore goods held in trust; for instance, if they are claimed for the purpose of fighting against one's country [as in Éomer's peculiar and problematic case that brings his conscience, based on the universal notion of Good, to choose to let Aragorn, Gimli and Legolas go]. And this principle will be found to fail the more, according as we descend further into detail" (*Summa Theologica* I - II. 94.4).

he says he is more interested in multiplicity rather than unity. If we substitute dialectics with a structure that analogically distinguishes different levels and can reunite them in a unitary conception, however, then we will be able to fully grasp the greatness of the vision Tolkien follows in his mythopoeia where (unlike what Wu Ming 4 affirms[75]) the terms "pagan" and "Christian" are never conceived of as contradictory. Only if we acknowledge this will it be possible to understand how the fully pagan horizon of the *Legendarium* is in complete harmony with the supernatural level of Christian revelation.

---

75 See quoted email.

Part Two

The Synthetic Approach

Chapter Four

Synthesis: Tolkien's Work is Pagan and in Harmony with Christianity

4.1 Principles

Based on the analysis so far conducted, it seems we are faced with a problem that has no satisfactory solutions. Neither the Christian analysis nor its pagan antithesis nor the simultaneous co-existence of both do, in fact, succeed in explaining the complexity of Tolkien's work because they all result in a "reductionist" or contradictory reading of it. However, it is undeniable that the three points of view do all point to elements that are somehow based on Tolkienian texts, as in fact it would be impossible to understand the *Legendarium* without acknowledging both its pagan roots and its relation with the Christian revelation.

The question is whether there could exist a deeper and unitary perspective that might "fit" these tensions between paganism and Christianity into a coherent framework and, at the same time, develop a critical analysis of Tolkien's work that could include all these elements and discard none. This is, in my opinion, possible. The approach I propose, which I think could provide the key to solve the "Tolkienian problem" [Introduction] is based on a "logic" that rigorously distinguishes between two points of view in examining Tolkien's Secondary World and two conceptual levels in defining the structural framework of the *Legendarium*.

The two points of view are:

    a' an *internal* one, examining the supporting structure that encloses the stories and the challenges the various characters have to face in the sub-created world;

    b' an *external* one, which by means of a metanarrative analysis compares the work to the historical cultural development of our "real" world.

The two levels are:

> *a"* *Level of Nature:*[1] that is when actions, knowledge and the achievements of rational beings are attained thanks exclusively to their innate capacities and abilities (reason, will, language, art, etc.);
>
> *b"* *Level of Grace*: that is a supernatural level where Man receives some "gifts" (e.g. faith) or certain revealed truths (e.g. the One and Triune God, the incarnation and resurrection of Christ, the Final Judgement) that would be impossible to obtain solely with his natural abilities [cf. 6.1].

4.2 Definition and Use of the Term "Pagan"

The term pagan derives from the Latin *pagus* (village). Therefore, *pagan* literally means *villager*. The corresponding term in the Jewish culture is *gojim* (plural of *goj*) and it was used to designate those peoples who did not know the true God (*Jeremiah* 10:25; *Psalms* 78[79]:6), but also, in a more positive sense, to indicate the whole of humanity that respects the "cosmic" alliance between God and Noah (testified by the rainbow appearing after the deluge: *Genesis* 9:8). In the Gospels the term is used in a negative sense (*Mt* 5:47; 6:7; 6:31), although St Paul admits the possibility for pagans to have access to the knowledge of God (*Rm* 1:19-23; 2:14; cf. 6.1) to such an extent that in *The Acts of the Apostles* the hint is given that also non-Christian religions are included in God's salvific design (*Ac.* 14:16). The Latin term used in liturgy for this concept is *gens* (or *natio*). Later in the Christian world the term *paganus* was assigned to the followers of those cults which were traditionally practised among country folks. The term

---

[1] To talk about "nature" today is very problematic for a variety of reasons it would be impossible to analyse here. In this essay I use the term "nature" *to indicate all abilities and attitudes inherent in different entities*, be they material, vegetal, animal or human. This is the Aristotelian acceptation of the concept (Aristotle, *Physics*, Book II, c. 1 n. 192b 20), classifying as "natural", for instance, the physical-chemical properties of material objects, the growing process of vegetables, the perceptive capacity of animals and the abilities of men inherent in their intellectual faculties (knowing, choosing, producing and so on). This concept of nature *does not identify itself with the environment* (as it is the case in most of contemporary culture) and *is not in contrast with Man* (juxtaposition nature vs. culture) if we consider that some human aspects are natural. Instead, it distinguishes itself on the level of Grace: if a given entity performs activities that in some way "transcend" *its natural abilities*, we have to admit by consequence that these actions are performed thanks to something supernatural. To distinguish then what is natural from what is not (anything but predictable and banal) is not in the scope of this essay. On the concept of nature, see Abbagnano 1987, 'Nature' 605-608; Jonas 1991; Mondin 1991 'Nature' and 'Grace' (301-303).

was never used to indicate the Jews,² while it was used for the Muslims at least until the 16th century,³ although already in the 13th century Thomas Aquinas did not consider the Muslims as "pagan".⁴

In modern times, the term is generally used to indicate the followers of old, pre-Christian religions, which it would be better to define as "neo-pagan".

The English language has two terms to indicate pagans:

- *pagan*, of Latin origin [cf. *supra*]: according to the *Oxford English Dictionary* it is used as a synonym of *heathen* [cf. *infra*] and "non-Christian" or also to indicate the followers of a pantheistic cult of nature;

- *heathen*, an Anglo-Saxon name of Gothic origin defining in its etymology the inhabitants of open country or foreigners,⁵ mostly used, however, after the introduction of Christianity. In this respect, and according to the first meaning given in the *Oxford English Dictionary*, it is "applied to person or races whose religion is neither Christian, Jewish or Muslim". We can also find it used for Muslims, but it is mainly used for the followers of polytheism.

Tolkien uses these two terms as synonyms. In fact:

- in the essay 'Beowulf: the Monsters and the Critics' (*BMC*) the term *pagan* (and its derivatives) occurs 27 times and the term *heathen* 24 times, with synonymy particularly evident on pages 7-8 ("heathen heroic lay [...] pagan lays"), 36 ("pagan 'belief' [...] heathen practice and belief"), 38 ("pagan past [...] heathen past"), and 42 ("a certain part of pagan Danes – heathen priests");

- in *The Lord of the Rings* the term *heathen* is used twice, first by Denethor and then by Gandalf (we will discuss these uses in detail in 5.2.2 and 5.2.5);

- in *The History of Middle-earth*, *heathen* is used twice within the Tolkienian mythology, to indicate the etymon of Dunharrow⁶ and to designate the tem-

---

2 Tworuschka 1998, 517.
3 Tworuschka 1998, 517-518; Maurier 2000, 1569-1572.
4 Aquinas, *Summa Contra Gentiles*, Book I, ch. 2, n. 4; ID. *De Rationibus Fidei*, c. 7.
5 Cf. Holmes 2011, 122.
6 *WR* 267, the term is cited in 'Guide to the Names in *The Lord of the Rings*'.

ples of Númenor after Sauron's arrival,[7] whereas *pagan* is used in some notes refers to the Ainur as "pagan" gods[8] and Ælfwine as a "pagan Englishman".[9]

As for myself, I will apply the term *pagan* to "all those who are not included in the alliance of Abraham with Jesus",[10] in other words to *all those who are not Jews, Christians (schismatics or heretics as they might be) or Muslims (of all ages and confessions)* who believe, although with a different "degree", in the biblical revelation. From this perspective, since "the natural state of Man is paganism [...]. Man is pagan by nature",[11] all cultural and religious contents of the so-called "natural" or "cosmic" religion, which are accessible to men without the need of explicit supernatural revelations, are to be considered as *pagan*.[12] This explains why I will use the term *pagan as a synonym of "natural", "non-supernatural and non-Christian"* (since the Christian message includes both Old and New Testament) in order to define all the capacities, truths and values that are accessible to Man *naturaliter sumptum* (in other words, without biblical revelation or supernatural help).

Does it make sense to apply this term to a literary work? I think yes, at least when we are faced with the sub-creation of a world (more or less detailed and coherent) in which you can find cosmogonic [5.2.1], ethical-religious [5.2.2-5.2.3] or philosophical [5.4-5.5] contents regardless of the historical period it refers to (pre-Christian or not).

As for the relationship between the author and his sub-created world, we can distinguish four main possibilities:

1. a Christian author who sub-creates a world with Christian elements in harmony with the revelation: see C.S. Lewis and his *The Chronicles of Narnia* series and his science fiction trilogy;[13]

---

7   *SD* 258, 384 in the unpublished story "The Notion Club Papers".
8   In *BLT 1* 249 it is used three times.
9   *BLT 2* 322.
10 Danielou 1988, 14.
11 Danielou 1995, 9.
12 Danielou 1995, 15 ff.
13 Flieger 2012e, 224.

2. a non-Christian author who sub-creates a pagan/natural world (that is without supernatural elements) *not* in harmony with the revelation: this is exemplified in the trilogy *His Dark Materials* by Philip Pullman;[14]
3. a non-Christian author who sub-creates a pagan/natural world in harmony with the revelation: this is the case of George Lucas and his *Star Wars* films or Gene Rodenberry and *Star Trek*;
4. a Christian author who sub-creates a pagan/natural world in harmony with the revelation: this is the case of Tolkien, as we will see in the following section.

4.3 Enunciation of the Proposed Synthesis

If we bear in mind the distinctions and definitions I described above and we apply them to the Tolkienian world we can say:

- if we consider his work from the *internal structural point of view*, it follows that the story is conceived on a *natural level*, meaning that the knowledge, choices and works that typify its characters are the result of their natural capabilities without any explicit reference to the contents of supernatural Faith. It is for this reason that we have to say that *we are in the presence of a work without essentially Christian elements, and therefore pagan, where God is "immensely remote"* (*Letters* n. 168);
- however, if we consider the work from an *external point of view* and confront it with the development of Western culture, we have to say that, even in its dissimilarities, its contents are *in harmony with the supernatural level of the Christian revelation*. Paganism in the *Legendarium*, in fact, is a particular kind of paganism, very different from historical paganism or from the paganism of other fantasy works (Pullman, Howard) so much that it becomes compatible with the contents of the Gospels;
- to conclude, it is *because of the presence of both these elements* (pagan work because it is set on a natural level *and* in harmony with Christianity) *that we can consider Tolkien's work as a manifestation of a fundamentally Catholic culture*.

The synthesis I propose here can be summed up in three propositions:

---

14 Cf. Gray 2010; Wrigley 2005.

1. Tolkien's world manifests an essentially natural level and is therefore pagan because of the absence of specifically Christian elements;
2. however, from the external point of view, it is in harmony with the supernatural level of the Christian revelation;
3. for both these aspects, Tolkien's work is an expression of an authentically Catholic way of thinking.

This perspective takes its inspiration from those authors whose intuitions, although not systematically developed, seem somehow to be heading in this direction, among whom I would like to mention in particular Tom Shippey and John Holmes.[15] At the very base of Shippey's interpretative approach we find, among others, the thesis that Tolkien's aim as narrator is that of portraying the most positive characters as "virtuous pagans", namely non-Christians who, because of their human virtues, are not an antithesis to the universe of values represented in the biblical revelation,[16] a thesis that is also present in the Catholic theology [cf. 6]. According to Shippey, we also find the same approach in Tolkien the philologist, who had always considered the old Anglo-Saxon poems, written in the Christian era but still imbued with pagan culture, in great harmony with contents specifically pertaining to Christianity.[17] Along the same line we find Holmes, who underlines Tolkien's clear intent to assimilate the more positive aspects of pagan culture harmoniously within a Christian perspective, an intention that is typical of a truly Catholic culture.[18]

The two authors, however, base their analyses on the concept of *praeparatio evangelii*,[19] an idea that is implicitly hinted at in many other authors.[20] In this perspective, the more positive events in the *Legendarium* are considered as a sort of prefiguration of the Christian revelation to come, although this vision entails the limitation of enclosing the Tolkienian universe in a rigid "chronological" framework that is not suitable to explain the anachronistic presence

---

15 In certain passages Kocher, too, seems to get closer to this perspective: Kocher 1977. Other texts that I found valuable in this context are: Manni 2006; Garbowski 2004. See also Mitchell 2013 and Carruthers 2016 (published after Testi 2013).
16 Shippey 2005, 222 ff.; Shippey 2000.
17 See also references to Shippey's work in sections 5.1.3-5.1.4: Shippey 2007b-c-d-e-h.
18 Holmes 2011, 123.
19 Shippey 2005, 222; Holmes 2011, 124.
20 See, as example: Birzer 2009, xxiii ff.; Burns 2004, 163-178; Candler 2008, 137-168; Dickerson 2003, 76.

in the *Legendarium* of many utterly modern elements (Saruman's technically oriented mind, middle-class narrow-mindedness portrayed in the Hobbit Society, the use of certain modern words, etc.).[21] Instead, what is really pivotal in the analysis I propose here is the idea that Tolkienian mythology does not so much narrate a pre-Christian era as that it expresses (with its simultaneous presence of historically different perspectives) a "natural level", to serve as a backdrop for the representation of the problems of Man as such, whether these problems are related to a pre-Christian, Christian or post-Christian era.[22]

---

21 On the presence of typically modern elements and themes in Tolkienian mythology, see: Chance and Siewers 2005; Honegger and Weinreich 2006; Garbowski 2004, 121 ff.; Kraus 2004; Kreeft 2005, 222; Petty 2002; Wood 2010; Patchen 2005, and Curry 2014. On modernity in Tolkien as a writer, Verlyn Flieger maintains that he is essentially a post-modern writer (Flieger 2009), Purtill shows how Tolkien was perfectly aware of the post-modern context where the use of myth was embedded (Purtill 2003, 7 ff.), and Nagy gives an insightful explanation of how Tolkien uses ancient myths in order to outline contemporary themes (Nagy 2005) in analogy with Plato (Nagy 2004).
22 On the simultaneous presence of different historical periods in *The Lord of the Rings* see Manni 2009.

Chapter Five

Paganism in Tolkien's World and Its Harmony with Christianity

In this section I wish to demonstrate the first two expositions of the synthesis, namely that Tolkien's work is pagan in its core (1) and in harmony with Christianity (2). These two aspects can be drawn from two different kinds of sources:

- statements on the poetic and hermeneutic principles which Tolkien "applies" to his literary criticism or to his philological studies;
- actual application and implementation of these principles in the sub-creation of the *Legendarium*, from the cosmogony described in the 'Music of the Ainur' up to the Third and Fourth Age when *The Lord of the Rings* takes place.

5.1 Poetic and Hermeneutic Principles

5.1.1 *On Fairy-Stories*

Natural level and internal point of view in fantasy sub-creation

'On Fairy-stories' (lecture delivered 1939, text published in 1947) is a fundamental text for the understanding of Tolkien's work. Somehow he always considered this text to be "definitive"[1] to such an extent that he wrote *The Lord of the Rings* to give a tangible demonstration of the views expressed in it.[2] However, despite the title, it is not at all easy to define this essay, given the fact that it goes far beyond the world of fairy-stories. In accordance with Tolkien's distinct way of writing, it makes the eye extend its view from the very details of the trunk of a tree to its branches, leaves and up to much wider dimensions that are only apparently very distant from the initial perspective (such as the origin of myth

---

1 *Letters* n. 250 of 1959.
2 *Letters* n. 234 of 1961.

and language, the connection between Man, Nature and Death, the relationship between fantasy narrative and the Christian revelation). The recent "extended" edition of 'On Fairy-stories', in addition to the previous editions, also attaches the copious bibliography consulted by Tolkien when he was writing the essay (more than 130 texts), which by itself should testify to the depth of perspective that gave origin to the lecture and the text that followed.

As for the theme we are dealing with now, we should note that the essay develops mostly on an essentially "lay" and "non-confessional" level, given that no traces of explicit references to the Christian revelation are present in it with the sole exception of the crucial Epilogue where the fundamental connection between myth and Gospels is outlined.

In fact, Tolkien unmistakably denies that the wish for fairy-stories be necessarily connected to the world and tastes of children;[3] therefore, its origin does not derive from a specific historical phase in the development of mankind, being on the contrary *connatural to human nature* and as such having no age. In Tolkien's opinion, fairy-stories are a *"natural human taste"*[4] that responds to *"primordial human desires"*,[5] including the desire to "survey the depths of space and time",[6] "hold communion with other living things"[7] and "converse with other living things".[8] For this reason, fairies themselves (as well as all the other inhabitants of Faërie, the world of fairy-stories) are considered wholly *"natural"*[9] beings. Likewise, magic in fairy-stories shouldn't be confused with miracles, where the power "comes from outside the world, and is 'supernatural'".[10]

Consistent with the above mentioned statements, Tolkien thinks that fantasy (the human capability of creating fairy-stories) is natural to men and can positively cooperate with Reason:

> Fantasy is *a natural human activity*. It certainly does not destroy or even insult Reason; and it does not either blunt the appetite for, nor obscure the perception

---

3 *TOFS* 49 ff.
4 *TOFS* 56, italics added.
5 *TOFS* 34.
6 *TOFS* 35.
7 *TOFS* 35.
8 *TOFS* 73.
9 *TOFS* 28, italics added.
10 *TOFS*, Manuscript B, 253; see 258-259.

of, scientific verity.[11] On the contrary. The keener and the clearer is the reason, the better fantasy will it make. (*TOFS* 65, italics added)

Fantasy remains a *human right*. (*TOFS* 66, italics added)

In this respect, we could say that Fantasy is to Narrative what Reason is to Science and Philosophy; in other words, Fantasy is the creative power that originates (or, to say it better, sub-creates) myths and secondary worlds (that is the name given by Tolkien to distinguish them from the "primary" world), "giving to ideal creations the inner consistency of reality".[12] In fact, the *proprium* of Fantasy (that must be distinguished from Imagination, the "common" capability of portraying images of non-present objects[13]) is to succeed in sub-creating a secondary world where, for example, a "green sun" may seem credible,[14] that is a universe endowed with its own truth (although secondary if compared with ours) so much so that it will be possible to say:

If you have built your little world well, yes: it is true in that world. (*TOFS* 77)

Therefore the reader, as long as he adopts a point of view internal to the sub-creation, will have the Secondary Belief of "moving around" within an inner world that has its own reality and truth. Tolkien carefully differentiates such Secondary Belief both from credulity (believing a fairy-story could also be true in our primary world) and from the voluntary suspension of disbelief (a subterfuge carried out in the intent to pretend that something is true[15]):

What really happens is that the story-maker proves a successful "sub-creator." He makes a Secondary World which your mind can enter. Inside it, what he relates is "true": it accords with the laws of that world. You therefore believe it, while you are, as it were, inside. (*TOFS* 52)

---

11 It is not by chance that Tolkien is greatly appreciated among the scientific community, so much so that many of the names given to some new scientific discoveries are Tolkien-inspired (cf. Larsen 2007, 223-34). Henry Gee, editor of the magazine *Nature* and Tolkien expert, has even devoted a volume to demonstrate (not without a certain humour) the scientific plausibility of a few "fantastic" ideas of Tolkien's (for instance, the reproduction of the Ents, the fire of the dragons and so on) (Gee 2004).
12 *TOFS* 59.
13 *TOFS* 59. Emphasis has also been given to the fact that Tolkien has somehow overturned the romantic tradition set forth by Coleridge, who considered "imagination" as superior to "fancy". See Seaman 2000; Milburn 2010; Helms 1974; Fornet-Ponse 2008; and Eilmann 2017.
14 *TOFS* 61.
15 *TOFS* 52.

Here we have the explicit evidence of the importance of an internal point of view in the story [4.1 a'], without which the whole story itself would lose value and power over the reader.

Harmony between fairy-stories and the Gospels

We have already seen that mythopoeia as a natural outcome of Fantasy does not at all presuppose the level of revelation and faith. Nevertheless, it does not preclude it:

> The road to fairyland is not the road to Heaven; nor even to Hell. (*TOFS* 28)

In fact, Fairy-stories have three faces:

> the Mystical towards the Supernatural; the Magical towards Nature; and the Mirror of scorn and pity towards Man. The essential face of Faërie is the middle one, the Magical. But the degree in which the others appear (if at all) is variable. (*TOFS* 44)

With a certain probability the direct source of this first hint at a supernatural level (not essential to Faërie but somehow related to myth) may be traced in the volume *Progress and Religion*[16] by Christopher Dawson, in which the renowned Catholic historian, quoted by Tolkien, expounds the theory that religions are the main element in the development of a civilization and religious rites (the primitive ones in particular) try to express the confused intuition of a transcendent being,[17] also called the "ocean of supernatural energy".[18] This means that:

> It is man who is, in contrast to fairies, supernatural. (*TOFS* 28)

> There is a part of man which is not 'Nature'. (*TOFS* 81 note D)

Tolkien, however, goes one step further. In fact, he affirms that the natural capability of sub-creation is a reflection of the creative power of the primary Creator, almost as if to say that there is no separation between the natural and the supernatural, which are actually connected by a profound bond:

> We make in our measure and in our derivative mode, because we are made: and not only made, but made in the image and likeness of a Maker. (*TOFS* 66)

---

16 Dawson 1929.
17 Dawson 1929, 77.
18 Tolkien mentions explicitly this last concept in his first draft of *TOFS* 182, comment at 200.

Moreover, in the Epilogue to the essay he maintains that if fantasies are well-conceived they have "the inner consistency of reality",[19] and this is so much more true for the happy ending or "eucatastrophe" (or "good catastrophe", intended as a sudden, joyous turn of events[20]) that is part of the very essence of fairy stories:[21]

> In the 'eucatastrophe' we see in a brief vision that the answer may be greater – it may be a far-off gleam or echo of *evangelium* in the real world. (*TOFS* 66)

With admirable coherence, he thus connects the natural level of Fantasy (and its outcomes) to the level of Revelation, when he considers that:

> approaching the Christian Story from this direction, it has long been my feeling (a joyous feeling) that God redeemed the corrupt making-creatures, men, in a way fitting to this aspect, as to others, of *their strange nature*. The Gospels contain a fairy-story, or a story of a larger kind which embraces all the essences of fairy-stories. [...] But this story has entered History and the primary world; the desire and aspiration of sub-creation has been raised to the fulfilment of Creation. The Birth of Christ is the eucatastrophe of Man's history. The Resurrection is the eucatastrophe of the story of the Incarnation. (*TOFS* 78, italics added)

Thus, fairy-stories, a product of human nature, find themselves in perfect harmony with the supernatural level of the Christian revelation because the latter does not abolish the sub-creative activity but, on the contrary, accepts it, perfects it and sanctifies it:

> Evangelium has not abrogated legends; it has hallowed them, especially the 'happy ending'. (*TOFS* 78)

To sum up, 'On Fairy-stories' places myths and Fantasy on an essentially natural level, affirms the need for an internal point of view in order to grasp the truth of the sub-created worlds and, at the same time, establishes a complete harmony between all this and the supernatural level of revelation to the point that, in the end, Tolkien comes to the congruent conclusion that "God is the Lord, of angels, and of the men – and of elves".[22]

---

19 *TOFS* 77.
20 This is one of the many words coined by Tolkien that have entered *ex officio* the English language (cf. Gilliver et al. 2006, 123-124). On the theme of language in Tolkien, besides the already mentioned contributions by Flieger and Shippey, see Smith 2007, Solopova 2009, Zettersten 2011.
21 *TOFS* 75-76.
22 *TOFS* 78.

5.1.2 Mythopoeia

The first unabridged version of the poem "Mythopoeia" was published in 1988 and was edited by Christopher Tolkien, who had examined the previous seven editions written between 1931 and 1935.[23] The poem expresses in verse the same philosophy of myth analysed more in depth in 'On Fairy-stories', where a few verses of the poem are also quoted. The poem was composed after the famous conversation that took place on 19th-20th September 1931 between Tolkien, Hugo Dyson and C.S. Lewis, and it marked the turning point in C.S. Lewis' shift from a theistic position to the Christian faith which ultimately led him to join the Anglican church.[24] This conversation helped him to finally realize that the pagan myths he loved so much were not in contradiction to the Gospels but, on the contrary, prepared them and through them were accepted and preserved.[25] The title of the poem is significant in and of itself, because it is reminiscent of that "myth production" which Tolkien would later identify by the name "sub-creation". The dedication is specifically addressed to C.S. Lewis, reading: "To one who said that myths were lies and therefore worthless, even though 'breathed through silver'."[26] Even more significant is the clarification that the text is written by Philomythos for one Misomythos,[27] that is from the myth lover to the myth denigrator. Incidentally, the word Philomythos is used by Aristotle at the beginning of *Metaphysics*,[28] when, in contrast to his master Plato, he explains how there could be no contradiction between mythopoeia and philosophy (or, to be specific, between Fantasy and Reason [cf. *supra*]) because, the mythmaker makes wonderful things and the philosopher is moved by wonder.[29]

The poem, made up of eleven stanzas, opens with a reference to God's will to create, which brings into being the trees and the stars,[30] the natural world and Man himself:

---

23 *Tree* viii-ix; Hammond & Scull 2006b, 620-622.
24 On the many differences that separate Lewis from Tolkien see the remarkable article by Wood 2003b.
25 Cf. Green & Hooper 2002, 18, 118, 397; Carpenter 1979, 174 ff.; Wood 2003b, 333.
26 *Tree* 85. In two versions the reference is explicit, since the dedication reads "JRRT for CSL" (Hammond & Scull 2006b, 620-622).
27 *Tree* 85.
28 Aristotle, *Metaphysics*, book I ca. 2, 982b 17-20.
29 On the concept of myth in Tolkien and Plato, see Nagy 2004; cf. Ferrari 2007, 346-347.
30 *Tree* 85.

> God made the piteous rocks, the arboreal trees,
> tellurian earth, and stellar stars, and these
> homuncular men, who walk upon the ground.
> (*Tree* 86)

Man has the power to perceive the created world and most of all the power of "naming"[31] the created things and seeing them each time in a different light in accordance with the "history" in which they partake:

> there is no firmament,
> only a void, unless a jewelled tent
> myth-woven and elf-patterned.
> (*Tree* 87)

This prodigious power[32] Man has of seeing things within a story is analogous to God's power of creating things, and Tolkien calls him a "sub-creator"[33] who, even now, in spite of a state of decadence, still maintains his right to mythopoeia:

> Although now long estranged,
> Man is not wholly lost nor wholly changed.
> Dis-graced he may be, yet is not de-throned,
> and keeps the rags of lordship once he owned:
> Man, Sub-creator, the refracted Light
> through whom is splintered from a single White
> to many hues, and endlessly combined
> in living shapes that move from mind to mind.
> Though all the crannies of the world we filled
> with Elves and Goblins, though we dared to build
> Gods and their houses out of dark and light,
> and sowed the seed of dragons – 'twas our right
> (used or misused). That right has not decayed:
> *we make still by the law in which we're made.*
> (*TOFS* 65, italics added; see also *Tree* 87)

These verses, quoted also in 'On Fairy-stories',[34] reaffirm *the natural level where the "sub-creation" takes place* and hint at its link with the supernatural one. The theme returns in the final stanza, where explicit mention is made of Paradise (where Man will be able to see things in their original aspect) and most of all

---

31 *Tree* 86.
32 Cf. *Tree* 86.
33 *Tree* 87.
34 Actually we found in *TOFS* a few small, non-essential variations.

to Salvation, which does not destroy but preserves whatever positive aspects we may find in Man (gardener/young) and in his production (garden/play):

> Then looking on the Blessed Land 'twill see
> that all is as it is, and yet made free:
> Salvation changes not, nor yet destroys,
> garden nor gardener, children nor their toys.
> Evil it will not see.
> (*Tree* 90)

So, *the level of nature and of supernatural salvation find themselves in admirable harmony* to such an extent that Tolkien even hypothesizes that Man will continue this very activity of narration in Paradise:

> In Paradise they look no more awry;
> and though they make anew, they make no lie.
> Be sure they still will make, not being dead,
> and poets shall have flames upon their head,
> and harps whereon their faultless fingers fall:
> there each shall choose for ever from the All.
> (*Tree* 90)

Certainly these verses remain partly a mystery, but they are consistent with other hints given by Tolkien at the possibility that the narrator's sub-created worlds may somehow receive a primary and objective fulfilment in Paradise.[35]

5.1.3 *Beowulf*: Critics, Dwarfs and Giants

The pagan Beowulf as expression of human nature

Beowulf is the most important poem in the Anglo-Saxon language and probably Tolkien's most beloved literary work. His essay, 'Beowulf: The Monsters and the Critics', published in 1936, is, in my opinion, essential for the understanding of all of Tolkien's works dealing with Middle-earth, especially as far as the topic of this book is concerned.[36] I'm not so much interested now in demonstrating

---

35 See the short story *Leaf by Niggle*. See also Tolkien's letter to his son Michael where he affirms: "There is a place called 'heaven' where the good here unfinished is completed; and where the stories unwritten, and the hopes unfulfilled, are continued. We may laugh together yet" (*Letters* n. 45).
Among the few critics who noticed this "peculiar" theological notion, let's mention Rateliff 2006, 86. For a different, more psychologically oriented reading of these passages, see the excellent article by Roberto Arduini (Arduini 2012).
36 Shippey has masterfully demonstrated it in Shippey 2007e. See also M. Fisher 2006.

the scholarly foundations of his philological theories,[37] as in examining Tolkien's approach to the poem (and the poet), because the distinction between levels of nature and revelation and their reciprocal harmony is very evident in his analysis.

It is very important to notice the kind of perception Tolkien had of the poetical activity of the *Beowulf* poet, whom he saw as a Christian who intended to depict the nobility of ancient times instead of denying all worth to the pagan cultures that preceded Christianity:

> So far from being a confused semi-pagan [...] he brought probably first to his task a knowledge of Christian poetry [...] *secondly*, to his task the poet brought a considerable learning in native lays and traditions. (*MC* 26)

> A mind lofty and thoughtful. It is, one would have said, improbable that such a man would write more than three thousand lines (wrought to a high finish) on a matter that is really not worth serious attention. (*MC* 13-14)

Tolkien sees in *Beowulf* a magnificent attempt of preserving all that is good and true acquired by Man outside the Christian revelation with only the help of his reason and his mythopoeic fantasy, in

> his attempt to depict ancient pre-Christian days, intending to emphasize their nobility, and the desire of good for truth. (*MC* 27)

Even more noteworthy is the fact that the *Beowulf* poet did not describe ancient paganism nor did he superimpose Christian ideological elements onto it. He instead described characters who had already been "purified" from their many blemishes (polytheism, as an example):

> But if the specifically Christian was suppressed, so also were the old gods. (*MC* 22)

This is just to say that, if we use the distinctions proposed in our critical approach to Tolkien [4] and if we examine it from *an internal point of view*, we will see that the poem develops *on an essentially natural level* where the theme is exclusively that of the human condition *sic et simpliciter*:

> He [Beowulf] is a man, and that for him and many is sufficient tragedy. (*MC* 18)

> It [the poem] glimpses the cosmic and moves with the thought of all men concerning the fate of human life and efforts; it stands amid but above the

---

[37] On the reception of Tolkien's philological essays see Shippey 2007f.

petty wars of princes, *and surpasses the dates and limits of historical periods.* (*MC* 33, italics added)

But if *Beowulf* is the expression of an essentially pagan culture and, to a certain extent, the acknowledgement of its value, we should also recognize – in accordance with Tolkien's point of view – those elements that are in harmony with Revelation.

Harmony between pagan and Christian cultures

The essay contains a famous and beautiful allegory Tolkien uses to show up the limitations of the literary criticism to *Beowulf* that tends to undermine the unity of the poem with the analysis of its sources (cf. the "bones and soup" metaphor in *TOFS* [1.3]):

> A man [the *Beowulf* poet] inherited a field in which was an accumulation of old stone [verses of an old pagan poem], part of an older hall [pagan literature]. Of the old stone some had already been used in building the house in which he actually lived [Christian literature of his time], not far from the old house of his fathers. Of the rest he took some and built a tower [the poem *Beowulf*]. But his friends [modern critics] coming perceived at once (without troubling to climb the steps) that these stones had formerly belonged to a more ancient building. So they pushed the tower over, with no little labour, in order to look for hidden carvings and inscriptions, or to discover whence the man's distant forefathers had obtained their building material [critics tear up the unity of the poem looking for his sources].[...] They all said: 'This tower is most interesting'. But they also said (after pushing it over) 'What a muddle it is in' [...] But from the top of that tower the man had been able to look out upon the sea. (*MC* 7-8)

This passage reminds us immediately of the image given by Bernard of Chartres when he affirms "we [the moderns] are like dwarfs on the shoulders of giants",[38] thus showing a philosophy of culture in which paganism is not conceived as an antithesis to the Christian revelation. Tolkien places this attempt within a vast doctrinal frame:

> Almost we might say that this poem was (in one direction) inspired by the debate that had long been held and continued after, and that it was one of the chief contributions to the controversy: shall we or shall we not consign

---

38 John of Salisbury, *Metalogicon*, III, 4.

the heathen ancestors to perdition? What good will it do posterity to read the battles of Hector? *Quid Hinieldus cum Christo?* (*MC* 23)

The question in Latin is the famous one by Alcuin, an English monk of the 8th century who forbade his brethren from listening to pagan stories. In fact, Hinieldus (Ingeld) was the son of the benevolent king Froda and a minor character in *Beowulf*. Froda was – according to Saxo Grammaticus and Snorri Sturluson – contemporary to Christ and a king who hated war.[39] Fortunately, Alcuin's attitude was on the minority side in the history of Christian culture; Christian theology, as we will see in [6.1], is in fact characterized by a truly authentic rehabilitation of pagan culture. According to Tolkien, this is the attitude shown by the *Beowulf* poet, who:

> Showed forth the permanent value of that pietas which treasures the memory of man's struggles in the dark past, man fallen and not yet saved, *disgraced but not dethroned*. (*BMC* 23, italics added; see quotes from *TOFS* and 'Mythopoeia' on p. 83, where the same words are used).

The "passionate" emphasis of these phrases clearly shows how much Tolkien would partake of this attitude and appreciate the fact that the poet, firm in his Christian faith (he was not, as it has been said, half-pagan), succeeded in enhancing the consideration of the ethical achievements (e.g. the ethics of courage, for example [cf. 5.1.4]) of the Norse culture, no longer seen as antithetical to the Gospel message:

> I am interested in that time of fusion [between paganism and the Christian message] only as it may help us to understand the poem. (*MC* 20)

> But in England this imagination was brought into touch with Christendom, and with the Scriptures. The process of 'conversion' was a long one, but some of its effects were doubtless immediate: an alchemy of change (producing ultimately the medieval) was at once at work. (*MC* 21)

In fact, if we examine the poem from the external point of view [4.1. b'], we will see that it is in great harmony with the Christian message "to come", as is very well shown by the decisive role played by the monsters, enemies of Man, who will later become enemies of God as well:[40]

---

39 Shippey 2005, 283 ff., where he analyses the relationship between Frodo's name and the mythical king Froda.
40 Cf. Chance 2001, 16.

> For the monsters do not depart, whether the gods go or come. A Christian was (and is) still like his forefathers a mortal hemmed in a hostile world. The monsters remained the enemies of mankind, the infantry of the old war, and became inevitably the enemies of the one God. (*MC* 22)
>
> At this point new Scripture and old tradition touched and ignited [...] Man alien in an hostile world, engaged in a struggle which he cannot win while the world lasts, is assured that *his foes are the foes also of Dryhten* [God]. (*MC* 26, italics added)[41]

This perspective is also present in the series of the Oxonian lectures (given between 1933 and 1935) collected in the volume *Beowulf and the Critics* (*B&C*) that, according to the editor Michael Drout, "is one step in a lifelong intellectual project of recovering (as Tolkien believed the *Beowulf*-poet had) the old, lost stories and harmonizing them with the new Christian truth."[42] Therefore, it cannot be by chance that Tolkien, when faced with religious themes within the poem, talks explicitly of a "differentiation"[43] in the various ways of indicating "God", one that closely follows the distinctions between the natural and supernatural levels I proposed in 4. a"-4. b".[44] Tolkien distinguishes in particular the following positions:

- Beowulf, who through his speeches appears to be a "good pagan" and conscious of the idea of hell,[45] seldom speaks about God and, when he does, tends to assimilate Him with the idea of Fate.[46] The only considerable exception, besides line 571, is the passage in 2469 where he refers to the "light of God" which grandfather Hrethel heads for after his death. Tolkien, however, explains the passage as a concession to the theory the Poet agreed upon, that virtuous pagans can know God [cf. the texts by St Paul and St Thomas Aquinas in 6.1];
- Hrothgar is the poetic example of the natural/pagan ability of referring to God. In fact, although a pagan, he is portrayed as a believer in a monotheism that takes inspiration from the patriarchs and kings of the Old Testament.[47]

---

41 On this theme see, among the countless essays, Burke 2008.
42 *B&C* 27.
43 *MC* 39.
44 I am grateful to Michael Drout who suggested that I analyze this specific aspect of the essay.
45 *MC* 40.
46 Cf. lines 441, 2526, 1658-61, 570; *MC* 40-41.
47 *MC* 40.

Therefore, he – more than Beowulf – seems destined to set out on the path that leads to the supernatural level of revelation;

- this last level is testified by the *Beowulf* poet who, in his commentaries, outlines the harmony between the natural/pagan level and Christianity, seeing Beowulf's strength as the result of the "favour of God"[48] and knowing that the "good pagans" do not go to hell[49] [cf. 6.1] which is reserved for those pagans who maliciously venerate idols and practise old rites.[50] The poet, indeed, with great awareness and clarity of mind, continues to describe the context and the hero of the poem as essentially pagan, distancing himself from those scribes who tend to mix the two levels with their silly additions.[51]

Whether the poem *Beowulf* is among the sources for Tolkien's idea of the differentiation between natural/pagan and supernatural/revelation, or if he had already developed this concept and applied it to the analysis of the poem,[52] is difficult to establish. Either way we can conclude that in these texts we can trace the theory and the application of the two levels/two points of view seen in 4.1.

---

48 *MC* 40-43, line 65.
49 *MC* 38-39.
50 *MC* 42-43, lines 175-80.
51 *MC* 40, line 2186.
52 Richard W. Fehrenbacher, for example sees a great continuity between *The Lord of the Rings* and *Beowulf*. He thinks that, thanks to a spell, the pagan elegiac form of *Beowulf* (and of *The Battle of Maldon*) is transformed into a Christian fairy-story in *The Lord of the Rings* (Fehrenbacher 2006).

5.1.4 Beorhtnoth: The Heroic Pagan Spirit Between Duty and Overmastering Pride

Norse ethics: internal self-criticism and harmony with the Christian revelations

In Tolkien's opinion, one of the most important "ethical" contributions of pagan culture is the so called "theory of courage", already present in *Beowulf* but examined in detail in 'The Homecoming of Beorhtnoth, Beorhthelm's Son', a text conceived of at the beginning of the '30s and published in 1953 in the academic journal *Essays and Studies*. The text is quite peculiar, subdivided in three parts: an introduction, a poem in alliterative verse serving as an epilogue to *The Battle of Maldon*, and a discussion of the Old English term *ofermod*.

The Battle of Maldon is an Old English poem of the late 10th century that narrates how in AD 991 Beorhtnoth, duke of Essex, gave up a tactically advantageous position beyond an untraversable ford to face the Viking enemy in the open field, thus exposing his army to a defeat that could have easily been avoided. Tolkien gives a quite different interpretation of the text from the more "common" one proposed by his friend E.V. Gordon,[53] according to whom the centre of the poem is to be found in verse 312-313 that reads:

> Will shall be the sterner, heart the bolder,
> Spirit the greater as our strength lessens.
> (HBBS 124)

These words have been recognized as "the finest expression of the northern heroic spirit";[54] Tolkien, however, thinks that this reading is too simplistic and says:

> This 'northern heroic spirit' is never quite pure; it is of gold and an alloy.
>
> a *Unalloyed* it would direct a man *to endure even death* unflinching, when necessary: that is when death may help the achievement of some object of will, or when life can only be purchased by denial of what one stands for. But since such conduct is held admirable,

---

53 As for *Beowulf*, what interests me is understanding how Tolkien tackles these themes and not determining who between Gordon and Tolkien is right. Drout (2007b), for example, thinks that Gordon's reading has the stronger arguments.
54 HBBS 143.

b *the alloy of personal good name* was never wholly absent. [...] Yet this element of *pride*, in the form of the desire for honour and glory, in life and after death, tends to grow, to become a chief motive, *driving a man beyond the bleak heroic necessity to excess* – to chivalry. 'Excess' certainly, even if it be approved by contemporary opinion, when it *not only goes beyond need and duty, but interferes with it.* (HBBS 144, italics and divisions added)

By these words Tolkien very clearly states that the less noble metal, pride [b], can collide with and damage the purest part of this ethical vision, represented by the undaunted will that defies death in order to reach a goal superior to all other values [a]. This is why he thinks that lines 89-90 represent the essential nucleus expressing this kind of awareness:

Then the earl in his overmastering pride actually yielded
ground to the enemy, as he should not have done.
(HBBS 143)

Here Tolkien, going against a well established philological tradition that uses the term "overboldness", translates *ofermod* with the words "overmastering pride" as if to show how already within the poem we find a criticism of the possible ethical degeneration caused by the "absence of measure" (very similar to the Greek *hybris*[55]) brought about by the emphasis on the less noble metal.[56] To be noted is that the criticism here is exclusively addressed to the character of the "leader", who takes advantage of his subjects' devotion in pursuit of personal glory; warriors who followed orders until death are in fact not blamed, while those who fled from the battlefield are severely stigmatised both in *The Battle of Maldon* and in Tolkien's commentary:[57]

---

55 *Hybris* indicates a violation of measure that also takes on religious meanings in the form of envy of the gods (Cf. Jaeger 1984, vol. I, 290 and 314). See also Forest-Hill 2008b, 76-77.

56 Alison Milbank misunderstands Tolkien's thought on this matter: Aiming at demonstrating a closeness between Tolkien and G. K. Chesterton, she affirms that they both admired lines 312-313 expressing the essence of Norse heroism (Milbank 2007, xi ff.). But Tolkien not only refutes such an interpretation (he shifts the centre of *The Battle of Maldon* to lines 89-90) but explicitly affirms, writing about Chesterton's 'The Ballad of the White Horse', that Priscilla, his daughter, "has been wading through The Ballad of the White Horse for the last many nights; and my efforts to explain the obscurer parts to her convince me that it is not as good as I thought. The ending is absurd. The brilliant smash and glitter of the words and phrases (when they come off, and are not mere loud colours) cannot disguise the fact that G. K. C. knew whatever about the 'North', heathen or Christian" (*Letters* n. 80). In fact, in this work the Danes are portrayed as bloodthirsty and hostile to Christ and the Church, and therefore very distant from the "virtuous pagans" Tolkien admired so much.

57 On this theme, see the interesting essay by Bowman (Bowman 2010) where he argues that Tolkien thought flight from the battlefield was not always dishonourable. Just think of the "fly, you fools" addressed by Gandalf to the rest of the Fellowship when confronted with the Balrog (*LotR*, 'The Bridge of Khazad-Dûm', 374).

> It is the heroism of obedience and love, not the pride of wilfulness, that is the most heroic and the most moving. (HBBS 148).

The same perspective is expressed by Tolkien in the second part of the text, the poem 'The Homecoming of Beorhtnoth, Beorhthelm's Son', in which he narrates the retrieval of Beorhtnoth's corpse by Torhthelm (son of a minstrel and completely "imbued" with the old ballads about the heroes of Old Norse tradition) and Tídwald (an old farmer who has taken part in many battles and whose perception of heroic deeds is therefore much more critical and cynical).[58]

Tom Shippey, in a fundamental essay on the theme, sees in this dialogue the "parricide"[59] of the Norse heroic spirit, perpetrated from a Christian point of view at the same time that it was being perverted by the Nazis:

> Tídwald and Christianity and lines 89-90 of the poem were in the right, and Torhthelm and Beorhtwold and lines 312-13 and the critics including Gordon were in the wrong. (Shippey 2007h, 338)[60]

To speak of parricide, however, may appear far-fetched, and I'm more inclined to speak instead of a "double warning":

- on the one hand the heroic spirit should not rely too much on the less pure metal that might lead to a debasement of the gold. This is Tolkien's intent when he underlines the importance of verses 89-90 and translates the term *ofermod* with the expression "overmastering pride";
- on the other hand, the noble metal shouldn't be thrown away together with the less noble one, which in my humble opinion is what Tídwald does when he rightly criticizes Beorhtnoth for being too proud[61] but also derides Torhthelm, judging as despisingly "pagan" verses 312-313 which he quotes emphatically.[62] In this respect, Tídwald's attitude is reminiscent of Alcuin's prejudice when he asked "Quid Hinieldus cum Christo?", an attitude of

---

58 See Honegger 2007 for an analysis of the development of the scholarly argument from the poetic-fictional part of HBBS.
59 Shippey 2007h, 337.
60 Tom Shippey has written other essays on the theme of heroism: Shippey 2007b (where he takes up the theme of the virtuous pagans already examined in Shippey 2005); Shippey 2007c (where he describes Tolkien's love for the pagan heroes).
61 HBBS 137.
62 HBBS 141.

radical refusal of pagan culture Tolkien could certainly not agree with [cf. *supra* 5.1.3].

Pagan and Christian ethics: differences and sanctification

Tolkien had already criticized the *ofermod* of the leader who, in pursuit of his own glory, jeopardizes something much more important than honour itself:

- in *Beowulf*, where the hero faces Grendel with his bare hands and in the end, already made king, decides to defy the dragon alone, thus exposing his own reign to great risk;[63]
- in *Sir Gawain and the Green Knight* (the 14th century poem in Middle English), where at the beginning it is told how King Arthur accepts the Green Knight's most dangerous challenge to his honour, and such acceptance is promptly rebuked by the poet who reports in verse the thoughts which the Knights of the Round Table exchange:

> Before God 'tis a shame
> That thou, lord, must be lost, who art in life so noble!
> To meet his match among men, Marry, 'tis not easy!
> *To behave with more heed would have behoved one of sense*
> (HBBS 149, italics added)[64]

To sum up, we can say that in all these interpretations Tolkien

- on the one hand criticises the *ofermod* [cf. *supra*, a] because it can corrupt the most noble aspect of the Norse ethic of courage;
- on the other hand re-evaluates the pagan culture because he realizes that it had already begun to develop a sort of self-criticism and, most of all, because he is convinced that it contains the purest part of an ethic [cf. *supra* a] which is in great harmony with Christianity.[65]

In this sense Shippey suggests that:

> Tolkien was trying in his work to reconcile a Christian attitude and a heroic attitude, and would have liked very much to feel that his ancestors in the past had tried to do the same thing. (Shippey 2007h, 339)

---

63 HBBS 150.
64 Tolkien examines them in the essay about *Sir Gawain and the Green Knight*.
65 Lynn Forest-Hill, too, agrees on this interpretation of the term *ofermod* given by Tolkien, who tries to harmonise paganism and Christianity (Forest-Hill 2008). For HBBS as criticism of the limitations of the Germanic ethos, see also Drout 2007b.

Still, according to Shippey, it is exactly the closeness between "pure" Norse spirit and revelation that can in part explain the very fast conversion of Germanic peoples to Christianity.[66] According to Tolkien, this Germanic culture of courage has not been cancelled by Christianity. On the contrary, it has been integrated with its authentic essence of dauntless courage even when facing defeat:

> Nowhere, incidentally, was it [the northern spirit] nobler than in England, nor more early sanctified and Christianized. (*Letters* n. 45)

> You [Christopher Tolkien] and I belong to the ever-defeated never altogether subdued side. (*Letters* n. 77)

In view of this, it is not surprising nor can it be misunderstood that Tolkien defined himself as a "converted heathen"[67] and reaffirmed in his letters that his work is "less dissonant" from what he considers to be the truth[68] and "consonant with Christian thought and belief".[69] In fact, he will take up once more the same themes related to heroism in his stories (in particular *The Lord of the Rings*) [5.2.5].

5.1.5 Gawain Between Courtesy and Christian Morality

In the above mentioned 1953 essay on *Sir Gawain and the Green Knight* Tolkien returns to the theme of *ofermod* and draws attention to the poet's attempt to give a wider vision of themes that are of great interest for this study. Before going into a more detailed analysis I will briefly sum up the story the poem narrates.

We have already seen how the Green Knight shows up in the hall where the Knights of the Round Table are assembled and defies them with a challenge that appears to be completely absurd. One of them has to strike him with an axe and, if he survives, the challenged will have the blow returned in one year's time at his castle. Gawain, begging King Arthur to let him take his place, accepts the challenge, delivers the blow and beheads the Green Knight. However, the Green Knight picks up his own head which, even though detached from

---

66 Shippey 2007b, 28.
67 EW, 163.
68 *Letters* n. 211.
69 *Letters* n. 269.

his body, magically still talks and reminds Gawain of their fatal date. About one year later Gawain leaves in search of the appointed place and, during his journey, stops at a castle where the noble Bertilak de Hautdesert invites him to stay and play a strange game: he will go hunting, Gawain will remain at the castle and, in the evening, the two will exchange whatever they have obtained. During his stay, Gawain will be more than once tempted by the lord's wife and will receive from her kisses and a girdle, a gift which, at the lady's request, should remain a secret (reputedly having the magic quality of saving Gawain's life at the final encounter with the Green Knight). Gawain accepts the token but then confesses himself to a priest. Returning from hunting at the end of each day Bertilak gives Gawain a deer, a boar and a fox respectively, and receives back the same number of kisses Gawain has received from the dame. Gawain leaves the castle to reach his destination and meets up with the Green Knight at the Green Chapel. He bends to receive the fatal blow but, to his surprise, the Green Knight spares him. It is shown that the Green Knight is the very Bertilak de Hautdesert who had also devised all these tricks together with his wife and Morgana in order to test the nobility of the Knights of the Round Table. Although Bertilak praises Gawain for keeping his promise and avoiding adultery, he also scolds him for not having been completely loyal to him because he kept the girdle for himself. As a consequence, Gawain will always wear the girdle for the rest of his life as a sign of his cowardice and greed that were the cause of his failure to keep a promise.

These complex situations are masterfully analysed by Tolkien who, faithful to the poetic beliefs outlined in 'On Fairy-stories', affirms that this story is first of all a fairy-story, being a believable and realistic tale, and its characters not allegoric but "real" and endowed with a specific individuality.[70] He sees something deeper at work in the poem, and at first he distinguishes between two levels of narration that follow the distinction natural/pagan and supernatural/Christian mentioned in 4.1. a"-b":

---

70 SGGK 73, 78-79.

1. the level of the "rules of the game" (just remember the exchange of game and kisses) and of courtesy, traits that characterize the behaviour of a courtly society;[71]
2. the level of Christian ethics which, being eternal, goes beyond the "contingent" good manners typical of certain societies in a certain historical period.

In Tolkien's opinion, the essential theme of the poem is the relationship, problematic at times, that exists between these two levels:

> We have in fact reached the point of intersection of *two different planes*: of a real and permanent, and an unreal and passing world of values: morals on the one hand, and on the other a code of honour, or a game with rules. (SGGK 89, italics added)

> Both these poems [*Sir Gawain and the Green Knight* and *Troilus and Criseyde*], deal, from different angles, with *the problems that so much occupied the English mind: the relations* of Courtesy and love with morality and Christian morals and the Eternal Law. (SGGK 105, italics added)

According to Tolkien, the poet organizes this connection of levels in relation to the following elements:

1. inadequacy of the levels of "rules of the game" and courtly behaviour since they can at times collide. Indeed Gawain refuses adultery out of a sense of loyalty towards the lord and does not reveal that he received the belt from the lady out of a sense of loyalty towards her. His actions are ruled by his sense of loyalty but, at the same time, he is disloyal to the rules set by Bertilak which he had agreed to;[72]
2. subordination of the level of courtly rules to those of eternal ethics. In the name of the latter and thanks to his prayers to Mary, Gawain does not abide by the courtly code that required him to yield to the lady's advances:

---

71 He clearly distinguishes the rules of the game from the rules of courtesy, ethically superior to the game but inferior to morality.
72 SGGK 107.

> And with that [the adultery] we have the re-entry, for the first time since the pentangle and the shield of Gawain (that is here indeed alluded to), of *religion*, of something higher than and beyond a code of polite or polished manners which have proved, and are going again and finally [with the secret of the girdle] to prove, not only an ineffectual weapon in the last resort, but an actual danger, playing into the hands of the enemy. (SGGK 86)

3. harmony between the two levels, if hierarchically organized: this harmony is symbolised by the Pentangle on Gawain's shield.

> For the significance that the pentangle is to bear in this poem is made plain – plain enough, that is, in general purport: it is to betoken 'perfection' indeed, but perfection in religion (the Christian faith), in piety and morality, and the courtesy that flows therefrom into human relations; perfection in details of each, *and a perfect and unbroken bond between the higher and lower planes.* (SGGK 77, italics added)

In this analysis, too, we can see how Tolkien makes a hermeneutic "use" of those principles of distinction and harmony of levels between paganism and Christianity and between chivalry/honour and superior ethics [cf. 4], although in this late work the main stress is given to the difference and subordination of the two levels/codes.[73]

5.1.6 From Siegfried to the English Monks

There are other texts which I will briefly discuss later, in which it is possible to observe how Tolkien makes use of principles that somehow follow and confirm those I set forth in section 4.1.

---

73 As I've already said, I do not wish to go into a detailed critical evaluation of Tolkien's point of view on *Sir Gawain and the Green Knight*, because my exclusive intent is to analyse the principles he uses in his interpretation. However, I would like to draw attention to two aspects of that interpretation that, in my humble opinion, might appear controversial: 1) he gives emphasis to the confession made by Gawain after he receives the girdle from the lady. If during confession Gawain had admitted to accepting the girdle (as Tolkien seems inclined to think) he would have heavily sinned if he hadn't revealed it to Bertilak de Hautedesert; 2) Tolkien seems here to consider the commandment "Thou shalt not commit adultery" as revelation. It is indeed one of the Ten Commandments, but it is also important to underline that according to a widespread reading, the Commandments are in great part the expression of a "natural" law (see, for instance, Aquinas, *S. Th.* I-II q. 100 a. 8).

The Legend of Sigurd and Gudrún

In the early 1930s[74] Tolkien decided to give a rendition in verse of the ancient legend of Siegfried (*Sigurd*), in an attempt to "unify" and "organise"[75] the various versions of the old tradition. As far as our research is concerned, it is important to observe how this Tolkienian re-narration also shows an attempt to "harmonize" these old pagan sagas with elements of the Christian revelation. We can see this, for example, in the following excerpt where the character of Sigurd takes on characteristics reminiscent of the Saviour:

> Tolkien's Sigurd, divinely-descended but himself mortal, and required to endure death in order to save the world, does in those ways parallel the Christian Saviour […] [This] shows that in the early 1930s (if Christopher Tolkien's dating of the poem's compositions is correct), a kind of reconciliation, or imitation [between pagan and Christian mythology], was still in Tolkien's thoughts. (Shippey 2010b, 308)[76]

Finn and Hengest

In different periods of his university teaching and research (1930s, 1940s and 1960s) Tolkien devoted a great deal of attention to the fragment of 48 alliterative verses in Old English known as *The Fight at Finnesburg*, which is about a clash that took place between Danes and Frisians. The verses are one of the very few examples of "truly" pagan texts (we are not talking of a "re-writing" carried out by Christian poets, as is the case with *Beowulf*, where, incidentally, reference is made to this episode), and they have been preserved due to the efforts of monks in English monasteries.[77] Alan Bliss has collected the notes Tolkien

---

74 *LSG* 4-5.
75 *LSG* 6.
76 When I was writing this book, Tolkien's version of the Arthurian legend (nor *Kullervo* or *The Lay of Aotrou and Itroun*) was published. Tolkien's son, Christopher, edited the book *The Fall of Arthur* [*FA*], a poem in alliterative verse written by Tolkien in the 1930s where he recounts the death of the legendary king. I did not have the opportunity to analyse in depth the complex subject. However, it is important to observe that Tolkien did not completely remove the explicit references to Christianity (cf. *FA*, 39, 55), unlike what could have been expected in view of the considerations expressed in *Letter* n. 131 quoted in 1.1. This might be due to the fact that he considered the connection with Christianity already too deep-rooted in the Arthurian myth. I had an exchange of correspondence on the matter with Verlyn Flieger, who sees things differently and, consistent with her approach, affirms: "I think he [Tolkien] was always of divided mind about this. If you look closely at *Letters* and at the two big essays [*BMC* and *TOFS*], he appears to contradict (or at least argue against) himself in this area on several occasions" (email of 18th November 2013) On the same problem see also Rateliff 2016.
77 *FH* 3.

Chapter Five: Paganism in Tolkien's World and Its Harmony with Christianity   97

himself donated to him and published them in 1982 in the volume *Finn and Hengest*, who were respectively the king of the Frisians and, later, one of the leaders of the Germanic tribes who invaded England in the 5th century. Leaving aside the essentially philological issues dealt with in this volume, we refer now to the passage where Tolkien shows how proud he was that the assimilation of pagan culture within the English monasteries had become so deep-rooted that it acted as the catalyst for the monks to cross the sea and to convert the same pagans who were living on the continent. In fact Tolkien writes:

> The continental missions [are] one of the chief glories of ancient England, and one of our chief services to Europe even regarding our history. (*FH* 14)

Unpublished Manuscripts

Despite Alcuin's views, medieval culture was able to combine paganism and Christianity in a harmonious synthesis. The importance Tolkien attached to this aspect of medieval culture is also visible in some of his unpublished works.

In 2009 and 2013, I had the privilege to consult the *Special Collection* of the Bodleian Library in Oxford where many of the still unpublished writings of Tolkien are held. Those scholars who are authorized can consult (not photocopy and certainly not publish) those precious manuscripts only under a non-disclosure agreement. Therefore, I will not make quotations of those texts. However, I could observe that Tolkien had begun to write a history of the church in England (*Church in Ancient England*[78]) in which he underlines how Christianity saved and redeemed the preceding culture, a sign of the universality of the Roman Catholic Church.[79]

In a series of notes on English culture,[80] Tolkien is even more convinced that the most important contribution of the Anglo-Saxons to humanity was the synthesis they realized between Norse, Roman, and Catholic cultures which led to the English missionaries converting the peoples of the continent[81] [see *FH supra*].

---

78 Manuscript A 14/2 (2) page 129ff.
79 Manuscript A 14/2 (2) page 137.
80 Manuscript A 14/2 (2) pages 120-28.
81 Manuscript A 14/2 (2) page 121.

5.2 Paganism and Harmony with Christianity in Tolkien's Universe

These poetical and hermeneutic principles, and the intrinsic difference and harmony they show between nature and revelation, are consistently "used" by Tolkien in the sub-creation of his Secondary World. It would be impossible to examine the whole of Tolkien's work, therefore I will confine myself to the analysis of some of the key elements where the coexistence of these principles is clearly present.

5.2.1 Theology

Natural Theology in Tolkien's world

If we want to analyse the contents of the *Legendarium* from an internal point of view [4.1. a'], we should always keep in mind that this multifaceted body of writings was conceived by Tolkien's narrative genius as a composite ensemble of different points of view [cf. 3.1.1]. If we look specifically at the theological contents of his mythology we find important theological references in 'The Music of the Ainur' (Elvish point of view),[82] the myth of Númenor (human tradition),[83] and *The Lord of the Rings* (written by Hobbits).

These points of view, if with different degrees of detail, do *all* testify:
1. the existence of Eru/Ilúvatar/The One, who creates all things out of nothingness[84] by means of a mysterious Secret Fire;[85]

---

82 We have many versions of 'The Music of the Ainur' (or 'Ainulindalë'). See also the 'List of Abbreviations' in front of the 'Bibliography':
 • a first narration contained in *The Book of Lost Tales* dates from 1917-1920;
 • a manuscript from the 1930s (MuB);
 • a typed manuscript from 1946-48 (MuC*) based on MuB, published in *MR*;
 • a new version of the previous one written during the same period (MuC);
 • a last version of the 'Ainulindalë' written in 1951 (MuD).
83 Of the 'Drowning of Anadûnê', which narrates the story of Númenor, we have four versions (DA1, DA2, DA3, DA4) written between 1943-45 (*SD* 340, 357).
84 "Behold, Ilúvatar dwelt alone. Before all thing he sang into being the Ainur first" (*BLT1* 52); "There was Ilúvatar, the All-Father, and he made first the Ainur, the only ones, that were the offspring of his thought" (*LR*, MuB 156; and, in almost the same words, *MR*, MuC 8; MuD 30; MuC* 39); "Before the coming of Men there were many Powers that governed Earth, and they were Eru-bēnī, servants of God" (*SD*, DA1 341; see also. *SD*, DA2 357). Eru/the One is mentioned in *The Lord of the Rings* [quoted in 2.1].
85 *BLT 1*, Mu 55; *LR*, MuB 157, 159; *MR*, MuC 9; see also *MR*, MuD 30 and MuC* 39. In *The Lord of the Rings*, FR, 'The Bridge of Khazad-dûm' Gandalf affirms: "I am a servant of the Secret Fire".

2 the existence of the Ainur, powerful beings created by Eru and inferior in degree, who developed the musical themes set forth by Ilúvatar, from which Arda originated, and which made its growth possible. Some of the Ainur (Valar and Maiar) decided to descend into Arda in bodily form;[86] the existence of Elves and Men, called the "Children of Ilúvatar" because they were created by his will. They are made of *fëa* and *hröa*, part soul (directly derived from Eru) and part body.[87]

However, the theological assertions we find in the *Legendarium* have nothing specifically Christian; if we observe them from an external point of view [4.1 b'] and compare them to similar aspects of Western culture, we realize that the existence of the Principle "of all things from all things separated" had already been formulated at least in the pagan culture of Ancient Greece.[88] The same applies to the existence of distinct spiritual entities[89] and the immaterial nature of the human soul.[90]

On the other hand, the revealed truths, such as the incarnation of God in Jesus Christ or the Holy Trinity [cf. 4.1 b" and the texts by Thomas Aquinas quoted in 6.1], are exclusively Christian concepts, and they are never specifi-

---

[86] "Greatest is their power and glory of all his creatures within the world and without" *BLT 1*, 53. See also MuB 156; MuC 8; MuD 30; MuC* 39: For the human tradition see DA1 341; DA2 357. For *The Lord of the Rings* see TT, 'Of Herbs and Stewed Rabbit' ("May the Valar turn him aside!", says Damrod about a Mûmakil); RK, 'The Ride of the Rohirrim', where Gandalf "was borne up on Snowmane like a god of old, even as Oromë the Great in the battle of the Valar when the world was young"; RK, 'The Steward and the King', where Gandalf affirms at Aragorn's coronation: "Now come the days of the King, and may they be blessed while the thrones of the Valar endure"; AppD, about a day of the week dedicated by the elves to the Valar; AppA.1 (the word "Valar" occurs many more times in the appendices).

[87] "Eldar and Men were of Ilúvatar's devising only" (*BLT 1*, 57); "At the appointed hour Men were born into the world, and they were called the Eru-hín, the children of God" (*SD*, DA2 358); "Eldar and Men were devised by Ilúvatar alone" (MuB, *LR* 160); "the Children of Ilúvatar were conceived by him alone" (*MR*, MuC 11; cf. MuD 30 and MuC* 39).

[88] For example, Aristotle's demonstration of the existence of an Unmoved Mover (*Physics*, Book VII-VIII) that is Thought in the Thought (*Metaphysics*, Book XII) and Plotinus' The One.

[89] Cf. Plato's Demiurge (*Timaeus*) and Aristotle's *nous poietikos* (*Peri Psyché* Lib.III) or intelligences that move the celestial spheres (*Metaphysics*, Book XIII).

[90] Cf. Plato's *Phaedo* and Aristotle's *Peri Psyché*. For an introductory study on these themes, see entries "God", "Angels" and "Soul" in Abbagnano's *Dictionary of Philosophy* and in *Enciclopedia Garzanti di Filosofia*, Garzanti, Milano, 1981.

cally and unequivocally mentioned[91] in the *Legendarium* as Tolkien himself admits in 1956:

> There is no 'embodiment' of the Creator anywhere in this story or mythology [...] The Incarnation of God is an infinitely greater thing than anything I would dare to write. (*Letters* n. 181)

In comparison with the "official" theology of our Primary World, we still find some considerable differences already mentioned in 1.4, which is that the world created by Eru was marred by Melkor's sin even before the creation of the Elves and Men, and the existence of "angels" (Valar or Maiar as they may be), who can unite in marriage with each other (Manwë and Varda) or with Elves (Melian and Thingol) and have children with them.

The world of Middle-earth is therefore *"a monotheistic world of 'natural theology'"*[92] and, because of the substantial absence of information given, we have to say that *the theological perspective of the Legendarium is essentially pagan*.

Harmony with the Revelation

However, the pagan perspective of Middle-earth, although differing from the Christian perspective, is just as distant from the polytheistic religion [cf. 2.3] as from the atheistic position (both also present in our contemporary culture). As for polytheism, an implicit reference is made in letter n. 156, where Tolkien writes that Men:

> escaped from 'religion' in a pagan sense, into a pure monotheist world, in which all things and beings and powers that might seem worshipful were not to be worshipped, not even the gods (the Valar), being only creatures of the One. (*Letters* n. 156)

> God (Eru) was a datum of good Númenórean philosophy. (*Letters* n. 156)

---

91 We should also remember that Tom Shippey, in what in my opinion is an overstretched interpretation of the text, adumbrates a reference to Incarnation in the dialogue of *The Lord of the Rings* where Legolas tells Gimli that "The deeds of Men will outlast us" (*LotR*, RK, 'The Last Debate'; Shippey 2005 249 ff.), where I honestly do not see any clear proof of any reference to a Saviour. Agøy, instead, finds that the words pronounced by Finrod in 'Athrabeth' [cf. 3.1.3] contain an explicit reference to the Christian theology of Incarnation and not (as I myself propose) a superb example of natural theology (see Agøy 1998; Agøy 2011).
92 *Letters* n. 165. On the theme of religion among the Inklings, see Reilly 2006.

The theology of Middle-earth has even less in common with the atheistic perspectives of modern times. The existence of a Creator is undeniable, to the extent that atheism in the *Legendarium* is considered to be the "creed" divulged by Sauron in Melkor's honour:

> Sauron could not, of course, be a 'sincere' atheist, but he preached atheism, because it weakened resistance to himself (and he had ceased to fear God's action in Arda). As was seen in the case of Ar-Pharazôn. But there was seen the effect of Melkor upon Sauron: he spoke of Melkor in Melkor's own terms: as a god, or even as God. (*MR* 397)

This explains why *the pagan theology of the Legendarium, even in its dissimilarities, is in great harmony with the Christian theology*. In fact:

- the three theological principles described above – a distinctive Creator, triple hierarchy Eru/Ainur/Men-Elves, special origin and destiny of the human soul – are also present in a Christian context (God/Angels/Men);
- polytheism and atheism are totally rejected in both perspectives;
- a few references, by extension, may also be easily applied [cf. difference between interpretation and application in 1.2.] to elements that strictly belong to the sphere of revelation. For instance:
  - the Secret Fire can be associated with the Holy Spirit;[93]
  - the hope that the Author enters the Book [3.1.3] will be realized in the incarnation of the Son of God;
  - the hint that many things in Middle-earth do not happen by chance can be fittingly associated with the concept of Christian Providence [cf. 5.2.4].

5.2.2 Rites and Religious Cults

Absence of Supernatural Sacraments

I will deal with the theme of cults and rituals with the same method I used in the previous paragraph: I will observe the *Legendarium* from an internal point of view and give some emblematic examples taken from the different cultures of the Free Peoples.

---

93 Kilby 1977, 59, where the author quotes Tolkien's point of view on the subject.

A) *Elves*. Elvish culture appears to be somewhat "static" with respect to the passing of time, a circumstance that suits the Elves' wish to "preserve" things from corruption [cf. 2.4]. Tolkien's most important text on the theme is 'Laws and Customs among the Eldar', written in 1957-59 and published (in the two manuscript versions) in *MR*, in which, among others, he describes some of the Elvish customs in connection to specific moments in their life, such as:

- *betrothal*, it lasts at least one year and the exchange of two silver rings solemnizes the event;[94]
- *marriage*, it is usually celebrated after the coming of age, which is at the age of fifty. Varda and Manwë are invoked as witnesses with a formula that remains unknown, and it seems that Eru's name is also mentioned;[95] after that the betrothed return the silver rings and exchange rings of gold.[96] However, these ceremonies were not indispensable for the marriage to be considered "valid". Validity could occur even in the absence of witnesses or without a rite being celebrated;
- *choice of names*, a moment of the greatest importance in the life of an Elf. There are different types of names:

1. *name chosen by the father*: it is given soon after birth and is always kept as it is. The name is announced during a ceremony called *Essecarmë* (presentation of name);[97]
2. *name chosen by the mother*: it can be chosen based on the mother's intuition concerning the nature of the child's personality or contain a prediction of his future;[98]
3. *name chosen by the child for himself*: this usually happens when the child is ten years old (Elves begin to sufficiently master sounds and the meaning of words only when they are seven). The ceremony is called *Esseclimë* (name choice) and it is not a public event, the chosen name being indeed private even though not secret.[99] This name can be changed with time or take a broader meaning, but not annulled;[100]

---

94 *MR* 211.
95 *MR* 211.
96 *MR* 211.
97 *MR* 214.
98 *MR* 216; cf. 'Note on Mother-names' in *PME*, 339, 340.
99 *MR* 214.
100 *MR* 214.

Chapter Five: Paganism in Tolkien's World and Its Harmony with Christianity   103

4. *nicknames*: anybody can assign one; however, only the preceding names are considered "true names".[101]

B) *Men*. Here things are much more complicated because human rituals vary according to place and time in the history of Arda. We can delineate them as follows:

- At their appearance, Men do not seem to practise rites or special cults. However, if we consider the contents of the 'Tale of Adanel' [cf. 3.1.3], we learn that just after the "Fall" a few men began to worship Melkor;[102]
- a great transformation at the level of religion takes place when the Valar "raise" the island of Númenor, which will become the dwelling place of those Men who were most faithful in the war against Melkor. The religion practised by Númenóreans is pure monotheism[103] without special cults or temples, with the exception of an area on mount Meneltarma that was consecrated to Eru[104] to whom the earliest fruits and produce of the season were offered.[105] Of great relevance to our purpose is that even in the history of Númenor the idea of a cult has always negative connotations. The increasing number of tombs being built, for instance, signals a fear of death seen as a loss and not as a sign of hope for something that goes beyond the Circles of Arda.[106] The apex of this cultural development is reached when Sauron misleads the Númenóreans by introducing the cult of Melkor and has a mighty circular temple built in his honour:[107]

---

101 To be more precise, in *MR* 214 "true names" are said to be the first and third names, whereas in *PME* 339 the first and the second.
102 *MR* 347.
103 "The Númenóreans [...] were pure monotheists" *Letters* n. 153.
104 "In the midst of the land was a mountain tall and steep, and it was named the Meneltarma, the Pillar of Heaven, and upon it was a high place that was hallowed to Eru Ilúvatar, and it was open and unroofed, and no other temple or fane was there in the land of the Númenóreans" (*S*, Ak.). The idea of a high mountain called "pillar of heaven" is present in the *Legendarium* since the very first mention of the myth of Númenor in FN1 (1936-37), although the name has been changed many times. However, only from the third version of 'The Drowning of Anadûnê' onwards (*SD* 392; DA 1-2-3-4 written in 1945-46) do we find the idea that part of it, although not marked or covered by a roof, is dedicated to Eru.
105 *S*, Ak.
106 *S*, Ak. For a detailed analysis of this subject see: Ladavas 2012; Canzonieri 2012.
107 *S*, Ak. It seems that in describing the temple Tolkien had in mind the Radcliffe Camera in Oxford (Blackham 2008, 28).

> It [Númenor] had no building and no temple, as all such things had evil associations.
> (*Letters* n. 156)
>
> There was no temple in Númenor (until Sauron introduced the cult of Morgoth).
> (*Letters* n. 153)

- After the fall of Númenor, only a few traces of the rites practised by the ancient civilization remain in Middle-earth. A consecrated area reserved for the kings and forgotten by most still remains in Gondor, and it is that area where Aragorn finds a shoot of the White Tree.[108] A few signs of devotion are also preserved,[109] such as the well known gesture of a minute's silence observed by Faramir before supper while looking west.[110] However, Tolkien observes:

> There are thus no temples or 'churches' or fanes in this 'world' among 'good' peoples. They had little or no 'religion' in the sense of worship.
> (*Letters* n. 153)

Funeral practises are also very widespread.[111] Let's just consider:
- the laying of Boromir in a funerary boat with trophies from his last battle,[112]
- Théoden's funeral, celebrated four months after his death and therefore an unequivocal sign of the diffusion of embalming practises;[113]
- the wish expressed by Denethor to die burning on a pyre as the ancient "heathen kings" (cf. *infra*).

C) *Hobbits*. Rituals are altogether absent among Halflings. We only have a hint of them in *The Hobbit* when mention is made of the funeral traditions of Hobbit society.[114] We also know that the Hobbit calendar celebrates many festivities (Midsummer, New Year and Mid Year's Day)[115] and that the names

---

108 *LotR*, RK, 'The Steward and the King'. "It later appears that there had been a 'hallow' on Mindolluin, only approachable by the King, where he had anciently offered thanks and praise on behalf of his people; but it had been forgotten. It was re-entered by Aragorn, and there he found a sapling of the White Tree" (*Letters* n. 156).
109 *Letters* n. 156.
110 *LotR*, TT, 'The Window on the West'.
111 On this theme, see Reynolds 2008; Klinger 2011, where it is shown how tombs and mounds in Middle-earth are intended to show (albeit not openly) a supernatural dimension.
112 *LotR*, TT, 'The Departure of Boromir'.
113 *LotR*, RK, 'Many Partings'.
114 *H*, ii. In *H*, xviii Thorin is laid to rest within the Lonely Mountain. On the other hand, we have almost no information about the dwarves' religion.
115 *LotR*, AppD.

of the days of the week (six) were of Númenórean origin and ultimately of Elvish origin, dedicated to the Stars, the Moon and the Sun, the two trees Telperion and Laurelin, the Skies, and the Valar.[116] However, Frodo explicitly denies the existence among Hobbits of a tradition similar to the one observed by Faramir,[117] and Tolkien affirms:

> I do not think Hobbits practiced any form of worship or prayer (unless through exceptional contact with Elves). (*Letters* n. 153)

We can say therefore that there is a significant absence of ceremonies and rites among all the Free Peoples in Middle-earth, specifically among the Free Peoples of the Third Age when *The Lord of the Rings* takes place, and that, even for those cults that survived, their "taste" and their very literary sources are typical of a pagan society.[118] We can but underline the enormous difference that separates them from the liturgical quality of Christian tradition, where worship is essentially addressed to God and aims at a divinization by Man:

> Worship and Creation as a whole share the same purpose: divinization, a world of freedom and love. (Ratzinger 2001, 24)

Sacraments, for instance, "confer the grace that they signify"[119] and thanks to them men can truly partake of God's nature and reach "divinization". As we have seen in 1.3, the "ontological status" of the sacramental wine and bread (*true* blood and *true* body of Christ) greatly differs from the concepts of *miruvor* and *lembas*, food that most certainly has nothing of the supernatural.[120]

If we consider this difference of level with respect to the higher plan of revelation, we can conclude that *religion in the world conceived by Tolkien can be quite rightly defined as pagan.*

---

116 *LotR*, AppD.
117 *LotR*, TT, 'The Window on the West', 738.
118 Reynolds, in the essay already quoted, underlines the great influence of *Beowulf* and other pagan poems on the rites of Middle-earth (Reynolds 2008).
119 *Catechism of the Catholic Church* n. 1127.
120 On the importance of *lembas* in Elvish culture, see the essay with the same title in *PME* 403-408.

Harmony with Christianity

While the *Legendarium* deals with the aspect of cult practises only marginally, we observe on the other side the total absence of those pagan rites recorded by historians that required human sacrifices and ritual nudity [cf. 2.2. II]. Moreover, the rite of cremation is described in a very negative manner, probably because it would hardly conform to the dogma of the Resurrection of the Body.[121] In fact, in *The Lord of the Rings* Denethor affirms:

> We will burn like heathen kings before ever a ship sailed hither from the West. (*LotR*, RK, 'The Siege of Gondor', 825)

Then Gandalf reproaches him, saying:

> Only the heathen kings, under the domination of the Dark Power, did thus, slaying themselves in pride and despair, murdering their kin to ease their own death. (*LotR*, RK, 'The Pyre of Denethor', 853)

The two passages are extremely important not only for the condemnation of the "rite" of suicide and immolation, but also for the analysis of the ethical dimension of the *Legendarium* [5.2.5]. We are here in the presence of an authentic "anachronism" in the use of the term *heathen*, which Tolkien was most surely aware of [4.2].[122] He had already used it in a negative sense to refer to Númenórean temples after Sauron's arrival. The situation may appear paradoxical – we are within a pagan world where some ancient rituals and choices are judged "heathen" – but the true meaning of it becomes clear if we remember that the world Tolkien has sub-created is intended as the expression of a natural plan [4.1.a']; Man is granted both the possibility of distancing himself from polytheistic or atheistic stances by means of his rational capabilities (cf. *supra*) and of understanding the unnatural essence of certain rituals that are qualified as "heathen". As a result, we have a world where cult is limited but *in harmony with the supernatural level of Christian revelation*. This is also confirmed by Tolkien, who writes:

---

121 This is the thesis already proposed by Reynolds. We have to remember that cremation at the time Tolkien was writing was expressly forbidden by the *Codex Iuris Canonici* of the Catholic Church of 1917 and has been allowed only since 1963 and only on condition it was not practised with the intent of denying the dogma of the Resurrection of the Body (see Suchecki 1995, 167 ff.).

122 See Shippey 2005, 159 ff.; Hammond & Scull 2006b, 573.

> The only criticism that annoyed me was one that it 'contained no religion'.
> (*Letters* n. 165)

If confronted with the ancient and modern paganism of our primary world, the monotheistic religion of Middle-earth appears to be a first step on the path from the cult of false idols to the dimension of Christian revelation. This is confirmed in the invocations addressed to the Valar which, although with their specific differences, would be in harmony with the much more profound and complete significance of the Christian prayers:

> For help they may call on a *Vala* (as *Elbereth*), as a Catholic might on a Saint, though no doubt knowing in theory as well as he that the power of the Vala was limited and derivative.
> (*Letters* n. 153)

5.2.3 Philosophy of History

Fall, pessimism and uncertainty about the ultimate destiny

Three fundamental elements characterize the philosophy of history: beginning, development and end of time. If we look at its history, in its initial phases Arda is characterized by a series of dramatic falls:

- *The Fall of the Ainur:* this happens during the 'Music of the Ainur' and is confirmed in each of its versions. While the music is developed by the Ainur on Eru's invitation, Melkor begins to follow his own thoughts and introduces a "discord" in the melody that right away affects many other "angelic intelligences".

- *The Fall of the Elves:* this is also a constant since *The Book of Lost Tales*,[123] and it mainly refers to the rebellion of Fëanor who, after refusing to give the Silmarils to the Valar who needed them to save the Two Trees of Aman, leaves the Blessed Realm to chase Melkor, the Enemy who had killed his father and stolen the gems. Fëanor gets to the port of Alqualondë and commits a fratricidal massacre of the Teleri Elves, who had refused him the use of their ships.[124]

---

123 *BLT 1*, 162ff.
124 *S*, Qu, ix.

- *The Fall of Man:* this takes place in the remotest times, soon after the creation of Man and is already mentioned in MuC and MuD where Melkor is reported to be responsible for the mysterious substitution of hope with the fear of death.[125] This subject is explicitly mentioned in some notes related to the 'Drowning' (*SD* 401-403) and in the already mentioned 'Tale of Adanel' [cf. 3.1.3].

After these initial dramatic events, the development of history has a predominantly negative evolution, as can be easily seen in the progressive "fading of light" that characterizes the ages to come. In the beginning, light radiates on Arda from the Two Lamps burning continuously, but they are destroyed by Melkor. After their destruction, light radiates from the two trees, Laurelin and Telperion, which give light alternately, but they are also destroyed by Melkor. After this, the Sun becomes the only source of light for Arda, but it disappears by night leaving Arda in darkness.[126] This progressive abatement of the available light is also visible in the cosmological and demographic changes (the multitudes of Elves and Men divide progressively) and in the breaking up of languages (the tree of languages splits in an ever increasing number of branches). This fragmentation does not exclusively affect the light but the darkness too. As time passes, the cohorts of "evil" are subject to a constant loss of power as mentioned in his 'Notes on motives in the Silmarillion'[127], in which Tolkien affirms that at the beginning Melkor was much more powerful, and he expanded and increased his control over the Earth[128] driven by his craving for the annihilation of as much as he could possibly destroy;[129] unlike Sauron, who chose instead to concentrate his power in the One Ring, aiming at dominating things instead of annihilating them.[130] This explains why Sauron, at the peak of his power, was stronger than Melkor, not at the beginning of the First Age but at the end

---

125 "Death is their fate, the gift of Ilúvatar unto them, which as Time wears even the Powers shall envy. But Melkor hath cast his shadow upon it, and confounded it with darkness, and brought forth evil out of good, and fear out of hope" (*MR*, MuC 21). The passage is not present in MuC* (*MR* 43) but it will be kept in MuD (*MR* 37) and taken into *S*, Ainul.
126 See *S*, Ainul.
127 *MR* 394-408.
128 *MR* 394-395.
129 *MR* 397.
130 *MR* 395-396.

of it.¹³¹ However, when at the beginning of the Third Age Sauron regained his shape, he was weaker than in the First Age.

So, in Arda, the power of Good and Evil diminishes from Age to Age.¹³² This offers no possibility of an optimistic idea of progress in whatever sense we might interpret it.

As for the ultimate destiny of Elves, Men and the whole of Arda, the *Legendarium* remains quite vague:

- *The destiny of Elves* is, since the very beginning, connected indissolubly with the created world, even though the possibility and modalities of their return after death have different nuances according to the stages of development of Tolkien's mythology.¹³³ However, there is no mention of what will happen to them at the end of Arda [cf. 3.1.3].

- *The destiny of Men* (and of Hobbits¹³⁴) is even more uncertain. The idea of a copycat Inferno, Purgatory and Paradise was at once abandoned to avoid the effect of a second-rate parody [1.1]. Only the idea of a certain kind of survival of the soul is confirmed, but no detail is given as to what will hap-

---

131 *MR* 394.
132 Verlyn Flieger has masterfully written about this in her *Splintered Light*. For an excellent collection of essays see Agnoloni 2011. Particularly interesting in this collection is the essay by Roberto Arduini.
133 For the development of Tolkien's ideas which range from the Elves' rebirth in the children to their embodiment in a new body, see 2.2.2. In the *Legendarium* we also find the evolution of the role of Mandos (Valar of the otherworld) and the possible choice for the Elves of a return. The last version Tolkien gives on the issue dates back to 1957, when he "finds out" that Míriel, after giving birth to Fëanor, freely decides to abandon her body which, still intact, is left in Aman. The event is a cause of distress for the Valar (*MR*, LawsA 249-250). At this stage, according to Laws, an Elf is faced with two different ultimate possibilities: (a) the Elf dies of grief or by wounds (both in Valinor and in Middle-earth: *MR* 218, 221 in note) or (b) the Elf fades. This is the case of the *Lingerers*, who having delayed their return to the West are left with the *fëa* only, which has withered the *hröa* and can thus remain immortal in Arda up to its end (*MR* 223-4). In the first case (a) the Elf is called by Mandos and can either *accept the call* (a.1) or *refuse it* (a.2), thus becoming a houseless soul who wanders as a dangerous ghost in the land of the living (*MR* 223). If the Elf accepts the call (a.2), Mandos, after announcing his judgment in due time (*MR* 235), can hold him by himself (a.1.1.1: *MR* 223) or offer him (a.1.1) the double choice of rebirth (a.1.1.1: in the children and, since 1959, in a body created by the Valar) or of an eternal dwelling in his Halls (a.1.1.2: *MR* 249). The enigmatic reference to a return of the soul is no longer present in QS, and it is said that rebirth is the only way of return (*MR* 221). An exception to the return by rebirth is represented by Míriel, because her body remains incorrupt in the Blessed Realm and her *fëa* can return into it (a.1.1.3; *MR* 221). This synthesis introduces a threefold free choice (one for Mandos and two for the Elves) and a new shocking event (the case of Míriel) in the Elves' destiny. All the ideas expressed in Laws would be maintained in the following writings (*MR* 339, 342; NotesR). See also Testi 2012.
134 We shouldn't forget that for Tolkien the Hobbits are Men (*Letters* n. 131).

pen *post mortem*.¹³⁵ Humans are left in a state of *overwhelming anxiety and uncertainty* that surfaces with dramatic force in the history of Númenor, when the Men's envy for immortality pushes them to attack the Blessed Realm of the Valar.

- As for *the ultimate destiny that awaits Middle-earth and the whole of Arda*, we find a few hints to a positive albeit mysterious outcome. Since *The Book of Lost Tales*,¹³⁶ mention is made of the eventuality of a Great End, when the Valar will be involved in a great battle, a "vision" which will return in *The Silmarillion*.¹³⁷ Later in Q¹³⁸ and QS¹³⁹ the "renaissance" of Arda after the Great End will be adumbrated, and *Arda Healed* will be a central theme *in the next and final period*,¹⁴⁰ from the 'Athrabeth'¹⁴¹ to 'The Problem of Ros' of 1967.¹⁴²

All this philosophy of history, however, *has nothing essentially Christian*. In fact,

a. the concept of the Fall does not exclusively belong to the Judeo-Christian culture. It occurs, for example, in form of the decline from a Golden Age, as found in Hesiod' *Works and Days*,¹⁴³ or as the fall of Osiris in the *Book of the Dead*;¹⁴⁴
b. the ultimate destiny of Elves and Men remains vague. No reference is made to a life everlasting, to the resurrection of the body or other forms of ultimate destiny;
c. one of the sources of *Arda Healed* is without doubt the *Apocalypse* of St John, and we should also mention that the idea of a final palingenesis is also present in the Norse *Ragnarök*.¹⁴⁵ However, the eschatological aspect is not the motive that guides the choices made by the characters of the *Legendarium*.

---

135 See Grant 2001. Edoardo Rialti writes of an "almost tragedy" (Rialti 2004). Passaro, instead, tends to deny the presence of any otherworldly perspective in Tolkien (Passaro and Respinti 2004).
136 *BLT 1* 53; *BLT 2* 285.
137 *SME* 40.
138 *SME* 165.
139 *LR* 333.
140 *MR*, LawsA, 245, 251; Athrabeth 405 ff.
141 *MR* 326. On these developments see Whittingham 2007, 170-200; Drout 2007, 475.
142 *PME* 374.
143 Hesiod, *Works and Days*.
144 Kolpaktchy and Piantanida 2008, 23 ff.
145 See Whittingham 2007; Dimond 2004, 179-90.

If we keep a point of view internal to the *Legendarium* [4.1. a'] then we realize that the characters, unlike what happens in the Christian tradition, are not concerned with the idea of life beyond a finite history. Because of that distance from the contents of the revelation, which pertains to a different level than that of speculative rationality, *the philosophy of history in the Legendarium is essentially pagan*.[146]

Harmony with Christian eschatology

However, we should notice that:

a. unlike in Pullman's "theology",[147] Falls are not seen as positive events;
b. the pessimistic idea of history seen as a long defeat is not at all an antithesis to a Christian perspective,[148] neither should that cosmologic pessimism be confused with the unavoidable perspective (somehow also ethically decadent) of the various "twilights of the west";[149]
c. as for the theme of the end of times, the "Twilight of the Gods" of Norse mythology will come in the form of a mutual annihilation of the positive and negative powers which will give way to a new cycle of the world.[150] If compared to it, the concept of history in the *Legendarium* is linear and without any reference to a cyclic Eternal Return.

The way these ideas are told and handed down (initial fall, long defeat, linearity of history) is not antithetical to the Christian revelation which can be seen as the completion of the "partial" pagan vision of the *Legendarium*. The Christian

---

146 On the theme of eschatology and philosophy of history in Tolkien, see the fundamental contribution by Manni 2012.
147 See Gray 2010.
148 Cf. 2.2.2. Tolkien's pessimism differs from William Morris', who is more inclined towards an optimistic utopic vision (see Scoville 2005). Holmes, too, underlines how the Norse perception of time (that flows towards a final destiny where all things succumb) is not in opposition to the Christian philosophy of history as a long defeat (Holmes 2005).
149 "Tolkien's 'philosophy of history' is not as pessimistic as those in fashion at the time: Tolkien does express a feeling of melancholy for the disappearance of elvish beauty in the Age of Men, but does not deplore moral decay or other forms of decadence! When he speaks of the fading of elvish beauty (or the ents) and the coming of the Age of Men, Tolkien – unlike Spengler, Rosenberg or Husserl – does not give us a message of 'decadence', but instead one of 'finiteness'. His refusal to add to the already numerous 'twilights of the West' then in vogue is made explicit, for example, in the dialogue between Gimli and Legolas at Minas Tirith" (Manni 2012, 28-29). Manni refers to the dialogue between the dwarf and the elf in Minas Tirith, already quoted in 5.2.1. in note.90.
150 Chiesa Isnardi 2008, 186-192; Turville-Petre 1975, 280-86; Eliade 1968.

vision of history, from Genesis to Apocalypse and the so called "novissimi" (Death, Judgement, Hell, Purgatory and Paradise),[151] *although pertaining to the supernatural level [4.1.b"] is in harmony with the intuitions that pervade Tolkien's universe.*

5.2.4 Fate and Providence

Paganism of Elvish Fate

The theme of Fate and Providence in Tolkien is extremely vast and a whole book would be required in order to attempt an in-depth study of all its aspects. In fact, the theme is crucial for a full understanding of Tolkien's work, so much so that the most respected Tolkien scholars have written fundamental contributions on the theme.[152]

One of the most interesting comments we have on the subject was set down by Tolkien himself in some linguistic notes written around 1968 but published only in 2009 in FFW, regarding the Elvish themes of *ambar* (world) and *umbar* (fate) that appear in *The Lord of the Rings*. The text is important because it was written at a very advanced stage of development in the creation of the *Legendarium* and also because the "definitions" given by Tolkien synthetically explain the philosophical principles underlying these themes, the very principles which support the narration throughout the whole of *The Lord of the Rings*.

This is what Tolkien writes about MBAR, the linguistic stem of the two words:

> MBAR 'settle, establish' (hence also, settle a place, settle in a place, establish one's home) also to erect (permanent buildings, dwellings, etc.). (FFW 184)
>
> ordering of a region as a 'home' (of a family or people) (FFW 183)

This is the stem for the Quenya word *umbar*, or *amarth* in Sindarin, the word that more closely translates the idea expressed by "our" idea of Fate, even if it does not coincide with it (cf. *infra*):

---

151 On the subject, see again Manni 2012.
152 See Shippey 2005 170 ff.; Flieger 2009; Fornet-Ponse 2010 (in answer to Flieger's article); Dubs 2004; Birks 2011.

> [*Umbar* or *Amarth* mean] 'Fate' especially (when applied to the future): sc. the order and conditions of the *physical* world (or of *Eä* in general) as far as established and preordained at Creation, and that part of this ordained order which affected an individual with a *will*, as being immutable by his personal will. (FFW 185)

The same stem appears in the Quenya word *ambar*, or *amar* in Sindarin, with the meaning of "world" or "large home" (*oikoumene*[153]), especially in the sense of:

> established (physical) processes of the Earth[154] (as established at its Creation directly or mediately by Eru), which was part of Eä, the Universe. And so approached in some uses the sense 'Fate', according to Eldarin thought on the subject. (FFW 183)

We can say that *umbar/amarth* is the sum of those physical conditions established by Eru at the moment of creation which will determine a certain course of events in the created world, whereas *ambar/amar* designate the universe intended as a physical process that realizes the conditions and the events established in *umbar*.

Umbar and *ambar* do not affect the free will of Elves and Men (and Hobbits) and in a certain way they can even go against it. If an event is supposed to happen, it will happen in any case, and no free will has the power to avert it. However, should this event happen and concern someone endowed with free will, he can act in complete freedom and not be subject to predetermination. Tolkien provides us with very clear examples in this regard:

> They would probably also have said that Bilbo was 'fated' to find the Ring, but not necessarily to surrender it; and then if Bilbo surrendered it Frodo was fated to go on his mission, but not necessarily to destroy the Ring – which in fact he did not do. They would have added that *if* the downfall of Sauron and the destruction of the Ring was part of Fate (or Eru's Plan) then if Bilbo had retained the Ring and refused to surrender it, some other means would have arisen by which Sauron was frustrated. Just as when Frodo's will proved in the end inadequate, a means for the Ring's destruction immediately appeared – being kept in reserve by Eru as it were. [...] but the Eldar held that only those efforts of "will" were "free" which were directed to a fully *aware purpose*. On a journey a man may turn aside, choosing this or that way – e.g.

---

153 FFW 183.
154 In a wider sense it is also defined "process of Eä" (FFW 188 n. 5). *Eä* in Elvish language corresponds to the universe, *Arda* to our Solar System and *Imbar* to the Earth (*MR* 337-38).

> to avoid a marsh, or a steep hill – but this decision is mostly intuitive or half-conscious (as that of an irrational animal) and has only an immediate object of easing his journey. His setting-out may have been a free decision, to achieve some object, but his actual course was largely under *physical* direction – and it *might have* led to/or missed a meeting of importance. It was this aspect of "chance" that was included in *umbar* [See LotR AppA]: "a chance-meeting as we say in Middle-earth".[155] That was said by Gandalf of his meeting with Thorin in Bree, which led to the visit to Bilbo. [...] Gandalf was not "fated" to act as he did.
> (FFW 185)

Continuing with the last example, we can conclude that the decision taken by Gandalf and Thorin was free, but, their route being "unalterable" (and not so much determined by their own free will), the circumstance that they met in Bree did appear to them as the result of chance while it was indeed already ordained in *umbar* (and put into being by *ambar*).

Following a consistent line of reasoning, Tolkien affirms that, according to the Elves, not even Eru, the Shaper of *umbar*, can foreknow how free creatures will act in certain given situations. To better explain the concept, he uses the analogy (an evidently autobiographical one[156]) of an author of a story, who outlines the crucial elements of it but still doesn't know all the details, especially those concerning the main characters:

> They said that, though this likeness is only a 'likeness,' not an equation, the nearest experience of the Incarnates to this problem is to be found in the author of a tale. The author is not in the tale in one sense, yet it all proceeds from him (and what was in him), so that he is present all the time. Now while composing the tale he may have certain general designs (the plot for instance), and he may have a clear conception of the character (independent of the particular tale) of each feigned actor. But those are the limits of his 'foreknowledge.' Many authors have recorded the feeling that one of their actors 'comes alive' as it were, and does things that were not foreseen at all at the outset and may modify in a small or even large way the process of the tale thereafter. All such unforeseen actions or events are, however, taken up to become integral parts

---

155 See also *UT*, 'The Quest of Erebor'.
156 From Tolkien's letter to Auden: "That [the main idea of the story of *LotR*] arrived at in one of the earliest chapters still surviving (Book I, 2). It is really given, and present in germ, from the beginning, though I had no conscious notion of what the Necromancer stood for (except ever-recurrent evil) in *The Hobbit*, nor of his connexion with the Ring. [...] So the essential Quest started at once. But I met a lot of things on the way that astonished me. Tom Bombadil I knew already; but I had never been to Bree. Strider sitting in the corner at the inn was a shock, and I had no more idea who he was than had Frodo..." (*Letters* n. 163); "always I had the sense of recording what was already 'there', somewhere: not of 'inventing'" (*Letters* n. 131).

of the tale when finally concluded. Now when that has been done, then the author's 'foreknowledge' is complete, and nothing can happen, be said, or done, that he does not know of and will/or allow to be. Even so, some of the Eldarin philosophers ventured to say, it was with Eru. (FFW 186-87)

However, Eru is "outside" *umbar* and *ambar* and can therefore interfere in ways that are not originally ordained in *umbar* and are considered "miraculous", e.g. 'The Downfall of Númenor'.[157]

To sum up, the Elves' views on these themes testify that:
- the physical events are established in *umbar*;
- *ambar* is the process that will realize them;
- these events are the ones that happen by "chance";
- the reaction of a free will (*lēle*)[158] to these events is not ordained in *umbar*;
- not even Eru knows how a free will will react to an event that is ordained in *umbar*;
- Eru can always change *umbar/ambar*.

The Lord of the Rings, which, we must not forget, is written from a Hobbit-narrator point of view [3.1], acknowledges these most interesting principles of "elvish philosophy". The word *providence* never occurs, whereas the word *fate* appears 38 times (29 items in the text, and nine in the Appendices), the word *doom* is used 69 times in the text (without counting, for obvious reasons, toponyms such as Mount Doom, Crack of Doom *et similia*), and we don't even mention the many times the word *chance* is used between quotation marks, that is to say the denial of *chance* itself (such as in the case of the "chance" encounters of the hobbits with Gildor[159] and Tom Bombadil,[160] and the already mentioned encounter between Gandalf and Thorin).

Restricting the analysis to the term *fate*, we find that it is used to indicate:
- the finding of the Ring by Bilbo (*LotR*, FR, 'The Shadow of the Past');
- the role played by Gollum in the events to come (*LotR*, FR, 'The Shadow of the Past');

---

157 FFW 185-86.
158 FFW 188 n. 5.
159 *LotR*, FR, 'Three is Company'.
160 *LotR*, FR, 'In the House of Tom Bombadil'.

- the absence of a permanent dwelling for Aragorn (*LotR*, FR, 'Flight to the Ford');
- Frodo's "lucky" escape from the Black Riders (*LotR*, FR, 'Many Meetings');
- Balin's end (*LotR*, FR, 'The Bridge of Khazad-dûm');
- Lórien's destiny (*LotR*, FR, 'The Mirror of Galadriel');
- future events seen as "tides of fate" (*LotR*, FR, 'The Mirror of Galadriel');
- Frodo's necessity to choose about what is to be done after the departure from Lórien (*LotR*, FR, 'The Breaking of the Fellowship');
- the bond between Frodo and the Ring (*LotR*, FR, 'The Breaking of the Fellowship', *LotR*, FR, 'The Departure of Boromir');
- the terrible day when the Fellowship breaks (*LotR*, FR, 'The Departure of Boromir');
- the arrow that hits Grishnákh while he is attempting to kill the hobbits (*LotR*, TT, 'The Uruk-hai');
- the failure of Wormtongue's mission (*LotR*, TT, 'Flotsam and Jetsam');
- the fate of the Palantír of Gondor (*LotR*, TT, 'The Palantír');
- the possible help of Gollum to Frodo (*LotR*, TT, 'The Black Gate is Closed');
- the choice Frodo is forced to make about the way to reach Mordor (*LotR*, TT, 'The Black Gate is Closed');
- Faramir's role (*LotR*, TT, 'Of Herbs and Stewed Rabbit');
- Frodo's silence about Boromir's destiny (*LotR*, TT, 'The Window on the West');
- the destiny of the Fellowship of the Ring (*LotR*, TT, 'The Window on the West');
- Boromir's death (*LotR*, TT, 'The Window on the West');
- the meeting between Aragorn and Halbarad (*LotR*, RK, 'The Passing of the Grey Company');
- what awaits Théoden in Gondor (*LotR*, RK, 'The Muster of Rohan');
- the use of the sword of Tyrn Gorthad against the Witch King (*LotR*, RK, 'The Battle of the Pelennor Fields');
- the landing of the pirate ships at the Battle of the Pelennor Fields (*LotR*, RK, 'The Battle of the Pelennor Fields');
- the destiny of Frodo and Sam (*LotR*, RK, 'The Field of Cormallen').

This list, which would need further analysis, shows how the term *fate* in *The Lord of the Rings* is used consistently with what is expounded in FFW, being applied exclusively to "physical" events or to qualify the situations that the main characters do sometimes experience.

In my opinion, this conception is *essentially pagan* for at least the following reasons:

a) the terminology used in the *Legendarium* is pagan because the term "Providence" is never used. It is true that, in the development of Western thought, the concept of "fate" is what moves closer towards the idea of Christian Providence, but Augustine of Hippo admonishes:

> And if any one attributes their [the historical events] existence to fate, because he calls the will or the power of God itself by the name of fate, let him keep his opinion, but correct his language.
> (Augustine of Hyppo, *The City of God*, Book V.1, 323)

b) the idea of an intelligence that somehow ordains events in accordance with a pre-established plan (as is the case for *umbar*) is not exclusively Christian. Plato had already masterfully elaborated it in *Timaeus*, in which it is explained how Cosmos had been arranged by the Demiurge's intellect,[161] and the concept was even more present in the ancient *Stoa*:

> Reason forces us to admit that everything happens by fate, and fate I call what the Greeks call *eimarméne*, that is a chain of causes and effects that give origin to all things. This is an eternal truth that has its roots in eternity; therefore nothing has ever happened that was not bound to happen and, likewise, nothing will happen that has not already in nature the causes that will determine its happening.
> (Cicero, *De Divinatione*, I 55, 125 cit. in Reale 1987 vol. III, 327)[162]

c) the Elvish concept of fate, although it tends towards the idea of Christian Providence, considerably differs from it. In fact, according to Christian theology, which, as far as this theme is concerned, has in Thomas Aquinas its highest systematic expression, Providence extends to all things, men's free choices included:

---

161 Reale 1987, vol III, 370.
162 *Eimarméne* stands for cosmic destiny, whereas *moira* refers either to a sort of goddess superior, even to Zeus, or to the fact that some events were to happen exactly the way they happened (Dodds 1962, 7 ff.).

> But since the very act of free will is traced to God as to a cause, it necessarily follows that everything happening from the exercise of free will must be subject to divine providence.
> (Aquinas, *Summa Theologica*, I pars q. 22 art. 2 ad 4)

This statement may be shocking to most, especially at a time when authentic metaphysics is seldom taught and even less understood, but it is the application of the simple principle that *all things* have been created by God and each single entity, be it a grain of dust, a man or even his choices, completely depends on Him for its existence and preservation. The Catholic catechism states:

> The truth that God is at work in all the actions of his creatures is inseparable from the faith in God the Creator. God is the first cause who operates in and through secondary causes: "For God is at work in you, both to will and to work for his good pleasure" (Phil 2:13). (*Catechism of the Catholic Church* n. 308)

The horizon embraced here is therefore much wider than that of the Elvish *umbar*. In fact, if we recall the example we have already mentioned, in the Elves' point of view *umbar* establishes that Bilbo will find the Ring, but Bilbo's choice about whether he should give it back or keep it is outside *umbar*; instead, a Christian theologian would say that both the finding of the Ring and *Bilbo's choice of giving it to Gandalf are part of the design of Providence and part of the same design as each and every entity, event and choice which happens to be*. One should be aware that Christian Providence does not violate the freedom of choice, but on the contrary it establishes its very foundations. In fact, events in the world do happen with two different modalities:

- *by necessity*: for instance, an object thrown upward must necessarily fall downward;
- *by contingency*: contingency defines those entities or events that may or may not occur; contingent are all the choices made by rational beings, such as in the case of Bilbo who can choose to keep or not to keep the Ring.

However, God is beyond the categories of necessity and contingency, just as much as He is beyond the chain of events in the material world, which He governs from the outside while maintaining everything in being. This is why there is no contradiction when we say that God's Providence establishes that Bilbo freely chooses to give the Ring back, whereas this would be unacceptable in the pagan language of the *Legendarium*. For Catholic theology, God's will creates (and therefore respects) the manner (necessary and contingent) in which events unfold:

> The effect of divine providence is not only that things should happen somehow; but that they should happen either by necessity or by contingency. Therefore whatsoever divine providence ordains to happen infallibly and of necessity happens infallibly and of necessity; and that happens from contingency, which the plan of divine providence conceives to happen from contingency. (Aquinas, *Summa Theologica*, I pars q. 22 art. 4 ad 1)

In the light of what we have seen, we have to conclude that the concept of fate in the *Legendarium* is *the result of an Elvish philosophy that has almost nothing to share with the supernatural level of the Christian revelation and, as a consequence, is essentially pagan.*[163]

Harmony with Christian Providence

We must not forget that, under certain aspects, the concept of *umbar* has similarities with Christian Providence. In fact:

a) *umbar* implies a total refusal of "chance" as the supreme architect of events. This is once more a pagan concept – typical, for instance, of Epicurus who believed that the gods were unconcerned with the chance events of the world[164] – and is not compatible with Christianity;

b) on the other hand, Elvish philosophy of fate does not imply the opposite of the complete supremacy of chance, which is that everything is determined and controlled by necessity. This was the concept of the first atomists[165] and stoics,[166] who ultimately denied free will to men;

---

163 In this regard, I have to admit I disagree with Shippey when he says that the main theme in *The Lord of the Rings* is Providence. His masterful analysis is mainly based upon the fact that, especially from the moment the Fellowship breaks, the development of the chain of events is not at all due to chance but appears to be orchestrated by a Superior Mind, which is why when Elves and Men try to guess their future, accessible only to Eru, they make serious mistakes. In fact, Shippey says that "And the totality of other people's actions forms a design which is set by Providence. But the bits we see of it, in our partial vision, we call "luck", or "chance", or in Anglo-Saxon, *wyrd*" (Shippey 2014, 63; Shippey 2005, 170 ff.). When Shippey affirms that even free will is part of the predetermined design, he applies, in my opinion, a Christian concept that goes beyond Elvish fate and what Tolkien writes about it. Irène Fernandez seems to share the same mistake (Fernandez 2003, 61 ff.).
164 Reale 1987 vol. III, 225 ff.
165 Reale 1987 vol. I, 179.
166 Reale 1987 vol. III, 375-378.

c) to a certain extent, the difference between *umbar/ambar* replicates the theory of Providence and Fate proposed by Boethius. Tolkien was by all means aware of this distinction, which was also analyzed by Alfred the Great.[167] The Roman philosopher affirms that:

> *Providence* is the Divine reason itself, established by the highest ruler of all things the reason that orders everything that exists; *fate* is the disposition that is inherent in each of these things, through which providence bonds all things together, each in proper order.
> (Boethius, *The Consolation of Philosophy*, IV.5.7, 132-133, italics added)

Although not in contradiction, the concept of Christian Providence is therefore on a superior level to the Elvish idea of fate, because He who devises fate (God, Eru, the Demiurge, gods) is "detached" from the ideas of necessity/contingency. In fact, He is the most simple and perfect being who, as if looking from the top of a mountain, encompasses the unwinding of history in one single "simultaneous" glance[168] that "perceives" what happens by necessity and what happens out of free will. This clarifies the relation between divine project and freedom [*supra*], a problem which, according to Tolkien, had not found a solution in the Elvish perspective:

> But the ultimate problem of Free Will in its relation to the Foreknowledge of a Designer (both of the plane of Umbar and of the Mind and the blending of both in Incarnate Mind), Eru, "the Author of the Great Tale," was of course not resolved by the Eldar. (FFW 186)[169]

We do not have sufficient proof that Tolkien at this stage of development of his work was hinting at the fact that the problem was "solved" by Thomistic theology. Either way, it is a "fact" that the Elves' conceptions, even with their differentiations, *are a partial insight into the ampler Christian perspective and, as a consequence, are in harmony with it.*

---

167 See Shippey 2014, where he studies these themes with special reference to Boethius and Alfred the Great.
168 We find this image in Thomas Aquinas (*In Peri Hermeneias*, Book I, lect xiv n. 194).
169 On the theme of free will in the *Legendarium*, see also Dickerson 2003; Fisher 2006; Fornet-Ponse 2006.

5.2.5 Ethics of the Hero

Not martyrs, but virtuous pagans

Once again, the theme of the hero in the *Legendarium* is so vast that a separate study would be needed for an exhaustive analysis. However, for the purpose of this book, a few considerations will be sufficient. In Tolkien's world we can essentially distinguish two different kinds of heroes:[170]

- the epic hero, exemplified in Aragorn: he has specific origins[171] and powers (he has been endowed with long life like Siegfried and with healing powers like Galahad), he has spent his early years in isolation (like King Arthur), he was assigned the specific quest of saving his reign and marrying a princess, he has a sword called Narsil that is reminiscent of Excalibur and, all things considered, his story ends with a sort of happy ending;
- the ordinary hero, represented at its best by Frodo: he is of humble origins, his assignment is an anti-quest (the destruction of the One Ring), he is not endowed with any particular power and, at the end of his eventful journey, he goes back to the land he came from without any form of happy ending and, because of the wounds, both physical and spiritual, he has received, he is forced to leave the Shire.[172]

We observe also that the ultimate aim that pushes both categories of hero into action is totally "mundane", with no reference to Eru or other gods.

Aragorn, a more complex character than usually thought,[173] is pushed into action mainly by three motives:

---

170 For these distinctions, see Flieger 2004. See also Auden 2004; Colebatch 2003; Glenn 1991; Honegger (forthcoming a and forthcoming b); Christensen 1977; Clark 2000; Wu Ming 4 2010; Rosebury 2003, 32 ff. (where he maintains that the real main character in *The Lord of the Rings* is Middle-earth).
171 We must not forget that he is the descendant of the two elvish and half-elvish strands and will "reunite" them thanks to his marriage with Arwen (*LotR*, App A.1).
172 This is seen by Flieger as a reminder of the tragic destiny of some epic heroes (Arthur, or Beowulf), proving that the Tolkienian heroes are not just sketched out (Flieger 2004, 145). About Frodo, see also 1.2 and 2.4.
173 On this theme, the pages Paul Kocher writes about Aragorn (chapter 5 in Kocher 1977) have become a sort of "classic". See also the recent study by Stephen 2012.

- by a sort of "duty" imposed on him by his lineage, as we see at the Council of Elrond when he, in a gesture of great nobility, unsheathes Narsil, the sword that was broken, just "invoked" by Boromir;[174]
- by his intention to rescue Gondor and the rest of the Free Peoples from Sauron's clutches;[175]
- by his love for Arwen, whom her father Elrond had forbidden him to marry until the time he would be worthy of her.[176]

Frodo's motives are essentially two:

- the main motive is his love for the Shire which he wants to save from the danger looming over it: "'I should like to save the Shire, if I could [...] And I suppose I must go alone, if I am to do that and save the Shire";[177]
- the second is a "great desire", which he does not openly confess to Gandalf, "to follow Bilbo, and even perhaps to find him again".[178]

From these emblematic examples we can observe that the plane within which the characters of the *Legendarium* act is totally different from that of the Christian heroes. These latter heroes can be identified as the saints and martyrs[179] of the Church, whose radical choices are primarily determined by their love for a transcendent God, the wish to reunite with Him and testify their faith in self-sacrifice. St Teresa of Avila expressed with the following words her desire for a complete reunion with God which was so strong that she experienced her not being dead as a cruelty:

Aquella vida de arriba	That life from above,
Es la vida verdadera:	That is true life,
Hasta que esta vida muera,	Until this life dies,
No se goza estando viva:	Life is not enjoyed.
Muerte, no me seas esquiva:	Death, be not aloof;
Vivo muriendo primero,	In dying first, may life be,
Que muero porque no muero.	I die because I do not die.[180]

---

174 *LotR*, FR, 'The Council of Elrond'. The Ring of Barahir has the same function (*LotR*, App A.5).
175 It is not by chance that during his childhood in Rivendell he was called Estel, "hope" in Sindarin (*LotR*, App A 5).
176 "She shall not be the bride of any Man less than the King of both Gondor and Arnor" (*LotR*, App A.5).
177 *LotR*, FR, 'The Shadow of the Past'.
178 *LotR*, FR, 'The Shadow of the Past'.
179 On the difference between Christian and pagan heroes see Fromm 1976, 122 ff.
180 Teresa of Avila 1985, 376.

We are here within a perspective unknown to the heroes of *The Lord of the Rings*, and even if some of its characters are able to accept sacrifice (Frodo, and Boromir too) their noble actions are performed without any reference to Eru/God or the supernatural level of faith. According to Kierkegaard, Faith is on a superior level in comparison to the strictly ethical level of "the common good"; hence, the sacrifice of Isaac, which Abraham was about to perform on God's command, is radically different from the sacrifice of Iphigenia, which Agamemnon was ready to undertake with the sole aim of conjuring favourable winds for the Greek fleet in the war against Troy.[181]

In consideration of the totally immanent and "secular" level on which the choices of the characters in the *Legendarium* take place, and without any specific reference to God and the supernatural level of Faith, we conclude that *Tolkien's heroes, virtuous as they may be, are nevertheless entirely pagan.*

Harmony with the Gospels

However, we should also remember that these heroes are different from characters of other fantasy sagas. Think for instance of Conan by Robert E. Howard or Skafloc, the main character of the novel *The Broken Sword* by Poul Anderson (published in 1954 just like *The Fellowship of the Ring*), whose goal is to kill, even with the use of sorcery, his half-brother Valgard. During his various adventures, he has incestuous intercourse with his sister Freda, and even after he has learnt about their kinship, he still wants to spend his life with her to the point that Freda decides to follow her love for her lover/brother and abandon her Christian faith.[182]

Nor do we find in Middle-earth the same ethics of bravery typical of the Norse culture, where *ofermod*, as we have seen in 5.1.4, may lead to an overmastering pride to the detriment of the "common good". The strong condemnation already expressed by Tolkien towards "his" pagan heroes, Beowulf and Beorhtnoth, is also present in the *Legendarium*.[183] For instance:

---

181 Kierkegaard 2006.
182 Freda, kneeling in front of the Crucifix, breaths: "Forgive me if You can, that I love him more than You" (Anderson 1954 ch.27).
183 Clark 2000.

- towards Túrin, who out of pride refuses many times to reconsider his decisions, thus turning his life into a tragedy;[184]
- towards Boromir, who craves the Ring because he thinks he can use it to free Gondor and return home as a hero;[185]
- towards the suicidal act of the "heathen" Denethor, induced by pride in order to avoid the humiliation of the defeat he thinks inevitable [5.2.3].

In the Tolkienian world, however, we can also find "pagans" who realize the purest part of the Northern heroism without ever letting the *overmastering pride* prevail. For instance:

- Gandalf, who, unlike Beorhtnoth (or Beowulf), faces the Balrog staff in hand on the bridge of Khazad-dûm without giving him way, and in the end urges the Fellowship to flee because he cares more for the success of the mission, the common good of Middle-earth, than for his personal pride,[186]
- the Rohirrim, who perfectly embody the ideal of faithfulness by fulfilling their promise to come to the aid of Gondor.[187] Even though this means certain defeat, they remain undaunted and, unlike Denethor, refuse to yield to passive resignation. At Helm's Deep, Théoden thinks he has no escape nor hope of rescue but, despite this, decides to seek "an end as will be worth a song"[188] together with his knights;
- the Rohirrim again, who, in the Pelennor Fields, after witnessing the end of their king Théoden and the young Éowyn, start the last charge raising the shout "Death, death, death!"[189] referring to themselves and not the enemies they are going to face.[190]

---

184 See West 2000.
185 See the well-documented essay by Forest-Hill 2008b. The author shows how Boromir's death was not the result of *ofermod* but only of his will to save the hobbits, as is proven by Aragorn's "absolving" him for his attempt at stealing the Ring from Frodo.
186 Bowman 2010.
187 The more positive characters are usually aware of the importance of being true to their word, a typical trait of Germanic culture that is also in great harmony with the Judeo-Christian idea of alliance. Think of the terrible destiny faced by the dead of Dunharrow just because they were not faithful to their word (see: Holmes 2004).
188 *LotR*, TT, 'Helm's Deep'.
189 *LotR*, RK, 'The Battle of the Pelennor Fields'.
190 For the role of the Rohirrim as the perfect example of the embodiment of German heroism in its noblest aspect, see Honegger 2011, Fehrenbacher 2006.

This pagan culture of courage, "purged" of *ofermod* in the more positive characters of the *Legendarium*, was not cancelled out by *Christianity* which, as we have already seen [5.1.4], *has kept in great harmony its authentic essence*, which is the tireless will of pursuing a superior good even in the face of history[191] perceived as a long defeat.

---

191 On the theme of the various ethics in the *Legendarium* see also Raddatz 2005.

Chapter Six

Catholicism and the Works of Tolkien

In this section I am going to demonstrate the third enunciation of the synthesis I proposed in 4.3, but first I will try to define what the essence of "Catholic" culture is [6.1]. Then I will show why, in my opinion, the works of Tolkien can be considered an expression of this kind of culture [6.2].

6.1 Clarification of the Term "Catholic"

An attempt at defining the essence of such a complex, thousand-year old tradition is inevitably bound to give only partial results. Despite the odds, however, the challenge is not impossible, all the more so because, in this context, I will confine the scope of my analysis to the cultural impact of Catholicism, *an endeavour that can be tackled either from the point of view of a believer or a non-believer.*

In the aim of culturally defining Catholicism, we may say that throughout its history Catholicism has been the advocate of the *principle of harmony between nature and Grace*. As a consequence, the two levels are only apparently separate, while in actual fact they coexist in reciprocal harmony: "grace does not destroy nature but perfects it",[1] as the famous Thomistic adage reads. This perspective bestows great dignity on the pagan man, that is a man living outside the Judeo-Christian revelation [cf. 4.1], because he is deemed to possess such natural abilities as allow him access, partial as it may be, to the real Truth and real Beauty of the Christian revelation. It is undeniable that the history of Catholicism has preserved a large part of the Classical[2] and Norse[3] culture in

---

1 "*Gratia non tollit naturam, sed perficit*" In II Sent. d. 9 a. 8 ag 3. Cf.: *ibid.* ad 3; In III Sent. d. 24, q. 1, a. 3A; S. Th. I.62.5,co; *De Malo* q. 2 a. 11
2 On the continuity of pagan and Christian culture see Danielou 1995; Dronke 2003; see also the entries "Classicismo" and "Mitologia" in *Enciclopedia Medioevale* (Vol. V and VIII).
3 It is a well known fact that after the fall of the Roman Empire Western culture was in a great part saved thanks to the Benedictine amanuenses. For orientation's sake in the vast subject see Billanovich et al. 1987; Cavallo 1987; Penco 1991, 79-81 and 175 ff.

works of art[4] and in its liturgy, *de facto* realizing the assimilation of paganism. The most evident example is the celebration of Christmas, "the most pagan of all festivities",[5] which was established in continuity with the celebrations of previous solar cults.[6] Tolkien was fully aware of this continuity and had begun to write a history of the Church in England in which he tackled this theme [cf. 5.1.6]. He also indulged in writing the famous *Father Christmas Letters*, destined for his children, where the use of the term "Father Christmas" instead of Santa Claus, and the fact that Yule is Father Christmas's grandfather,[7] do speak for themselves.

The foundations of this harmonic perspective are already present in the Old Testament, in which we find hints about the salvation of all[8] people and meet some biblical persons like Abel, Noah, Melchizedec and the Queen of Sheba, who can be defined as "pagan saints",[9] that is "just" men and women who have not yet received the revelation. The theme of the books of Jonah and Job, which were in part translated by Tolkien for the English version of the *Bible of Jerusalem*,[10] is that of the salvation of the pagan city of Nineveh and the sanctification of a pagan by means of innumerable trials.

In the New Testament it becomes even more clear that salvation is meant for all men, as we can see in the preaching of Christ, which goes far beyond the borders of orthodox Judaism, or in his descent into Hell to save those who died before his coming.[11] Moreover, St Paul affirms as well the possibility for the natural rationality of man to acknowledge the existence of God without the need for an explicit revelation:

---

4 As reference book, see Ries 2009; on the continuity with Norse paganism, see Boyer 1992; on the persistence of pagan elements within Christian liturgy, see Eliade 1968.
5 Danielou 1995, 30.
6 Danielou 1995, 30.
7 *FCL*, Letter dated 24/12/1930.
8 "Among those who know me I mention Rahab and Babylon; behold, Philistia and Tyre, with Cush, 'This one was born there' they say. 'This one and that one were born in her' for the Most High himself will establish her" (*Psalm* 87/86:4/6). "For you are not sent to a people of foreign speech and a hard language but to the house of Israel – not too many peoples of foreign speech and a hard whose words you cannot understand. Surely I, if I sent you to such, they would have listened to you" (*Ez* 3:6).
9 See Danielou 1988.
10 Hammond & Scull 2006b, 439.
11 "For just as Jonah was three days and three nights in the belly of the great fish, so will the Son of Man be three days and three nights in the heart of the earth. The men of Nineveh will rise up at the judgment with this generation" (*Matthew* 12:40; see also 27:52); "God, being put to death in the flesh but made alive in the spirit, in which he went and proclaimed to the spirits in prison" (1 *Peter* 3: 18-19). Note that Jesus' descent into hell is an article of the Apostles' Creed.

For what can be known about God is plain to them because God has shown it to them. For his invisible attributes, namely, his eternal power and divine nature, have been clearly perceived, ever since the creation of the world, in the things that have been made (*Romans* 1:19-20; see *Wisdom* 13:6).

This is the message St Paul brings at the Areopagus, thus bringing about the conversion of some of the philosophers who were listening to him.[12]

Having these Scriptures as reference, the Church Fathers accepted since the very beginning some of the achievements of pagan culture, from Justin[13] to Clement of Alexandria,[14] from Eusebius of Caesarea[15] to Augustine of Hippo.[16] We can see it especially from their positive evaluation of ancient culture; the idea of *praeparatio evangelii*,[17] salvation as being accessible to "virtuous" pagans,[18] and the use of the categories of Greek philosophy for the understanding of the Scriptures[19] are all "consequences" of the harmony between nature and Grace.

Thomas Aquinas, one of the pillars of Catholic theology,[20] offers the clearest distinction between the different orders that exist within the one Truth, so that some truths that can be grasped by natural rationality become preambles and prerequisites for the fulfilment of faith:

---

12 *Acts* 17, 16-34.
13 "All that has been expressed correctly in each one of them [Platonists and Stoics] belongs to us Christians" (*II Apologia*, 13,4); "All who lived according to the Word, of which all men do partake, are Christians, even if they were considered atheists such as, among the Greeks, Socrates, Heraclitus and the like and, among the Barbarians, Abraham, Elias and many others" (*I Apologia*, 45, 2-5; Cf. *II Apologia* 10, 2 and *I Apologia*, 60).
14 "Philosophy opens the road that Christ completes" (*Stromata* I, c. 5,6); "philosophy prepares for the reception of truth" (*Strom.* I c. 16 n. 5); "now, the truth is one, and the 'barbarian' philosophical schools each pretend that the part of the truth they received be the whole truth" (*Strom.* I, c. 13, 57; Cf. *Strom.* V, c. 10, 66, 3 e *Protrettico*, 74, 7).
15 Author of the famous *Praeparatio Evangelii*.
16 "It is necessary to count in the Church also all the saints that lived before Christ came and believed he was going to come as we believe he has come" (*De catechizandis rudibus* 3, cit. in Danielou 1988, 20).
17 Danielou 2009; Danielou 1988; de Lubac 1997; see also the essay on de Lubac by Morali 1999.
18 On these themes and the related evolution of the principle *Extra Ecclesia Nulla Salus*, see Caperan 1934; Hardon 1967, 502-504; Sullivan 2002; Müller 2007; Mazzoleni 2008.
19 Danielou 2010; Jaeger 1966. See also the interesting reflections by Divo Barsotti on the works of Euripides, that distinguish themselves from the more explicitly religious Greek tragedies for a deeper "humaneness" that paradoxically brings them closer to the Christian message (Barsotti 1991).
20 Documents of the Second Vatican Council, *Optatam Totius* n. 807; *Gravissimum Educationis* n. 10. The first to affirm Tolkien's "speculative" closeness to the Aristotelian-Thomistic perspective was Paul Kocher (Kocher 1977), while on similar positions we have the already mentioned Franco Manni (Manni 2006). Completely dedicated to the comparison between Tolkien and the Thomistic metaphysics is the book by McIntosh 2017, which is based on his thesis (McIntosh 2009); cf. also McIntosh 2010. On Tolkien and Aquinas see also: Milbank 2007, 20; Milbank 2008; Birzer 2007, 21-22; Nimmo 2001.

The existence of God and other like truths about God, which can be known by natural reason, as it is said in Rom. I, are not articles of faith, but are preambles to the articles; for faith presupposes natural knowledge, even as grace presupposes nature, and perfection supposes something that can be perfected. (Aquinas, *Summa Theologiae*, I.2.2. ad 1; see also *In Boethii De Trinitate*, Lect. I q. 1 a. 3).

Some truths about God exceed all the ability of the human reason. Such is the truth that God is triune. But there are some truths which the natural reason also is able to reach. Such are that God exists, that He is one, and the like. In fact, such truths about God have been proved demonstratively by the philosophers, guided by the light of the natural reason. (Aquinas, *Summa Contra Gentiles*, Book 1 ch. 3).

That said, it does not come as a surprise that Aquinas, who would draw from the Neo-Platonic or Aristotelian pagan philosophy [cf. 2.2.2.] to develop a Christian theology, affirms – as St Ambrose had already done – that: "every truth, no matter who utters it, comes from the Holy Spirit".[21] This explains his belief that salvation be accessible to those pagans who have followed the rational and ethical principles rooted in human nature, as is the case of the pre-Abrahamic patriarch Enoch,[22] the Sibyls[23] and Trajan,[24] whom he considered to be "potentially"[25] part of the Church. As for Trajan, an old legend, originated at the time of St Gregory the Great and adopted by John of Salisbury in the *Policraticus*, tells that, despite the fact that he was a persecutor of Christians, he was nevertheless saved because of his virtues and thanks to a miraculous rebirth which allowed him to be baptized and die as a Christian.[26] Dante, too, takes up the legend,[27] placing in Paradise other illustrious pagans such as Ripheus, who had sacrificed his life to save Aeneas,[28] and in Limbo the most famous poets and philosophers of antiquity.[29] These themes were well known to Tolkien, who explicitly criticized Alcuin [5.1.3] and certainly knew the story

---

21 "*Omne Verum a quocumque dicatur, a Spiritu Sancto Est*", commentary to the Gospel of St John c. 8.
22 *Commentary on the Sentences*, Book III, d. 18 a.6b ad 1; *Commentary on the Sentences*, book IV d. 45 q. 1 a. 3 arg. 5. Enoch, as well as Elijah, are in the Garden of Eden and not yet in the Celestial Paradise.
23 *Summa Theologica* II-II q. 2 a. 7 ad 3.
24 *De Veritate* q. 6 a. 6 ad 4.
25 *Summa Theologica* III.8.3 ad 1.
26 *De Veritate* q. 6 a. 6 ad 4.
27 *Divine Comedy*, Paradiso, c. XX, vv. 103 ff.
28 *Divine Comedy*, Paradiso, c. XX, vv. 103 ff.
29 *Divine Comedy*, Inferno, c. IV. However, the International Theological Commission 2007 has established that the existence of Limbo as a theological hypothesis is no longer valid.

Chapter Six: Catholicism and the Works of Tolkien

of St Erkenwald,[30] extant in a Middle English poem from the 14th century, and derived from the legend of Trajan. Indeed, Thomas Honegger and I found out that Tolkien owned a volume containing this legend,[31] attributed by some scholars to the author of *Pearl* and *Sir Gawain and the Green Knight*.[32]

Since then, the idea of a possible salvation for the unbelievers has always been part of the Catholic theology:

> The damnation of all pagans that have never heard of Jesus Christ has never been a Catholic doctrine [...]. To those who do their best, God does not refuse Grace; this principle, that Protestants have so harshly reproached to the Scholastic, [...], was applied by Catholic theologians as a benefit to the infidels. (Caperan 1934, 592)[33]

We should point out that the concept of harmony between reason and faith (that is one of the "corollaries" of the harmony between nature and Grace) is not a *proprium* of Muslim[34] or Orthodox[35] culture, nor of the Lutheran Reformation that refuses it completely (*sola fide, sola scriptura*, in Luther's words) to the

---

30 Cf. Shippey 2005, 225.
31 Horstman 1881, 264-274, held in the English Faculty Library of Oxford (coll. VC272).
32 Shippey 2005, 225-226.
33 Sullivan writes: "It is only those who are *culpably* outside the Catholic Church who are thereby excluded from salvation [...] The profound difference between the medieval view and the doctrine of Vatican II on the salvation of non-Catholics is that instead of a presumption of guilt, the attitude expressed by the Council involves a presumption of innocence [...]. But if we presume that those outside are inculpable, then we must conclude that they can be saved" (Sullivan 2000, 151).
34 In Islamic culture, philosophy and science intended as disciplines separate from the religious sphere had their maximum development during the Middle Ages, when the relation between reason and faith had been studied by eminent scholars among whom we mention al-Kindi (d'Ancona 2005, 289-295), Avicenna (d'Ancona 2005, 585), Maimonides (d'Ancona 2005, 646) and Averroes (d'Ancona 2005, 734 ff.). This lively current of thought came to a standstill because of the criticism pronounced by Al-Ghazālī, who rejected the autonomy of knowledge from the Quran (d'Ancona 2005, 153), and the much debated ban on interpreting the Quran that occurred in the 12th century (cf. Campanini 2005, 157-159 and, for the scientific aspect, Grant 2001, 263-277; Jaki 186, 192-218). Therefore, we can say that the harmony between reason and faith is certainly *not* a characteristic of Muslim culture, and this even if we take notice of the fundamental studies of Henry Corbin (Corbin 1989), which show how it is not correct to affirm that the apex of Muslim culture took place during the middle ages. In fact, there is a "prophetic philosophy" that continued to develop in the East, especially in Iran, up to the beginning of the 20th century. However, this philosophy does not welcome the "metaphysical secularization" of the Middle Ages (Corbin 1989, 23), has its justification in the Quran (Corbin 1989, 51), has marked esoteric characteristics (Corbin 1989, 51), does not have "consciousness" of the autonomy of reason from faith and, therefore, cannot harmonize the two spheres.
35 "What is certain, anyway, is that through Byzantium Russia was Christianized but not Hellenized" and as a consequence philosophy was not an autonomous discipline up to the 18th century (Tagliagambe 2006, 19). It is not without reason that the great Russian philosopher Pavel Florenskij does not hesitate to analyse philosophically (and not exclusively theologically, as Thomas Aquinas would have done) the concept of the Trinity and Trinitarian logic within his philosophical perspective (cf. Florenskij 1974, 83 ff.).

extent of rejecting the very concept of *praeparatio evangelii*[36] and, in contrast to Zwingli, even the possibility of salvation for the "virtuous pagans":[37]

> Tell me now any one of you who wants to be a Christian, what need is there for Baptism, the Sacrament, Christ, the Gospels or the Prophets and the Holy Scriptures if such godless heathens, Socrates, Aristides [and Antigone, Cato and Hercules, mentioned earlier] [...] are saved and sanctified together with the Patriarchs, Prophets and Apostles in Heaven, though they knew nothing about God, Scripture, the Gospels, Christ, the Sacrament or the Christian faith? [...] I abandoned every hope of improvement of these followers [of Zwingli] (to the point I do not even pray for them). (Luther, *Kurze Bekenntnis vom heiligen Sakrament*, 26)

---

36 Luther explicitly rejects it in In *Ps* XIV, pp. 144-145 (quoted in Caperan 1934, 235).

37 Luther reproaches Zwingli for granting the opportunity of salvation to Socrates, Antigone and other virtuous pagans (Caperan 1934, 243) and attacks Erasmus for his positive evaluation of pagan culture (O'Rourke Boyle, 1981). In *On the Enslaved Will* Luther affirms: "it was given unto them [the pagans] to hear and know Christ, when before, they could not even think of Him, much less seek Him, or prepare themselves for Him" (Luther, *De Servo Arbitrio*, CLV, 171). I had an exchange of ideas on the subject with Professor Lubomir Zak, a scholar widely respected for his profound knowledge of the Reformation, who wrote me the following: "as for your reading of Luther, I have to say that his thought is complex and difficult to grasp because of its paradoxical structure. As soon as he affirms something you can be sure that at a given moment he will come out with the exact opposite. The examples are innumerable [...]. As for the theme of *praeparatio evangelii*, your reading coincides with the prevailing interpretation and is widespread among most of the Catholic scholars, but also among the Evangelical ones. Nevertheless, there are also scholars who show how Luther was for obvious reasons the proponent of the necessity of the transition from the absence of faith to faith as condition for the knowledge of God and, at the same time, admitted that a certain knowledge of God was also possible even before the gift of the faith in Christ. In this regard, it will be interesting to examine what Luther says about the centurion Cornelius in *On the Bondage of the Will* (WA 739; *ibid*. 325 ff.), where he admits Cornelius received the Holy Spirit even before having heard of Jesus Christ and being baptized. Another interesting passage is Luther's remark on Rm 2, 14 (about the laws of the heart) in his *Commentary*. Once again, the cause he embraces forces him to reiterate the necessity of the *sola fide*; however, as in every argumentation of Luther's, this example too shows its complexity and a structure of reasoning based on the paradox. We must say that the development of the Lutheran evangelical theology after the death of the Reformer did lose, at least in part, the dialectical and paradoxical complexity of Luther and, especially for certain themes, took up a monodirectional orientation. The theme of *praeparatio*, resoundingly rejected mainly by the Calvinist Barth also with the support of many Lutheran-Evangelicals, is one of them. In my opinion, the number of commonplaces we register on Luther and his theses (as for instance the one that denies the possibility of *praeparatio*) is due to the interpretation that has been given of Luther and continues to be given by some theologians and schools of theology within the world of the Reformation" (Zak, e-mail of 7th April 2012).

This position was followed by other protestant theologians from the 16th century[38] to the 1900s.[39] This casts even more light on the "catholicity" of the thesis in support of the harmonies nature/Grace and reason/faith, which were reaffirmed in Catholic theology[40] up to the Second Vatican Council[41] and beyond[42] with the continuity of teaching that characterizes the Catholic culture within which Tolkien was educated, having attended a college founded by John Henry Newman, author of the famous work *Essay on the Development of Christian Doctrine*, an essay where these themes are also dealt with.[43]

6.2 Why Tolkien's Work is "Fundamentally Catholic"

The hermeneutical criteria of Tolkien's texts proposed here are essentially based on the distinction between two levels, pagan-natural and Christian-supernatural, and on their mutual harmony [4-5].

We have also seen how the "cultural" essence of Catholicism is based on this very distinction and the harmony between the level of nature and the level of Grace [6.1].

Therefore, we conclude that the principles on which the *Legendarium* is based are the same as those of the "philosophy of culture" that Catholicism has always postulated and defended since its very beginning, and I hope this overview has helped to elucidate the third enunciation of the synthesis I proposed in 4.1.3.

---

38 In Wittenberg, the professors publicly protested: "as for me, I would not like to be in Zwingli's heaven [where virtuous pagans such as Socrates, Antigone, Cato and Hercules were admitted too]" (Conradi Schlusselburgii 1594, 56, quoted in Caperan 1934, 214). On the theme see also the classic Möhler 1984, 113 ff., where it is shown that according to the Catholic doctrine of original sin Man *post peccatum* is not completely evil and his nature still keeps "spiritual energies" (*ibid*. 114) which make him tend towards God and truth "in the whole ancient world we find a search for the truth" *ibid*. 117) in a completely different perspective in respect to the reformers we have just examined (as an example, Melancton compares the Platonic and Aristotelian concepts used in theological studies to a cancer, *ibid*. 116).
39 Salvation of the Gentiles remains problematic in the world of Protestantism up to the present day (Sullivan 2002, 169 ff. on Barth and Kraemer, cf. Caperan 1934, 585 and 593). Also the famous thesis on demythification by Bultmann, is aimed at clearing away the incrustation of myth and metaphysics of other cultures from the authentic Christian message. On this extremely vast problem see for instance Jaspers and Bultman, 1995.
40 See, for example, the already mentioned works by de Lubac and Danielou.
41 *Lumen Gentium*, n. 16.
42 John Paul II, *Fides et Ratio*, Benedict XVI, *Faith, Reason and University*; Francis, *Lumen Fidei*.
43 As we all know, at the end of this study Newman converted to Catholicism. On Tolkien and Newman see Fornet-Ponse 2010b, 172-87; Andreini 2003.

Likewise, if we adopt this perspective, we can understand the true meaning of letter n. 142, so often quoted but in my opinion only seldom analyzed and adequately understood, where Tolkien affirms:

> *The Lord of the Rings* is of course a fundamentally religious and Catholic work; unconsciously so at first, but consciously in the revision. That is why I have not put in, or have cut out, practically all references to anything like 'religion', to cults or practices, in the imaginary world. For the religious element is absorbed into the story and the symbolism. (*Letters* n. 142, dated 2 December 1953)

I will now analyse it in detail and comment on each passage:

- "*The Lord of the Rings*": the letter is an answer to his Jesuit friend Robert Murray, who just finished reading the book; Tolkien refers therefore to it, but I think his evaluations can also apply to the *Legendarium* as a whole, in that *The Lord of the Rings* is an essential part of it;
- "fundamentally": this is, in my opinion, the *decisive adverb*, too many times found between parenthesis or simply ignored. It indicates that the adjectives "religious" and "Catholic" do not refer to a superficial aspect that can be traced under an explicit or allegorical form but to an aspect that lies at the very foundations of Tolkien's works;
- "religious [...] work": here Tolkien refers to a characteristic of his universe that, as we have seen, is imbued with religion [5.2.2];
- "and Catholic": I believe that in light of what was written in 6.1 it should be easy to understand the meaning of this term. Given the absence of ecclesiastic institutions in Middle-earth, it is quite clear that the scope of this passage is neither strictly confessional nor hierarchical. Tolkien, in my opinion, was using this term to indicate the importance of the Catholic Church in Western culture, an importance that, as we have seen, derives from its accepting and defending the principle of harmony between Nature and Grace, of which the *Legendarium* happens to be a wonderful literary example;
- "at first" Tolkien began to write *The Lord of the Rings* between the 16th and 19th of November 1937;[44]

---

44 Cf. *Letters* n. 20 of 16th Dec. 1937 (in which we find out Tolkien had not yet begun *The Lord of the Rings*) and n. 21 of 19th Dec. 1937 (that informs Stanley Unwin he had begun the first chapter, A Long-expected Party).

Chapter Six: Catholicism and the Works of Tolkien   135

- "unconsciously": it means that the book was not conceived with the aim of proving a religious doctrine of some sort,[45] but "only" "to have as one object the elucidation of truth, and the encouragement of good morals";[46]
- "consciously in the revision": Tolkien finished the book in 1949,[47] even if it was published five years later;
- "That is why": meaning because of the fundamentally religious and Catholic character of the book;
- "I have not put in": in the published text we do not find any special mention of confessional cult or practices (*infra*);
- "or have cut out": it is difficult to say to what kind of cuts Tolkien refers. In the various version of *The Lord of the Rings* published in *The History of Middle-earth* (volumes VI-IX) these cuts are not traceable, nor do we have proof that they were made in the original manuscripts or during the revision of the drafts.[48] He might refer to thoughts he discarded before writing them down;
- "practically": because some religious and cultural elements have been maintained, such as the reference to the One [5.2.1], Faramir's gesture and the prayers to the Valar [5.2.2];
- "all references to anything like 'religion'": meaning prayers directly addressed to God;
- "to cults or practices": here Tolkien probably refers to the abandonment of cults due to the spread of rational monotheism reached by the more advanced peoples;
- "For the religious element": that is the reference to something "beyond" the mundane level;
- "is absorbed into the story": in the sense that the many decisive moments in *The Lord of the Rings* (the finding of the Ring by Bilbo, the fall of Gollum into the Crack of Doom, Frodo's voyage, Aragorn's death) all indicate the existence of a "beyond", even if it is not well defined;

---

45 *Letters* n. 211 (cf. *supra*).
46 *Letters* n. 153.
47 Cf. Hammond & Scull 2006b, 540.
48 The drafts were revised by Tolkien in 1953-54 and we do not know of any special change from the manuscript version of 1949 (cf. Hammond & Scull 2006b, 545).

- "and the symbolism": Tolkien refuses any sort of allegoric reading of his work [1.2], although he accepts the concept of "symbol" meant as the embodiment of some ideas in the story [2.4].

We have to affirm then that *the fundamental Catholicity* of Tolkien's work should not be traced in explicit references to Faith or internal allegories, but that it *paradoxically resides in the distinctive non-Christianity of his world*, a universe that is essentially the pagan expression of a level of nature that is nevertheless in harmony with the supernatural level of Revelation.

Conclusion

Conclusion

To conclude this work, I would emphasize that this can be defined a "synthetic" approach, because it somehow goes beyond the thesis (Tolkien's work is Christian), the antithesis (his work is pagan) and the simple juxtaposition of the two (Tolkien's work is Christian and pagan), reaching a unitary and consistent perspective. This reading differs from all the others I happen to know (and I can say I've read a significant number of articles and essays on the subject). In fact, on a level of logical reasoning:

- this interpretation is based on *few and clear principles* (two points of view and two levels) and can be summed up in only three enunciations [4.1]. To my knowledge this is the first time the analysis has been developed so systematically;
- this reading is *complete*, because it takes into consideration almost *all* of Tolkien's writings[1], be they philological or narrative;
- the approach is *consistent*, because it does not – or better said I think it does not – show internal contradiction.

Finally, from the point of view of criticism, this interpretation "goes beyond" other critical reviews because it does not diminish Tolkien's perspective. In fact:

Unlike the explicitly Christian interpretations [1]:

1. it does not violate Tolkien's Razor, but on the contrary makes consistent use of it;
2. it does not confuse application, allegory and interpretation because there is no longer the need for explicit Christian references within Tolkien's various narrations;
3. likewise, it has no longer the need for confusing a source with its representation;

---

1 The "minor" works are excluded, but only for lack of space.

4. nor does it need to ignore the differences between the *Legendarium* and Revelation, on the contrary requiring them because of the natural – not supernatural – level on which the story of Middle-earth unfolds.

Unlike the Pagan readings [2],

1. it does not overlook those texts where the connection between the *Legendarium* and Christianity comes to the surface, explaining them in light of the harmony between these two worlds;
2. it does not require the search for improbable and erroneous contrasts between Tolkienian narration and Christian revelation;
3. it explains the dissimilarities between paganism in Middle-earth, placed on the level of Nature and therefore non-historical, and its better known historical forms;
4. and, lastly, it avoids the application of symbolisms which does not belong in the Tolkienian texts.

Unlike the interpretations that accept the Pagan-Christian contradiction within the Legendarium [3], it solves the lack of consistency in the final synthesis and, at the same time, maintains the tension between the two levels and points of view which is vital for the whole Tolkienian body of work.

Unlike readings similar to this synthetic approach, it is based on the idea of an almost non-historical natural level – which can as such contain both ancient and contemporary elements – and therefore distinguishes itself from those interpretations that are centred on the "historic" perspective of the *praeparatio evangelii*, which is inadequate to explain the many modern elements in the *Legendarium* [4.1].

Finally, I really hope that this book, written with no polemic intent whatsoever, may contribute to the understanding of Tolkien's greatness and the complexity of his artful mythology, which has been admired all over the world and by every culture and was written neither for a single nation (England[2]) nor a specific religion, but for "all of Mankind"[3] capable of sensing with their natural abilities that beyond the Circles of the World there is "more than memory".[4]

---

2 Cf. Introduction,
3 Honegger 2006, 26.
4 *LotR*, App. A.I.5; see West 2006.

Afterword by Tom Shippey:

On Coincidence, and Harmony

It is no surprise that the relationship of paganism and Christianity in Tolkien's work has proved a lasting problem for critics. Both, in very different ways, and at different moments, come to unexpected prominence within a narrative, in religious terms, generally neutral.

Thus, Tolkien declared that the most stirring moment of *The Lord of the Rings*, for him, was the moment when the horns of the Rohirrim are heard at cockcrow, coming to the rescue of Gondor (*Letters*, n. 165). It is a moment which captures the essence of "the creed of unyielding will" which Tolkien linked explicitly to "the tradition of pagan imagination" (*BMC*, 262). The best word for it is perhaps "dauntless". Théoden at that moment has every reason to be daunted, and just before he seizes his horn from Guthláf there are a string of words which powerfully suggest the possibility: ""dread ... shrink ... cowed ... doubt ... quail ... slink". But with the horn-blast and the charge Théoden appears "fey" (a word from pagan tradition), and even "like a god of old" (*LotR*, RK. V.5). "The Northern Gods", wrote W.P. Ker, quoted by Tolkien (*BMC*, 263), "have an exultant extravagance in their warfare", and Tolkien caught that quality perfectly.

By contrast the most moving moment in *The Lord of the Rings*, for many, may well be the moment when Sam Gamgee wakes from unconsciousness, after the destruction of the Ring. Sam and Frodo had fallen among the fumes of the destruction, to be swept up by the eagles and carried, still unconscious, to Ithilien. When Sam wakes up in the sunlight, he smells the fragrance, wonders where he is – and the first person he sees is Gandalf the Grey, "robed in white": *whom he knows to be dead* (*LotR*. RK. VI.4). It is not surprising that Sam thinks for a moment that he too has died. Does he think he has gone to Heaven? As a Christian might?

One can be sure that this is a moment exactly of "eucatastrophe," to use Tolkien's own term. But does it carry also a hint or echo of that greater "eucatastrophe", the *evangelium*, as Tolkien hinted such things might (*TOFS*, 66)? Sam's words in the scene just quoted suggest as much: "is everything sad going to come untrue? What's happened to the world?"

Even more pointed, I would argue, is the date carefully and immediately indicated by Gandalf, "the New Year will always now begin upon the twenty-fifth of March when Sauron fell". That is the date of the Crucifixion, by old tradition, including Anglo-Saxon tradition, as of the Fall of Man which it annulled.[1] This does not, of course, turn Sam, or even Frodo, into a Christ-figure, and the hint of resemblance is a very indirect one: few nowadays have any idea of the old tradition. But can we just call it "a coincidence"?

I believe not, but my point in this "Afterword" is that while the co-existence of pagan and Christian elements in *The Lord of the Rings* is relatively demonstrable, that co-existence, in a work and a body of work so clearly "polyphonic" (see 47 above), *is not the same as harmony*. And harmony is what this book has demonstrated.

It is an important demonstration, for reasons both historical and contemporary. To take the historical one first, the issue of "virtuous pagans" has been an important one for Christian thinkers many times, exercising (as pointed out above, 128) St Aquinas on Trajan and Dante on Ripheus, as well as the *Beowulf*-poet on his entire cast of heroes (above, 86-87). It gains immediacy at various times of crisis – missionary endeavour, external challenge. It also seems to have exercised English writers in particular, perhaps because of the culture's strong sense of tradition and of loyalty to the ancestors. Claudio Testi has noted above (129) the recurrence of the theme in the poem *St Erkenwald*, often linked to the Gawain-poet, and there is a story similar to that of Trajan in *The Earliest Life of Gregory the Great*, composed by an English monk of Whitby close to the year 710, and so almost certainly contemporary with the *Beowulf*-poet.[2] No

---

1 See *Byrhtferth's Manual*, ed. S.J. Crawford (Early English Text Society Original Series 177). London: Oxford University Press, 1929, 82-5. It is interesting that Gandalf immediately converts the date of Sam's awakening into Shire reckoning, the eighth of April. 25th March Old Style would have been 6th, or even 7th April in 1955, when *The Return of the King* was published. In which case (given that Sam might have been unconscious for a day), Tolkien was indicating the date in both traditional and contemporary terms, as contemporaneously relevant.

2 For the Whitby monk, see Bertram Colgrave, ed., *The Earliest Life of Gregory the Great*. Repr. Cambridge: Cambridge University Press, 1985, 48, 52. For a reaffirmation of Tolkien's view of the date of *Beowulf*, see Leonard Neidorf, ed., *The Dating of Beowulf: A Re-assessment*. Cambridge: D.S. Brewer, 2014.

learned source for the story in the *Earliest Life* has ever been found, and the simplest explanation is that the Whitby monk invented it himself, in response (as perhaps was *Beowulf*) to a felt need in a missionary milieu.

Nor does that exhaust the list of English speculations, and a well-known one much closer to us in time comes in the last of C.S. Lewis's "Narnia" stories, *The Last Battle* (1956). This gives a very clear picture of the salvation of a pagan, one might even say, a demon-worshipper (though one who knew no better). Lewis however took his solution from a much earlier Englishman, Uthred of Boldon, who first framed the hypothesis of the *clara visio* at the moment of death which determines the fate of all in the hereafter, believers and non-believers alike.[3]

One can be sure that Tolkien, for all his admiration of the earlier authors mentioned, would not have endorsed this speculation of Lewis: but such speculations seem to have arisen spontaneously and independently several or many times, and the motive for them is surely both clear and creditable. Tolkien noted the "Mirror of scorn and pity" which fairy-stories turned towards humanity (*TOFS*, 44), and one might apply the phrase to the varied reactions which Christian thinkers applied to pagans and their narratives.

The scorn is there, for instance, in Alcuin's derisive *Quid Hinieldus cum Christo?* (quoted above, 90) Tolkien's reaction, by contrast, was pity, as one sees from his poem on "King Sheave" (*LR*, 87-91). This takes its origin from the opening lines of *Beowulf*, which describe the arrival in Denmark of the child Scyld son of Sceaf, "whom God sent for the comfort of the people".[4] In his poem Tolkien indicates that the comfort was not merely political (as *Beowulf* seems to say). Rather, it was a rescue from the "dark shadow", the "dread" in which the people live, the hopelessness of the pagan world, on which Tolkien's poem lays great stress. The poem still awaits detailed commentary, but it is surely

---

3 The claim may see unlikely, Uthred's speculation having been effectively forgotten for centuries, but in 1951, i.e. shortly before the publication of *The Last Battle*, a lecture on him was given to the British Academy by Dom David Knowles, "The censured opinions of Uthred of Boldon", *Proceedings of the British Academy* 37 (1951): 306-42. It seems probable that this caught Lewis's attention.

4 *Beowulf*, lines 13-14, translated as above by Tolkien in his *Beowulf: a translation and commentary*. London: HarperCollins, 2014,13. On p. 138 Tolkien indicates that he thinks Sceafing was intended by the poet as a patronymic, son of Sceaf, while noting the alternative explanation, "provided with a sheaf". Why Tolkien shifted the miraculous arrival from son to father, and used what he considered the less-likely meaning, would require detailed comment. A further point is that in line 44 of *Beowulf* Scyld is described as sent not by God, but by "those", a plural form. This apparent contradiction must surely have furnished a hint for the Valar, agents of The One, beyond the Sundering Sea.

no "coincidence" that it is 153 lines long: 153 being, in both learned and folk tradition, "the number of salvation".[5] King Sheave cannot bring salvation, any more than Sam and Frodo could: but he and the hobbits bring a hint of salvation. A hope, or perhaps an inkling.

The pagan world, to sum up, *always* was in harmony with the Christian universe, and within the purview of Providence. And, Tolkien would surely wish us to go on to add, *it still is*. A point of more than literary or academic interest.

Turning to the contemporary, the issue of pagans, and virtuous pagans, has once again gained immediacy. England in the twenty-first century is by no means a pagan country, but it could well be described as "post-Christian". The trend was visible even in Tolkien's lifetime two generations ago. Churches are used for marriages and funerals, but more rarely for baptisms, and church-going for worship is at best unusual.

Yet the morality shaped by and inherited from Christianity remains powerful, despite many challenges. Is it possible to have morality without the ultimate sanctions of theology? The hobbits seem to manage the feat. But while it would be too much to say that the modern world, like the Númenóreans, has been left in "a state of overwhelming anxiety and uncertainty" (above, 109), it is perhaps only the word "overwhelming" which needs to be removed.

What Tolkien has given us – as this book so clearly demonstrates – is an image, through narrative, of "harmony between nature and Grace" (above, 125), as between Providence and free will, as well as pagan and Christian. I would suggest, finally, that such difficult mediations may well be best expressed (for human minds) through narrative, rather than through abstract reasoning.

Thus, the relationship between Providence and free will has certainly defeated this author in time past (see note 163 on page 119 above), and left him in the same condition as Milton's rebel angels, who "reasoned high ... Of providence, foreknowledge, will and fate ... And found no end, in wandering

---

5 For the learned tradition, see (among others) *St. Augustine: tractates on the Gospel of John 11-27*, trans. John W. Rettig. Washington: Catholic University of America Press,1988, Tractate 27: 10, 284-6. I can offer no authority for folk tradition other than what was told me in childhood, perhaps by a grandmother: but as Celeborn remarks, "oft it may chance that old wives keep in memory word of things that once were needful for the wise to know" (*LotR* FR. II. 8).

mazes lost".⁶ It is illuminated, though, by a strangely philological and even Tolkienian moment in another of Lewis's works, *Perelandra* (1943). Here the hero Ransom, on Venus, and attempting to avert a second Fall by a second Eve, caused once again by the Tempter Satan, sees his duty – which is to attack the devil-possessed Un-man – but fears to do it.

Then he hears a voice which says, "It is not for nothing that you are named Ransom" (ch. 11). Now Ransom – a philologist, generally accepted to be modelled on Tolkien himself – knows quite well that his name derives from "Ranolf's son": it has nothing to do with the idea of ransoming a captive, and never has had. Then the Voice says, "My name also is Ransom". I refrain from theological comment on this (it takes even Lewis several pages to draw out its significance), but in brief, *Ransom's name is not a coincidence* (any more than March 25, or the number 153). All three were meant – to use Gandalf's word⁷ – of course at immensely different levels.

How a human author does this is clear. How Providence does so is beyond our understanding. Not, however, beyond our appreciation. Many readers of Tolkien's *Lord of the Rings* must have felt the harmony at its core, without being able to explain it: it is one of the sources, perhaps the greatest of them, of his near-universal appeal. Inability to explain that harmony beneath polyphony may even account in part for the many hostile reactions to Tolkien, born of bafflement and frustration.

Both admirers and critics, however, have now been helped to a better and truer understanding of Tolkien's work by this admirable exposition, the deepest appreciation yet written of Tolkien's Catholicity,⁸ and one he himself would certainly have welcomed and approved.

---

6 John Milton, *Paradise Lost* II: 558-61.
7 *LotR* FR I.2, "I can put it no plainer than by saying that Bilbo was meant to find the Ring, and not by its maker. In which case you also were meant to have it." However plainly Gandalf can put it, Frodo replies – and see my remark in the second sentence following – "I am not sure that I understand you".
8 Though rivalled by the collection edited by Roberto Arduini and Claudio A. Testi, *The Broken Scythe: Death and Immortality in the Works of J.R.R. Tolkien*. Zurich and Jena: Walking Tree Publishers, 2012. (English translation of *La Falce Spezzata*. Milano: Marietti 1820, 2009).

Abbreviations

Abbreviations for Tolkien's works

ATB *The Adventures of Tom Bombadil and Other Verses from the Red Book,* London: George Allen & Unwin, 1962.

AW 'Ancrene Wisse and *Hali Meiðhad.*' *Essays and Studies* 14 (1929): 104-126.

BLT 1 *The Book of Lost Tales, Part One.* Edited by Christopher Tolkien. London: HarperCollins, 2002.

BLT 2 *The Book of Lost Tales, Part Two.* Edited by Christopher Tolkien, London: HarperCollins, 2002.

B&C *Beowulf and the Critics by J.R.R. Tolkien.* Michael D.C. Drout. Medieval and Renaissance Texts and Studies 48. Tempe AZ: Arizona Center for Medieval and Renaissance Studies, 2002.

BMC *Beowulf: The Monster and the Critics.* Proceedings of the British Academy 22 (for 1936), 1937. Reprinted in *MC*.

EW 'English and Welsh.' *Angles and Britons: O'Donnell Lectures.* Cardiff: University of Wales Press, 1963. 1-41. Reprinted in reprinted in *MC*.

FA *The Fall of Arthur.* Edited by Christopher Tolkien. London: HarperCollins, 2013.

FCL *The Father Christmas Letters.* London: HarperCollins, 2004.

FFW 'Fate and Free Will.' Two annotations written in 1968 and published in *Tolkien Studies* 6 (2009): 183-188.

FGH *Farmer Giles of Ham.* Edited by Christina Scull and Wayne G. Hammond. London: HarperCollins, 1999.

FH *Finn and Hengest: The Fragment and the Episode.* Edited by Alan Bliss, London: George Allen & Unwin, 1982.

GN 'Guide to the Names in *The Lord of the Rings.*' *A Tolkien Compass.* Edited by Jared Lobdell. La Salle IL: Open Court, 1975. 153-201.

H *The Hobbit: or, There and Back Again.* Edited by Douglas A. Anderson. London: HarperCollins, 2001.

HBBS	'The Homecoming of Beorhtnoth Beorhthelm's Son.' *Essays and Studies* N.S. vol. 6 (1953): 1-18. Reprinted in *Tree*.
HoMe	*The History of Middle-earth*. Twelve volumes edited by Christopher Tolkien, containing: *LT I-II, LB, SME, LR, RS, TI, WR, SD, MR, WJ, PME*.
Letters	*The Letters of J.R.R. Tolkien*. Edited by Humphrey Carpenter, with the assistance of Christopher Tolkien. London: HarperCollins, 1999.
LB	*The Lays of Beleriand*. (*The History of Middle-earth* 3). Edited by Christopher Tolkien. London: HarperCollins, 2002.
LN	'Leaf by Niggle.' *Dublin Review* (January 1945): 46-61. Reprinted in *Tree*.
LotR	*The Lord of The Rings*. 50th anniversary edition. Boston: Houghton Mifflin, 2004.
LR	*The Lost Road and Other Writings: Language and Legend before The Lord of the Rings*. (*The History of Middle-earth* 5). Edited by Christopher Tolkien, London: HarperCollins, 2002.
LSG	*The Legend of Sigurd & Gudrún*. Edited by Christopher Tolkien. London: HarperCollins, 2009.
LTP	*La trasmissione del pensiero e la numerazione degli Elfi*. Milano: Marietti 1820, 2008.
MC	*The Monsters and the Critics and Other Essays*. Edited by Christopher Tolkien, London: George Allen & Unwin, 1984.
MR	*Morgoth's Ring*. (*The History of Middle-earth* 10). Edited by Christopher Tolkien, London: HarperCollins*Publishers*, 2002.
OOE	*The Old English Exodus: Text, Translation and Commentary,*. Edited by Joan Turville-Petre. Oxford: Clarendon, 1981.
P	*Pictures by J.R.R. Tolkien*. Edited by Christopher Tolkien. London: George Allen & Unwin, 1979; republished London: HarperCollins, 1991.
PME	*The Peoples of Middle-earth*. (*The History of Middle-earth* 12). Edited by Christopher Tolkien. London: HarperCollins, 2002.
Preface	'Prefatory Remarks' *Beowulf and the Finnesburg Fragment: A Translation into Modern English* by J.R. Clark Hall. London: George Allen&Unwin, 1940. ix-xliii. Reprinted in *MC* as 'On Translating *Beowulf*.'
RGEO	*The Road Goes Ever On: A Song Cycle*. Poems by J.R.R. Tolkien, music by Donald Swann. London: HarperCollins, 2002.
RS	*The Return of the Shadow*. (*The History of Middle-earth* 6). Edited by Christopher Tolkien, London: HarperCollins, 2002.

S	*The Silmarillion.* Edited by Christopher Tolkien. London: George Allen & Unwin, 1977; reprinted London: HarperCollins, 2001.
SD	*Sauron Defeated.* (*The History of Middle-earth* 9). Edited by Christopher Tolkien, London: HarperCollins, 1992.
SGGK	'Sir Gawain and the Green Knight.' (W.P. Ker Memorial Lecture given on 15 April 1953.) Reprinted in *The Monster and the Critics and Other Essays.* Edited by Christopher Tolkien. London: HarperCollins, 1997. 109-161.
SGPO	*Sir Gawain and the Green Knight, Pearl and Sir Orfeo.* Translated by J.R.R. Tolkien, edited by Christopher Tolkien. London: George Allen & Unwin, 1975.
SME	*The Shaping of Middle-earth.* (*The History of Middle-earth* 4). Edited by Christopher Tolkien, London: HarperCollins, 2002.
SP	*Songs for the Philologists.* By J.R.R. Tolkien, E.V. Gordon and others, printed by the Dept. of English. London: University College, 1936.
SWM	*Smith of Wootton Major.* Edited by Verlyn Flieger. London: HarperCollins 2005.
Tales	*Tales from the Perilous Realm.* Containing *Giles, TB,* and *Smith.* London: HarperCollins, 2002.
TI	*The Treason of Isengard.* (*The History of Middle-earth* 7). Edited by Christopher Tolkien. London: HarperCollins, 2002.
TOFS	*Tolkien On Fairy-Stories.* Edited by Verlyn Flieger and Douglas A. Anderson. London: HarperCollins. 2008. Originally published as 'On Fairy-Stories.' *Essays Presented to Charles Williams.* Edited by C.S. Lewis. London: Oxford University Press, 1947. 38-89.
Tree	*Tree and Leaf.* London: HarperCollins, 2001; containing: HBBS, OFS and LN.
UT	*Unfinished Tales of Númenor and Middle-earth,.* Edited by Christopher Tolkien. London: HarperCollins, 2001.
WJ	*The War of the Jewels.* (*The History of Middle-earth* 11). Edited by Christopher Tolkien. London: HarperCollins, 2002.
WR	*The War of the Ring.* (*The History of Middle-earth* 8). Edited by Christopher Tolkien. London: HarperCollins, 2002.
YWES	*The Year's Work in English Studies.* Containing the chapter 'Philology, General Works.' Vols. 4-6 (1923-1925), cited by no. of volume and page.

Abbreviations for some parts of *S* and *LotR*:

Ainul	'Ainulindalë'
Val	'Valaquenta'
Qu	'Quenta Silmarillion'
Ak	'Akallabêeth'
RiPo	'Of the Rings of Power and the Third Age'
FR	*The Fellowship of the Rings*
TT	*The Two Towers*
RK	*The Return of the King*
App	'Appendix'
TAA	'The Tale of Aragorn and Arwen'

Abbreviations connected with *The History of Middle-earth*

AAm1	'Annals of Aman', written in 1951-52 as revision of AV2, chronology for LQ1[1], published in *MR*.
AAm2	Typescript written in 1957-58 of the 'Annals of Aman'[2], published in *MR*.
AB1	'Annals of Beleriand', written in 1930[3] as a chronology for Q, published in *Shaping*.
AB2	Second version of AB1, written in 1930-37[4] as a chronology for QS, published in *LR*.
AB3	See GA1[5].
Aman	'Aman', written about in 1959, before 'Athrabeth'[6], published in *MR*.
Athrabeth	'Athrabeth Finrod ah Andreth', manuscript written in 1959-60[7], published in *MR*.

---

1 *MR* 433, *Jewels* 3.
2 *MR* 432, *Jewels* 4.
3 *Shaping* 262, 294; *Jewels* 3.
4 *LR* 107-8; *MR* 47; *Jewels* 3.
5 *Jewels* 3-4.
6 *MR* 424 and *MR* 361.
7 *MR* 303-304, 352, 433.

Abbreviations 151

Athrabeth B-C	Amanuensis typescripts of 'Athrabeth Finrod ah Andreth', written in 1959-60[8], cited in *MR*.
AV1	'Annals of Valinor', written in 1930[9] as a chronology for Q, published in *Shaping*.
AV2	Second version of AV1, written in 1930-37[10] as a chronology for QS, published in *LR*.
Commentary	'Commentary to Athrabeth' written in 1960[11], published in *MR*.
Converse A-B-C	Three different versions of 'Converse' published in Michaël Devaux. *J.R.R. Tolkien, l'effiges des Elfes*. Bragelonne, Paris, 2014.
Converse	'Converse between Manwë and Eru', written in 1959-60 and before the 'Commentary to Athrabeth'[12], published in *MR*.
DA1	'Drowning of Anadûnê', typescript of extreme unevenness, written in 1945-46[13], published in *SD*.
DA2	Typescript written with care of 'The Drowning of Anadûnê', written in 1945-46[14], published in *SD*.
FM1	'The Tale of Finwë and Míriel', written in 1957-58[15] before LawsA, published in *MR*.
FM2	'The Tale of Finwë and Míriel', written in the late '50s, after FM1 and before LawsB[16], published in *MR*.
FM3	'The Tale of Finwë and Míriel', written in the late '50s, after LawsB[17], published in *MR*.
FM4	Final text of 'The Tale of Finwë and Míriel', written in the late '50s after LawsB[18], published in *MR*.
FN1	'Fall of Númenor', written in 1936-37[19], inserted in 'Lost Road' and published in *LR*.
FN2	Written in 1937-41 but after FN1[20] and published in *LR*.

---

8 *MR* 303-304, 352, 433.
9 *Shaping* 262, 294; *Jewels* 3.
10 *LR* 107-9; *MR* 47; *Jewels* 3.
11 *MR* 303-304, 352, 433.
12 *MR* 424, 361.
13 *SD* 147, 340, 357.
14 *SD* 147, 340, 357.
15 *MR* 300, 433.
16 *MR* 141, 199, 300, 433.
17 *MR* 141, 199, 300, 433.
18 *MR* 141, 199, 300, 433.
19 *LR* 9, 34.
20 *LR* 9, 34.

FN3	Written in 1937-41 but after FN2[21] containing some corrections related to DA1-2 and NCP, published in *SD*.
GA1	'Grey Annals', written in 1951-52[22], revision of AB2, chronology of LQ1, published in *Jewels*.
GA2	Written in the early '50s, clean manuscript, second version of GA1[23], published in *Jewels*.
GA3	'Grey Annals', written 1957-58, connected to LQ2[24], published in *Jewels*.
LawsA	'Laws and Customs among the Eldar', manuscript written in the late '50s[25], published in *MR*.
LawsB	Typescript written in the late '50s, after LawsA[26] published in *MR*.
Lost Road	'The Lost Road', unfinished tale written in 1936-37[27], published in *LR*.
LQ1	'Later Quenta Silmarillion', revision of QS, dated 1950-51[28], published in *MR*.
LQ2	'Later Quenta Silmarillion', written in 1958 as revision of QS[29], published in *Jewels*.
LT	*The Book of Lost Tales*, written in 1917-20 and published *LT I-II*.
MuB	'The Music of the Ainur/Ainulindalë', written in the 1930s[30], published in *LR*.
MuC*	'Ainulindalë' already in existence in 1948, far-reaching revision of MuB[31], published in *MR*.
MuC	'Ainulindalë', written after MuC*[32] and before 1951, published in *MR*.

---

21 *SD* 331.
22 *Jewels* 3-4.
23 *Jewels* 3-4.
24 *MR* 432, *Jewels* 4.
25 *MR* 300.
26 *MR* 300.
27 *LR* 7-9.
28 *MR* 141, 433.
29 *MR* 141, 433.
30 *MR* 3-7, 432.
31 *MR* 432.
32 *MR* 4, 7, 432.

MuD	'Ainulindalë', written after MuC and before 1951[33], published in *MR*.
NCP	'The Notion Club Papers', written in 1945-46[34], containing FN3, published in *SD*.
NOO	'A Note on Óre', written in 1968, published in *Vinyar Tengwar* 41 (July 2000): 11-19 (translated into Italian in *LTP*).
NotesR	'Some notes on 'rebirth', reincarnation by restoration, among Elves. With a note on the Dwarves.' Draft written in 1972[35] and published in Michaël Devaux. *J.R.R. Tolkien, l'effiges des Elfes*. Bragelonne: Paris, 2014.
OK	'Ósanwe-kenta', written in 1959-60 as appendix of 'Quendi and Eldar', edited with introduction, glossary, and additional notes by Carl F. Hostetter and published in *Vinyar Tengwar* 39 (July 1998): 21-34 (translated in Italian in *LTP*).
Q	'Quenta Noldorinwa' written in 1930[36], expansion of Sk, published in *Shaping*.
QS	'Quenta Silmarillion', written in 1930-37[37], expansion of Q, published in *LR*.
Reincarnation	Text written in 1960, after the 'Athrabeth' and (according to Christopher Tolkien) before 'Comment' (with a note dated 1966), cited in *MR*[38] and published in Michaël Devaux. *J.R.R. Tolkien, l'effiges des Elfes*. Bragelonne: Paris, 2014 (including the text 'The Númenórean Catastrophe & End of 'Physical' Arda').
Sk	'Sketch of the Mythology', written in 1926, published in *Shaping*.

---

33 *MR* 432.
34 *SD* 147.
35 *Peoples* 390-391.
36 *Shaping* 76.
37 *Shaping* 76, *LR* 199.
38 *MR*, 363-65.

Citations

For *S* and *LotR*, the abbreviations refer to the part and the chapter of the part:

E.g. *S*, Qu.1 refers to the first chapter of the 'Quenta Silmarillion', contained in *The Silmarillion*;

E.g. *LotR*, FR.II.3 refers to the third chapter of Book Two of *The Fellowship of the Ring*, contained in *The Lord of the Rings*;

E.g. *LotR*, App A.5 refers to the fifth part of Appendix in *The Lord of the Rings*, that is 'The Tale of Aragorn and Arwen'.

For the *Letters*, the reference is to the number of the letter:

E.g. *Letters* n. 131 refers to letter number 131, contained in *The Letters of J.R.R.Tolkien*.

E.g. *Letters* nn. 131, 156 refers to the letters n. 131 and n. 156, contained in *The Letters of J.R.R.Tolkien*.

For all the other references the last number indicates the number of the page.

MR 195 refers to p. 195 of *Morgoth's Ring*, 10th volume of *The History of Middle-earth*;

MR, Athrabeth 332 refers to p. 332 of 'Athrabeth Finrod ah Andreth' contained in *Morgoth's Ring*, 10th Volume of *The History of Middle-earth*;

Flieger 2002, 28 refers to p. 28 of Verlyn Flieger's *Splintered Light*;

ibid. 30 refers to the same book or text: here p. 30 of Verlyn Flieger's *Splintered Light*;

Flieger 2002, 28 ff refers to p. 28 and following of Verlyn Flieger's *Splintered Light*.

Bibliography

ABBAGNANO, Nicola. *Dizionario di Filosofia*. Turin: UTET, 1987.

AGNOLONI, Giovanni (ed. and trans.). *Tolkien. La Luce e l'Ombra*. Frascati: Senzapatria Editore, 2011.

AGØY, Nils Ivar. 'The Fall and Man's Mortality: An Investigation of Some Theological Themes in J.R.R. Tolkien's 'Athrabeth Finrod ah Andreth'.' *Between Faith and Fiction: Tolkien and the Powers of His World.* Ed. Nils Ivar Agøy. Oslo: The Arda Society, 1998. 16-27.

'The Christian Tolkien: A Response to Ronald Hutton.' *The Ring and The Cross*. Ed. Paul Kerry. Madison NJ: Fairleigh Dickinson University Press, 2011. 71-89.

ALESSIO, Giancarlo (ed.). *Dall'Eremo al Cenobio*. Milan: Libri Scheiwiller, 1987.

ALIGHIERI, Dante. *The Divine Comedy*. New York: New American Library, 2003.

ANDERSON Douglas. 'Richard C. West: A Checklist.' *Tolkien Studies* 2 (2005): 11-14.

'Obituary.' *Tolkien Studies* 2 (2005b): 217-224.

'Brian Rosebury on Tolkien: A Checklist.' *Tolkien Studies* 5 (2008): 21.

ANDERSON, Paul. *The Broken Sword*. New York: Ballantine Books, 1954.

ANDREINI, Alessandro. 'Newman e i 'suoi'.' *Comunità Di San Leonino. Una creatività per il Vangelo*. Panzano di Chianti: Edizioni Feeria, 2003. 67-74.

ARDUINI, Roberto. '*Lo Hobbit*: stilemi fiabeschi dell'opposizione tra luce e ombra.' *La Luce e l'Ombra*. Ed. Giovanni Agnoloni. Ascoli Piceno: Senzapatria, 2011. 17-43.

'Tolkien, Death and Time: The Fairy Story within the Picture.' *The Broken Scythe. Death and Immortality in the Works of J.R.R.Tolkien*. Eds. Roberto Arduini and Claudio A. Testi. Zurich and Jena: Walking Tree Publishers, 2012. 69-102.

and Claudio A. TESTI (eds.). *The Broken Scythe. Death and Immortality in the Works of J.R.R.Tolkien*. Zurich and Jena: Walking Tree Publishers, 2012.

(English translation of *La Falce spezzata*. Eds. Roberto Arduini and Claudio A. Testi. Milan: Marietti 1820, 2009.)

and Claudio A. Testi (eds.). *Tolkien and Philosophy*. Zurich and Jena: Walking Tree Publishers, 2014. (English translation of *Tolkien e la Filosofia*. Eds. Roberto Arduini and Claudio A. Testi. Milan: Marietti 1820, 2011.)

and Cecilia Barella, Giampaolo Canzonieri and Claudio A. Testi (eds.). *Tolkien e i Classici*. Cantalupa: Effatà Editrice, 2014.

Aristotle. *The Complete Works of Aristotle*, Vol. 1-2. Ed. J. Barnes. Princeton NJ: Princeton University Press, 1984.

Auden, Wystan Hugh. 'The Quest Hero.' *Understanding the Lord of the Rings. The Best of Tolkien Criticism*. Eds. Neil Isaacs and Rose Zimbardo. New York: Houghton Mifflin, 2004. 31-51.

Augustine of Hyppo. *De Civitate Dei*. In *Opera Omina di S. Agostino*, Vol. V.1. Florence: La Città Nuova, 1990.

Bakhtin, Michail. *Problems of Dostoevsky's Poetics*. Minneapolis MI: University of Minnesota Press, 1984.

Dostoevskij. Turin: Einaudi, 2002.

Barbiano, Paolo. 'Tolkien scrittore cattolico?' *Tolkien e la Terra di Mezzo*. Ed. Franco Manni. Brescia: Grafo, 2003. 85-92.

Baroni, Pietro, Caterina Isoldi, Edoardo Rialti, and Mattia Lupo (eds.). *Uno sguardo fino al mare*. Rimini: Il Cerchio, 2004. 15-18.

Barsotti, Divo. *Dal Mito alla Verità*. Turin: Pietro Gribaudi Editore, 1991.

'Il Signore degli Anelli più vero della storia vera.' Appendix, edited by Paolo Gulisano, to the Italian translation of Joseph Pearce. *Tolkien l'Uomo e il Mito*. Milan: Marietti 1820, 2010. 221-222.

Bassham, Gregory and Eric Bronson (eds.). *The Lord of the Rings and Philosophy*. Chicago IL: Open Court, 2004.

Becker, Alida (ed.). *The Tolkien Scrapbook*. New York: Grosset & Dunlap, 1978.

Benedict XVI. *Fede, ragione e università*. 2006. http://www.vatican.va/holy_father/ benedict_xvi/speeches/2006/september/documents/hf_ben-xvi_spe_20060912_university-regensburg_it.html (Accessed 21/3/2014).

Bernard of Clairvaux. 'De Laude novae militiae ad milites Templi liber.' *Il Movimento Crociato*. Florence: Sansoni, 1972. 90-91.

Bertani, Greta. *Le radici profonde: Tolkien e le Sacre Scritture*. Città di Castello: Il Cerchio, 2011.

BERTO, Francesco. *Che cos'è la dialettica hegeliana*. Padua: Il Poligrafo, 2005.

The Holy Bible. Wheaton: Crossway, 2001.

The Jerusalem Bible. New York and London: Doubleday, Darton, Longman & Todd, 1966.

BILLANOVICH, Giuseppe, Claudia VILLA and Giancarlo ALESSIO (eds.). 'Tradizione classica e cultura letteraria.' *Dall'Eremo al Cenobio*. Milan: Libri Scheiwiller 1987. 279-320.

BIRKS, Annie. 'Augustinian and Boethian Insights in Tolkien's Shaping of Middle-earth: Predestination, Prescience and Free Will.' *Hither Shore* 8 (2011): 132-147.

BIRZER, Bradley. 'Aquinas.' *Tolkien Encyclopedia*. London: Routledge, 2007. 21-22.

J.R.R. Tolkien's Sanctifying Myth. Wilmington: ISI book, 2009.

'The 'Last Battle' as a Johannine Ragnarök.' *The Ring and The Cross*. Ed. Paul Kerry. Madison NJ: Fairleigh Dickinson University Press, 2011. 259-282.

BLACKHAM, Robert. *Tolkien's Oxford*. Stroud: The History Press, 2008.

BOETHIUS. *The Consolation of Philosophy*. Cambridge MA: Harvard University Press, 2008.

BOLOGNA, Tullio. 'Tolkien e gli altri.' *J.R.R. Tolkien Creatore di Mondi*. Eds. Mario Polia et al. Rimini: Il Cerchio, 1992. 79-100.

BONECHI, Simone. 'Per una definizione di magia.' *Endóre* 6 (2003): 29-35.

BONVECCHIO, Claudio (ed.). *La Filosofia del Signore degli Anelli*. Milan: Mimesis, 2008.

'Frodo o del destino dell'eroe.' *La Filosofia del Signore degli Anelli*. Ed. Claudio Bonvecchio. Milan: Mimesis, 2008b. 23-57.

BOWMAN, Mary R. 'Refining the Gold: Tolkien, *The Battle of Maldon*, and the Northern Theory of Courage'. *Tolkien Studies* 7 (2010): 91-115.

BOYER, Régis. *Il Cristo dei Barbari*. Brescia: Morcelliana, 1992.

BRATMAN, David. 'The Literary Value of *The History of Middle-earth*.' *Tolkien's Legendarium*. Eds. Verlyn Flieger and Carl Hostetter. Westport CT and London: Greenwood Press, 2000. 69-94.

'The Year's Work in Tolkien Studies 2005.' *Tolkien Studies* 5 (2008): 271-297.

BRUNER, Kurt and Jim WARE. *Finding God in The Lord of the Rings*. Carol Stream IL: Tyndale House Publishers, 2001.

BURKE, Jessica. 'Fear and Horror: Monsters in Tolkien and *Beowulf.*' *The Mirror Cracked. Fear and Horror in J.R.R. Tolkien's Major Works*. Ed. Lynn Forest-Hill. Newcastle Upon Tyne: Cambridge Scholars Publishing, 2008. 15-52.

BURNS, Marjorie. 'Norse and Christian Gods: The Integrative Theology of J.R.R. Tolkien.' *Tolkien and the Invention of Myth*. Ed. Jane Chance. Lexington KY: University Press of Kentucky, 2004. 163-178.

Perilous Realms. Celtic and Norse in Tolkien's Middle-earth. Toronto: University of Toronto Press, 2005.

'Saintly and Distant Mothers.' *The Ring and The Cross*. Ed. Paul Kerry. Madison NJ: Fairleigh Dickinson University Press, 2011. 246-258.

CALDECOTT, Stratford. 'Over the Chasm of Fire.' *Tolkien: A Celebration*. Ed. Joseph Pearce. London: HarperCollins, 1999. 17-33.

Secret Fire: The Spiritual Vision of J.R.R. Tolkien. 2nd ed. London: Darton, Longman and Todd, 2003.

'Tolkien's Project.' *Tolkien's The Lord of the Rings. Sources of Inspiration*. Eds. Stratford Caldecott and Thomas Honegger. Zurich and Jena: Walking Tree Publishers, 2008. 211-232.

and Thomas HONEGGER (eds.). *Tolkien's The Lord of the Rings. Sources of Inspiration*. Zurich and Bern: Walking Tree Publishers, 2008.

CALVINO, Italo. *Perché leggere i classici*. Milan: Mondadori, 1995.

CAMPANINI, Massimo (ed.). *Dizionario dell'Islam*. Milan: BUR, 2005.

CANDLER, Peter. 'Frodo or Zarathustra.' *Tolkien's The Lord of the Rings. Sources of Inspiration*. Eds. Stratford Caldecott and Thomas Honegger. Zurich and Jena: Walking Tree Publishers, 2008. 137-168.

CANTONI, Pietro. *Cristianesimo e Reincarnazione*. Torino: Elledici, 1997.

CANZONIERI, Giampaolo. 'A Misplaced Envy.' *The Broken Scythe. Death and Immortality in the Works of J.R.R.Tolkien*. Eds. Roberto Arduini and Claudio A. Testi. Zurich and Jena: Walking Tree Publishers, 2012. 193-210.

CAPERAN, Louis. *Le problem de la salut des infedeles*. Toulouse: Grand Seminarie, 1934.

CARDINI, Franco. *Il Movimento Crociato*. Florence: Sansoni, 1972.

CARPENTER, Humphrey. *J.R.R. Tolkien: A Biography*. London: George Allen & Unwin, 1977.

The Inklings. Boston MA: Houghton Mifflin, 1979.

CARRUTHERS, Leo. *Tolkien et la religion*. Paris: Pups, 2016.

CARTER, Susan. 'Galadriel and Morgan le Fey: Tolkien's Redemption of the Lady of the Lacuna.' *Mythlore* 25.3-4 (2007): 71-90.

CASSERI, Gianluca, 'Frodo Baggins, l'eroe che non ha fallito.' *'Albero' di Tolkien*. Ed. Gianfranco de Turris. Milan: Bompiani, 2007. 183-198.

CAVALLO, Guglielmo. 'Dallo 'scriptorium' senza biblioteca alla biblioteca senza scriptorium.' *Dall'Eremo al Cenobio*. Ed. Giancarlo Alessio. Milan: Libri Scheiwiller, 1987. 321-424.

Catechism of the Catholic Church, 1972. www.vatican.va/archive/ENG0015/_ P33.htm (Accessed 20/12/2016).

CHANCE, Jane. *Tolkien's Art. A Mythology for England*. Lexington KY: University Press of Kentucky, 2001.

(ed.). *Tolkien the Medievalist*. New York: Routledge, 2002.

(ed.). *Tolkien and the Invention of Myth*. Lexington KY: University Press of Kentucky, 2004.

and Alfred K. SIEWERS (eds.). *Tolkien's Modern Middle Ages*. New York: Palgrave Macmillan, 2005.

CHATMAN, Seymour. *Storia e discorso. La struttura narrativa nel romanzo e nel film*. Pratiche Editrice: Parma, 1981.

CHESTERTON, Gilbert Keith. *The Ballad of the White Horse*. San Francisco CA: Ignatius Press, 2001.

CHIESA ISNARDI, Gianna. *I Miti Nordici*. Milan: Longanesi, 2008.

CHRISTENSEN, Bonniejean. 'Tolkien's creative Technique: *Beowulf* and *The Hobbit*.' *Mythlore* 15.3 (1977): 4-10.

CHRISTOPHER, Joe R. 'Tolkien's Lyric Poetry.' *Tolkien's Legendarium*. Eds. Verlyn Flieger and Carl Hostetter. Westport CT and London: Greenwood Press, 2000. 143-160.

CILLI, Oronzo. *Tolkien e l'Italia*. Rimini: Il Cerchio, 2016.

CLARK, George. 'J.R.R. Tolkien and the True Hero.' *J.R.R. Tolkien and His Literary Resonances*. Eds. George Clark and Daniel Timmons. Westport CT and London: Greenwood Press: 2000. 39-52.

CLARK, George and Daniel TIMMONS (eds.). *J.R.R. Tolkien and His Literary Resonances*. Westport CT and London: Greenwood Press, 2000.

CLEMENT OF ALEXANDRIA. *Protrettico ai Greci*. Rome: Città Nuova, 2004.

Gli stromati. Milan: Paoline, 2006.

COLEBATCH, Hal G.P. *The Return of the Heroes: The Lord of the Rings, Star Wars, Harry Potter and Social Conflict*. Christchurch: Cybereditions, 2003.

COULOMBE, Charles A. 'The Lord of the Rings: A 'Catholic view'.' *Tolkien: A Celebration*. Ed. Joseph Pearce. London: HarperCollins, 1999. 53-66.

COMUNITÀ DI SAN LEONINO *Una creatività per il Vangelo*. Panzano di Chianti: Edizioni Feeria, 2003.

CORBIN, Henry. *Storia della filosofia islamica*. Milan: Adelphi, 1989.

CRISTOFARI, Cécile. 'Paganism in Middle-earth.' *Hither Shore* 8 (2011): 148-159.

CROFT, Janet Brennan. *War and the Works of J.R.R. Tolkien*. Westport CT: Greenwood Press, 2004.

— and Leslie A. DONOVAN (eds.). *Perilous and Fair: Women in the Works and Life of J.R.R.Tolkien*. Altadena CA: Mythopoeic Press, 2015.

CUCCI, Giovanni and Andrea MONDA. *L'Arazzo rovesciato*. Assisi: Cittadella Editrice, 2010.

CURRY, Patrick. *Defending Middle-earth*. London: HarperCollins, 1997.

— 'Review of *Ents, Elves and Eriador*.' *Tolkien Studies* 4 (2007): 238-243.

— *Deep Roots in Times of Frost*. Zurich and Jena: Walking Tree Publishers, 2014.

CURTIUS, Ernst R. *Letteratura europea e medioevo latino*. Florence: La Nuova Italia, 2002.

D'ANCONA, Cristina (ed.). *Storia della filosofia nell'Islam medievale*. Vol. 2. Turin: Einaudi, 2005.

DANIELOU, Jean. *I santi pagani nell'antico testamento*. Brescia: Queriniana, 1988.

— *Miti pagani e mistero cristiano*. Rome: Arkeios, 1995.

— *Dio e noi*. Milan: BUR, 2009.

— *Messaggio evangelico e cultura ellenistica*. Padua: EDB, 2010.

DAWSON, Christopher. *Progress and Religion*. London: Sheed and Ward, 1929.

DE KOSTER, Katie (ed.). *Readings on J.R.R. Tolkien*. San Diego CA: Greenhaven Press, 2000.

DE LUBAC, Henri. *Paradosso e Mistero della Chiesa*. Milan: Jaca Book, 1997.

DE TURRIS, Gianfranco. 'Il caso Tolkien.' *J.R.R. Tolkien Creatore di Mondi*. Eds. Mario Polia et al. Rimini: Il Cerchio, 1992. 7-28.

— (ed.). *'Albero' di Tolkien*. Milan: Bompiani, 2007.

'Tolkien tra tradizione Modernità.' *'Albero' di Tolkien*. Ed. Gianfranco de Turris. Milan: Bompiani, 2007b. 133-142.

'Il Signore degli Anelli come itinerario iniziatico.' *La Filosofia del Signore degli Anelli*. Ed. Claudio Bonvecchio. Milan: Mimesis, 2008. 57-70.

'La Terra di mezzo, un mondo immaginario?' Preface to Paul Kocher. *Il Maestro della Terra di mezzo*. Milan: Bompiani, 2011.

'Le radici sacre e simboliche della letteratura fantastica.' *Antares* 3 (2012): 6-8.

'Alla ricerca della radici della narrativa tolkieniana.' *J.R.R. Tolkien. Tradizione e modernità nel Signore degli Anelli*. Ed. Stefano Giuliano. Milan: Bietti, 2013. 7-18.

DEL CORSO, Lucio and Paolo PECERE. *L'Anello che non tiene*. Rome: Minimum fax, 2003.

DENZINGER, Heinrich. *Enchiridion Symbolorum*. Bologna: EDB, 1985.

DEVAUX, Michaël. 'L'effiges des Elfes.' *J.R.R. Tolkien, l'effiges des Elfes*. Ed. Michaël Devaux (ed.). Paris: Bragelonne, 2014. 23-93.

DI CESAREA, Eusebio. *La preparazione evangelica*. Vatican City: Libreria Editrice Vaticana, 2001.

DICKERSON, Matthew. *Following Gandalf*. Grand Rapids MI: Brazos Press, 2003.

and Jonathan EVANS. *Ents, Elves and Eriador. The Environmental Vision of J.R.R. Tolkien*. Lexington KY: The University Press of Kentucky, 2006.

DIMOND, Andy. 'The Twilight of the Elves: Ragnarök and the End of the Third Age.' *Tolkien and the Invention of Myth*. Ed. Jane Chance. Lexington KY: University Press of Kentucky, 2004. 179-190.

Dite 'amici' ed entrate. Turin: Elledici, 2004.

DODDS, Eric R. *The Greeks and the Irrational. Sather Classical Lectures*. Berkeley CA et al.: University of California Press, 1962.

DRONKE, Peter. *Imagination in the Late Pagan and Early Christian World*. Florence: Edizioni del Galluzzo, 2003.

DROUT, Michael. 'A Mythology for Anglo-Saxon England.' *Tolkien and the Invention of Myth*. Ed. Jane Chance. Lexington KY: University Press of Kentucky, 2004. 229-248.

'Tolkien's Prose Style and its Literary and Rhetorical Effects.' *Tolkien Studies* 1 (2004b): 139-163.

'Toward a better Tolkien Criticism.' *Reading The Lord of the Rings*. Ed. Robert Eaglestone. London and New York: Continuum, 2005. 15-28.

The J.R.R. Tolkien Encyclopedia: Scholarship and Critical Assessment. London: Routledge, 2007.

'J.R.R. Tolkien's Medieval Scholarship and its Significance.' *Tolkien Studies* 4 (2007b): 113–176.

and Patrick H. Wynne. 'Tom Shippey's *J.R.R. Tolkien: Author of the Century* and a Look Back at Tolkien Criticism since 1982.' *Envoi* 9.2 (2000): 101-167.

Dubs, Kathleen E. (2004), 'Providence, Fate and Chance: Boethian Philosophy in *The Lord of the Rings*.' *Tolkien and the Invention of Myth*. Ed. Jane Chance. Lexington KY: University Press of Kentucky, 2004. 133-144.

du Chaillu, Paul B. *The Viking Age*. Two volumes. First published 1889. Elibron Classics, 2005.

Eaglestone, Robert (ed.). *Reading The Lord of the Rings*. London and New York: Continuum, 2005.

Edwards, Raymond. *Tolkien*. London: Robert Hale, 2014.

Eliade, Mircea. *Il mito dell'eterno ritorno*. Rome: Borla, 1968.

Enciclopedia dell'Arte Medievale. Ed. Angiola Maria Romanini. Rome: Istituto Treccani, 1997.

Enciclopedia di Filosofia. Milan: Garzanti, 1981.

Evans, Jonathan. 'Review of *The Ring and The Cross*.' *Tolkien Studies* 9 (2012): 97-105.

Evola, Julius. I*mperialismo Pagano. Il fascismo di fronte al pericolo euro-cristiano*. Rome: Edizioni Mediterranee, 2004.

Fabro, Cornelio. *La nozione Metafisica di partecipazione*. Milan: SEI, 1939.

Fascina, Vito. *Alberi e Miti. In ascolto di J.R.R. Tolkien*. Bari: L'arco e la corte, 2007.

Fehrenbacher, Richard W. '*Beowulf* as Fairy-story: Enchanting the Elegiac in The Two Towers.' *Tolkien Studies* 3 (2006): 101-115.

Fernandez, Irène. *Et si on parlait du Seigneur des Anneaux*. Paris: Presses de la Renaissance, 2003.

Ferrari, Franco. *I Miti di Platone*. Milan: BUR, 2007.

Filmer-Davies, Kath. 'An Allegory Unveiled.' *Mythlore* 50 (1987): 19-21.

Fimi, Dimitra. *Tolkien, Race and Cultural History: From Fairies to Hobbits*. Basingstoke: Palgrave Macmillan, 2008.

FISHER, Jason. "'Man does as he is when he may do as he wishes.' The Perennial Modernity of Free Will.' *Tolkien and Modernity 1*. Eds. Thomas Honegger, and Frank Weinreich. Zurich and Jena: Walking Tree Publishers, 2006. 144-175.

Tolkien and the Study of His Sources. Jefferson NC and London: McFarland, 2011.

FISHER, Matthew. 'Working at the Crossroads: Tolkien, S. Augustine and the *Beowulf* Poet.' *The Lord of the Rings 1954-2004: Scholarship in Honour of Richard E. Blackwelder.* Eds. Wayne G. Hammond and Christina Scull. Milwaukee, WI: Marquette University Press, 2006. 217-230.

FLIEGER, Verlyn. *A Question of Time.* Kent OH: The Kent State University Press, 1997.

'J.R.R. Tolkien and the Matter of Britain.' *Mythlore* 87 (2000): 47-59.

Splintered Light: Logos and Language in Tolkien's World. 2nd ed. Kent OH: The Kent State University Press, 2002.

'Frodo and Aragorn: The Concept of Hero.' *Understanding the Lord of the Rings. The Best of Tolkien Criticism.* Eds. Neil Isaacs and Rose Zimbardo. New York: Houghton Mifflin, 2004. 122-145.

Interrupted Music. Kent OH: The Kent State University Press, 2005.

'A Post-modern Medievalist?' *Tolkien's Modern Middle Ages.* Eds. Jane Chance and Alfred Siewers. New York: Palgrave Macmillan, 2005b. 17-28.

'The Curious Incident of the Dream at the Barrow: Memory and Reincarnation in Middle-earth.' *Tolkien Studies* 4 (2007): 99-112.

'Gilson, Smith, and Baggins.' *Tolkien's The Lord of the Rings'. Sources of Inspiration.* Eds. Stratford Caldecott and Thomas Honegger. Zurich and Bern: Walking Tree Publishers, 2008. 85-98.

'The Music and the Task: Fate and Free Will in Middle-Earth.' *Tolkien Studies* 6 (2009): 151-182.

Green Suns and Faërie: Essays on J.R.R. Tolkien. Kent OH: The Kent State University Press, 2012.

'Whose Myth Is It?' Verlyn Flieger. *Green Suns and Faërie: Essays on J.R.R. Tolkien.* Kent OH: The Kent State University Press, 2012b. 102-109.

'A Mythology for Finland: Tolkien and Lönnrot as Mythmakers.' Verlyn Flieger. *Green Suns and Faërie: Essays on J.R.R. Tolkien.* Kent, OH: The Kent State University Press, 2012c, 179-184.

'Allegory versus Bounce.' Verlyn Flieger. *Green Suns and Faërie: Essays on J.R.R. Tolkien.* Kent OH: The Kent State University Press, 2012d. 165-178.

'Missing Person.' Verlyn Flieger. *Green Suns and Faërie: Essays on J.R.R. Tolkien.* Kent OH: The Kent State University Press, 2012e. 223-232.

'The Footsteps of Ælfwine.' Verlyn Flieger. *Green Suns and Faërie: Essays on J.R.R. Tolkien.* Kent OH: The Kent State University Press, 2012f. 74-88.

'Mito e verità nel Legendarium di Tolkien.' *Divus Thomas* 1 (2014): 163-177.

'But What Did He Really mean?' *Tolkien Studies* 11 (2014b): 149-166.

and Carl HOSTETTER (eds.). *Tolkien's Legendarium.* Westport CT and London: Greenwood Press, 2000.

FLORENSKIJ, Pavel. *La Colonna e il Fondamento della Verità.* Milan: Rusconi, 1974.

FOREST-HILL, Lynn. *The Mirror Cracked. Fear and Horror in J.R.R. Tolkien's Major Works.* Newcastle Upon Tyne: Cambridge Scholars Publishing, 2008.

'Boromir, Byrhtnoth, and Bayard: Finding a Language for Grief in J.R.R. Tolkien's *The Lord of the Rings*.' *Tolkien Studies* 5 (2008b): 73-97.

FORNET-PONSE, Thomas. "*The Lord of the Rings* is of Course a Fundamentally Religious and Catholic Work': Tolkien zwischen christlicher Instrumentalisierung und theologischer Rezeption.' *Hither Shore* 1 (2004): 53-70.

'Tolkiens Theologie des Todes.' *Hither Shore* 2 (2005): 157-186; 193-194 (English summary).

'Freedom and Providence as Anti-Modern Elements?' *Tolkien and Modernity 1.* Eds. Thomas Honegger and Frank Weinreich. Zurich and Jena: Walking Tree Publishers, 2006. 176-206.

'Eucharist.' *The J.R.R. Tolkien Encyclopedia.* Ed. Michael Drout. London: Routledge, 2007. 177-178.

'Theology and Fairy-Stories: A Theological Reading of Tolkien's Shorter Works?' *Tolkien's Shorter Works.* Ed. Margaret Hiley and Frank Weinreich. Zurich and Jena: Walking Tree Publishers, 2008. 135-164.

(ed.). *Violence, Conflict and War in Tolkien.* (*Hither Shore* 6, 2009).

"Strange and Free': On Some Aspects of the Nature of Elves and Men.' *Tolkien Studies* 7 (2010): 67–89.

'Tolkien, Newman und das Oxford Movement.' *Hither Shore* 7 (2010b): 172–87, 231-32 (English summary).

FRANCESCO. 'Lumen Fidei.' 2013. http://www.vatican.va/lumen-fidei/it/html/index.html (Accessed 21/3/2014).

FROMM, Erich. *To Be or To Have?* New York: Bloomsbury Publishing, 1976.

FUSCO, Sebastiano. 'L'uso del simbolismo tradizionale in J.R.R. Tolkien.' *'Albero' di Tolkien*. Ed. Gianfranco de Turris. Milan: Bompiani, 2007. 69-74.

GARTH, John. *Tolkien and the Great War*. London: HarperCollins, 2003.

GARBOWSKI, Christopher. *Recovery and Transcendence for the Contemporary Mythmaker. The Spiritual Dimension in the Work of J.R.R. Tolkien*. Zurich and Berne: Walking Tree Publishers, 2004.

GEE, Henry. *The Science of Middle-earth*. New York: Cold Spring Press, 2004.

GEIGER, Louis Bertrand. *La Partecipation dans la philosophie de saint Thomas d'Aquin*. Paris: Vrin, 1942.

GILLIVER, Peter, Jeremy MARSHALL, and Edmund WEINER. *The Ring of Words. Tolkien and the Oxford English Dictionary*. Oxford: Oxford University Press, 2006.

GIULIANO, Stefano. *J.R.R. Tolkien. Tradizione e modernità nel Signore degli Anelli*. Milan: Bietti, 2013.

GLENN, Jonathan A. 'To translate a Hero: *The Hobbit* as *Beowulf* retold.' *Publications of the Arkansas Philological Association* 17 (1991): 13-44.

GLOFCHESKIE, Tanya. 'Life as a shared Story: Narrative Freedom in *The Lord of the Rings*.' *The Ring Goes Ever On. Proceedings of the Tolkien 2005 Conference*. Two volumes. Ed. Sarah Wells. Coventry: The Tolkien Society, 2008. Vol. 1, 133-139.

GRANT, Edward. *Le origini medievali della scienza moderna*. Turin: Einaudi, 2001.

GRAVES, Robert. *La Dea Bianca*. Milan: Adelphi, 1992.

GRAY, William. *Fantasy, Myth and Truth*. New York: Palgrave Macmillan, 2010.

GREEN, Roger L. and Walter HOOPER. *C.S. Lewis: A Biography*. London: HarperCollins, 2002.

GREEN, William H. *The Hobbit: A Journey into Maturity*. New York: Twayne Publishers, 1995.

HAMMOND, Wayne G. and Christina SCULL (eds.) *The Lord of the Rings, 1954-2004: Scholarship in Honour of Richard E. Blackwelder*. Milwaukee WI: Marquette University Press, 2006.

Reader's Companion. London: HarperCollins, 2006b.

HARDON, John A. *Salvation of Infidels*: New Catholic Encyclopedia, Vol .7. New York: McGraw-Hill, 1967.

HART, Trevor and Ivan KHOVACS. *Tree of Tales: Tolkien, Literature and Theology*. Waco TX: Baylor University Press, 2007.

HARVEY, David. *The Song of Middle Earth*. London: George Allen & Unwin, 1985.

HEIDEGGER, Martin. 'Lettera sull' 'umanismo'.' *Segnavia*. Milan: Adelphi, 1987. 267-315.

HEIN, David and Edward HENDERSON (eds.). *C.S. Lewis and Friends*. London: SPCK, 2011.

HEIN, Rolland. *Christian Mythmakers. C.S. Lewis, Madeleine L'Engle, J.R.R. Tolkien, George MacDonald, G.K. Chesterton & Others*. Chicago IL: Cornerstone Press, 1998.

HELMS, Randall. *Tolkien's World*. London: Thames and Hudson, 1974.

HESIOD. *Le opere e i giorni*. Milan: BUR, 1984.

HILEY, Margaret and Frank WEINREICH (eds.). *Tolkien's Shorter Works*. Zurich and Jena: Walking Tree Publishers, 2008.

HOLMES, John. 'Oaths and Oaths Breaking. Analogues of Old English Comitatus in Tolkien's Myths.' *Tolkien and the Invention of Myth*. Ed. Jane Chance. Lexington KY: University Press of Kentucky, 2004, 249-261.

'Tolkien, Dustsceawung, and the Gnomic Tense.' *Tolkien's Modern Middle Ages*. Eds. Jane Chance and Alfred Siewers. London: Palgrave Macmillan, 2005. 43-60.

"Like Heathen Kings': Religion as a Palimpsest in Tolkien's Fiction'. *The Ring and The Cross*. Ed. Paul Kerry. Madison NJ: Fairleigh Dickinson University Press, 2011. 119-144.

HONEGGER, Thomas (ed.). *Reconsidering Tolkien*. Zurich and Berne: Walking Tree Publishers, 2005.

'Tolkien Through the Eyes of a Mediaevalist.' *Reconsidering Tolkien*. Ed. Thomas Honegger. Zurich and Berne: Walking Tree Publishers, 2005b. 45-66.

'A Mythology for England – the Question of National Identity in Tolkien's Legendarium.' *Hither Shore* 3 (2006): 13-26.

'The Homecoming of Beorhtnoth: Philology and the Literary Muse.' *Tolkien Studies* 4 (2007): 191-201.

'Fantasy, Escape, Recovery, and Consolation in *Sir Orfeo*: The Medieval Foundations of Tolkienian Fantasy.' *Tolkien Studies* 7 (2010): 117-136.

'The Rohirrim: 'Anglo-Saxon on Horseback'? An Inquiry into Tolkien's Use of Sources.' *Tolkien and the Study of His Sources*. Ed. Jason Fisher. Jefferson NC and London: McFarland, 2011. 116-132.

'A Reviewer's Complaint.' *Hither Shore* 12 (2015): 276-277.

'Splintered Heroes – Heroic Variety and its Function in *The Lord of the Rings*.' *A Wilderness of Dragons: Essays in Honor of Verlyn Flieger*. Ed. John D. Rateliff. Wayzata MI: The Gabbro Head, (forthcoming a).

"We don't need another hero' – Problematic Heroes and their Function in Some of Tolkien's Works.' *J.R.R. Tolkien: Individual, Community, Society: Proceedings of the 5th International Conference on Tolkien in Hungary (Budapest, 3-4 September 2015)* (forthcoming b)

and Eduardo Segura (eds.). *Myth and Magic*. Zurich and Jena: Walking Tree Publishers, 2007.

and Frank Weinreich (eds.). *Tolkien and Modernity*. Zurich and Jena: Walking Tree Publishers, 2006.

Horstman, Carl (ed.). *Altenglische Legenden*. Heilbronn: Verlag Gebrüder Henninger, 1881.

Hostetter, Carl and Arden R. Smith. 'A Mythology for England.' *Proceedings of the J.R.R. Centenary Conference*. Ed. Patricia Reynolds. Milton Keynes and Altadena CA: The Tolkien Society and the Mythopoeic Press, 1996. 281-290.

Houghton, John. 'Neues Testament und Märchen: Tolkien, Fairy Stories, and the Gospel.' *Journal of Tolkien Research* 4.1 (2017): Article 9.

and Neal Keesee. 'Tolkien, King Alfred, and Boethius: Platonist Views of Evil in *The Lord Of The Rings*.' *Tolkien Studies* 2 (2005): 131-159.

Hutton, Ronald. *Triumph of the Moon*. Oxford: Oxford University Press, 2001.

Witches, Druids and King Arthur. London: Humbledon Continuum, 2006.

'Can We Still Have a Pagan Tolkien? A Reply to Nils Ivar Agøy.' *The Ring and The Cross*. Ed. Paul Kerry. Madison NJ: Fairleigh Dickinson University Press, 2011. 90-105.

'The Pagan Tolkien.' *The Ring and The Cross*. Ed. Paul Kerry. Madison NJ: Fairleigh Dickinson University Press, 2011b. 57-70.

International Theological Commission 'The Hope of Salvation for Infants Who Die without Being Baptised.' 2007. http://www.vatican.va/roman_curia/congregations/cfaith/cti_documents/rc_con_cfaith_doc_20070419_un-baptised-infants_en.html (Accessed 7/1/2017).

Isaacs, Neil and Rose Zimbardo. *Understanding The Lord of the Rings. The Best of Tolkien Criticism*. New York: Houghton Mifflin, 2004.

Jaeger, Werner. *Cristianesimo primitivo e paideia greca*. Florence: La Nuova Italia, 1966.

Paideia, Vol. I. Florence: La Nuova Italia, 1984.

JAKI, Stanley L. *Science and Creation.* Edinburgh: Scottish Academic Press, 1986.

JASPERS, Karl and Rudolf BULTMANN. *Il problema della demitizzazione.* Brescia: Morcelliana, 1995.

JEFFREY, David Lyle. 'Tolkien and the Future of Literary Studies.' *Tree of Tales: Tolkien, Literature and Theology.* Ed. Trevor Hart and Ivan Khovacs. Waco TX: Baylor University Press, 2007. 55-70.

JOHN OF SALISBURY. *Metalogicon.* Berkeley CA: University of California Press, 1955.

JOHN PAUL II. *Fides et Ratio.* Casale Monferrato: Piemme, 1988.

JOHNSON, Judith A. *J.R.R. Tolkien: Six Decades of Criticism.* Bibliographies and Indexes in World Literature 6. Westport CT: Greenwood Press, 1986.

JONAS, Hans. *Dalla fede antica all'uomo tecnologico.* Bologna: Il Mulino, 1991.

JONES, Leslie E. *Myth and Middle-earth.* New York: Cold Spring Press, 2002.

JUSTIN THE MARTYR. *Apologie.* Milan: Rusconi, 1995.

KANT, Immanuel. 'Attempt to Introduce the Concept of Negative Magnitudes into Philosophy.' *Theoretical Philosophy, 1755-1770.* Ed. David Walford. Cambridge: Cambridge University Press, 1992. 203-242.

KANE, Douglas Charles. *Arda Reconstructed. The Creation of the Published Silmarillion.* Bethlehem PA: Lehigh University Press, 2009.

KERRY, Paul (ed.). *The Ring and The Cross.* Madison NJ: Fairleigh Dickinson University Press, 2011.

'Introduction.' *The Ring and The Cross.* Ed. Paul Kerry. Madison NJ: Fairleigh Dickinson University Press, 2011b. 17-53.

and Sandra MIESEL (eds.). *Light Beyond All Shadows: Religious Experience in Tolkien's Work.* Madison NJ: Fairleigh Dickinson University Press, 2011.

KIERKEGAARD, Søren. *Fear and Trembling.* Cambridge: Cambridge University Press, 2006.

KILBY, Clive S. *Tolkien and the Silmarillion.* Wheaton IL: Harold Shaw, 1977.

KLINGER, Judith. 'Tolkien's Mythopoietic Transformation of Landscape: Tombs, Mounds and Barrows.' *Hither Shore* 8 (2011): 170-189.

KLOCZKO, Édouard J. *Lingue Elfiche.* Rome: Tre Editori, 2002.

KOCH, Ludovica (ed.). *Beowulf.* Turin: Einaudi, 1992.

KOCHER, Paul. *Master of Middle-Earth.* New York: Ballantine, 1972.

KOLPAKTCHY, Gregorio and Donato PIANTANIDA. *Il Libro dei Morti degli antichi egiziani*. Rome: Atanòr, 2008.

KRAUS, Joe. 'Tolkien, Modernism, and the Importance of Tradition.' *The Lord of the Rings and Philosophy*. Eds. Gregory Bassham and Eric Bronson. Chicago IL: Open Court, 2004. 137-149.

KREEFT, Peter J. *The Philosophy of Tolkien*. San Francisco CA: Ignatius Press, 2005.

LADAVAS, Alberto. 'The Wrong Path of the Sub-Creator.' *The Broken Scythe. Death and Immortality in the Works of J.R.R.Tolkien*. Eds. Roberto Arduini and Claudio A. Testi. Zurich and Jena: Walking Tree Publishers, 2012. 117-132.

LARSEN, Kristine. 'Sauron, Mont Doom, and Elvish Moths: The Influence of Tolkien on Modern Science.' *Tolkien Studies* 4 (2007): 223-234.

LIBRÁN-MORENO, Miryam. "A Kind of Orpheus-Legend in Reverse': Two Classical Myths in the Story of Beren and Lúthien.' *Myth and Magic*. Eds. Thomas Honegger and Eduardo Segura. Zurich and Jena: Walking Tree Publishers, 2007. 143-186.

LOBDELL, Jared (ed.). *A Tolkien Compass*. Chicago IL: Open Court, 2003.

LODIGIANI, Emilia. *Invito alla lettura di Tolkien*. Milan: Mursia, 1982.

LOMBARDO, Alberto. 'Il sentimento politeista di J.R.R. Tolkien.' *'Albero' di Tolkien*. Ed. Gianfranco de Turris. Milan: Bompiani, 2007. 99-115.

LONG, Rebekah. 'Fantastic Medievalism and the Great War in J.R.R. Tolkien's *The Lord of the Rings*.' *Tolkien's Modern Middle Ages*. Eds. Jane Chance and Alfred Siewers. New York: Palgrave Macmillan, 2005. 123-138.

LUTHER, Martin, *Servo arbitrio*. 1525. http://www.martinluthersermons.com/_of_the_free_Will.pdf (Accessed 7/1/2017).

Kurze Bekenntnis vom heiligen Sakrament. 1545. http://www.lutherdansk.dk/WA_54/WA_54_-_web.htm (Accessed 7/1/2017)

LYNCH, James. 'The Literary Banquet and the Eucharistic Feast.' *Mythlore* 18 (1978): 13-14.

McINTOSH, Jonathan S. *The Imperishable Flame*. Ann Arbor MI: UMI, 2009.

'Ainulindalë: Tolkien, St. Thomas, and the Metaphysics of the Music.' *Music in Middle-earth*. Eds. Heidi Steimel and Friedhelm Schneidewind. Zurich and Jena: Walking Tree Publishers, 2010. 53-74.

The Flame Imperishable. Tolkien, St. Thomas and the Metaphysics of Faërie. Kettering OH: Angelico Press, 2017.

MADSEN, Catherine. "Light from an Invisible lamp': Natural Religion in *The Lord of the Rings*.' *Tolkien and the invention of Myth*. Ed. Jane Chance. Lexington KY: University Press of Kentucky, 2004. 35-47.

'Eru erased: The Minimalist Cosmology of *The Lord of the Rings*.' *The Ring and The Cross*. Ed. Paul Kerry. Madison NJ: Fairleigh Dickinson University Press, 2011. 152-169.

MAIETTINI, Giulio. *La Discrezione di Dio*. Noci: Editore La Scala, 2011.

MANNI, Franco (ed.). *Tolkien e la Terra di Mezzo*. Brescia: Grafo, 2003.

Lettera a un amico della Terra di Mezzo. Brescia: Simonelli, 2006.

'Real and Imagined History in *The Lord of the Rings*.' *Mallorn* 47 (2009): 28-37.

'A Eulogy of Finitude.' *The Broken Scythe. Death and Immortality in the Works of J.R.R.Tolkien*. Eds. Roberto Arduini and Claudio A. Testi. Zurich and Jena: Walking Tree Publishers, 2012. 5-38.

MAURIER, Henri. 'Paganesimo.' *Grande dizionario delle religioni*. Ed. Paul Joseph Poupard. Casale Monferrato: Piemme, 2000. 1569-1572.

MAZZOLENI, Sandra. *Chiesa e Salvezza*. Rome: Urbaniana University Press, 2008.

MILBANK, Alison. *Chesterton and Tolkien as Theologians*. London: T&T Clark, 2007.

'Tolkien, Chesterton, and Thomism.' *Tolkien's The Lord of the Rings: Sources of Inspiration*. Eds. Stratford Caldecott and Thomas Honegger. Zurich and Berne: Walking Tree Publishers, 2008. 187-98.

MILBURN, Michael. 'Coleridge's Definition of Imagination.' *Tolkien Studies* 7 (2010): 55-66.

MINGARDI, Alberto and Carlo STAGNARO. *La Verità su Tolkien*. Rome: Liberal Edizioni, 2004.

MITCHELL, Philip I. "But Grace is Not Infinite': Tolkien's Explorations of Nature and Grace in His Catholic Context.' *Mythlore* 31.3, issue 121-122 (2013): 61-81.

MÖHLER, Adam Johann. *Simbolica*. Milan: Jaca Book, 1984.

MONDA, Andrea. *L'anello e la Croce*. Soveria Mannelli: Rubettino, 2008.

and Wu MING 4. 'Tolkien the Catholic Philosopher.' *Tolkien and Philosophy*. Eds. Roberto Arduini and Claudio A. Testi. Zurich and Jena: Walking Tree Publishers, 2014. 85-124.

and Saverio SIMONELLI. *Tolkien Il Signore della fantasia*. Cles: Frassinelli, 2002.

MONDIN, Battista. *Dizionario Enciclopedico del pensiero di San Tommaso d'Aquino*. Bologna: ESD, 1991.

MORALI, Ilaria. *La salvezza dei non cristiani*. Bologna: Emi, 1999.

MORILLO, Stephen. 'The Entwives: Investigating the Spiritual Core of *The Lord of the Rings*.' *The Ring and The Cross*. Ed. Paul Kerry. Madison NJ: Fairleigh Dickinson University Press, 2011. 106-118.

MORINI, Massimo. *Le parole di Tolkien*. Faenza: Moby Dick, 1999.

MOTHER TERESA and Brian KOLEDIEJCHUK. *Come Be My Light*. New York: Doubleday, 2007.

MÜLLER, Michael. *The Catholic Dogma 'Extra Ecclesia nullo omnino salvetur*. Hartford CT: Authors Press, 2007.

NAGEL, Rainer. 'Review of *Tolkien Studies 4*.' *Hither Shore* 4 (2007): 216.

NAGY, Gergely. 'The Great Chain of Reading: (Inter-)textual Relations and the Technique of Mythopoesis in the Túrin Story.' *Tolkien the Medievalist*. Ed. Jane Chance. New York: Routledge, 2002. 239-258.

'Saving the Myths: The Re-creation of Mythology in Plato and Tolkien.' *Tolkien and the Invention of Myth*. Ed. Jane Chance. Lexington KY: University Press of Kentucky, 2004. 81-100.

'The Medievalist('s) Fiction: Textuality and Historicity as Aspects of Tolkien's Medievalist Cultural Theory in a Postmodernist Context.' *Tolkien's Modern Middle Ages*. Eds. Jane Chance and Alfred K. Siewers. New York: Palgrave Macmillan, 2005. 29-42.

NAJOIVITS, Simson. *Egypt, Trunk of the Tree*. New York: Algora Publishing, 2003.

NIMMO, Andrew. *Tolkien and Thomism, Middle-earth and the States of Nature*, 2001. http://copiosa.org/Lord_Rings/lord_ring_tolkien.htm (Accessed: 16/2/2014).

O'ROURKE BOYLE, Marjorie. *Christening Pagan Myths: Erasmus in Pursuit of Wisdom*. Toronto: University of Toronto Press, 1981.

PAGGI, Marco. *Il Labirinto e la Spada*. Genova: ECIG, 1990.

PASSARO, Enrico. 'Tolkien Pagano.' *Minas Tirith* 9 (2000): 37-45.

and Marco RESPINTI. *Paganesimo e Cristianesimo in Tolkien*. Rome: Il Minotauro, 2004.

PATCHEN, Mortimes. 'Tolkien and Modernism.' *Tolkien Studies* 2 (2005): 113-129.

PEARCE, Joseph. *Tolkien: Man and Myth*. London: HarperCollins, 1998.

(ed.). *Tolkien: A Celebration*. London: HarperCollins, 1999.

'Foreword.' *J.R.R. Tolkien's Sanctifying Myth: Understanding Middle-earth*. Bradley J. Birzer. Wilmington DE: Intercollegiate Studies Institute, 1999b.

'True Myth: the Catholicism of *The Lord of the Rings.*' *Celebrating Middle-earth.* Ed. John West Jr. Seattle WA: Inklings Books, 2002. 83-94.

PENCO, Gregorio. *Il monachesimo tra spiritualità e cultura.* Milan: Jaca Book, 1991.

PETTY, Anne C. *One Ring to Bind them All. Tolkien's Mythology.* Tuscaloosa AL and London: University of Alabama Press, 2002.

PHELPSTEAD, Carl. *Tolkien and Wales.* Cardiff: University of Wales Press, 2011.

PLATO. *Fedone.* Bari: Laterza, 1987.

POLIA, Mario. *Omaggio a J.R.R. Tolkien.* Rimini: Il Cerchio, 1980.

and Gianfranco DE TURRIS, Adolfo MORGANTI, and Tullio BOLOGNA. *J.R.R. Tolkien Creatore di Mondi.* Rimini: Il Cerchio, 1992.

POPPI, Angelico. *Sinossi dei Quattro Vangeli, Introduzione e commento.* Padua: Edizioni Il Messaggero, 1990.

POUPARD, Paul Joseph. *Grande dizionario delle religioni.* Casale Monferrato: Piemme, 2000.

PURTILL, Richard. *J.R.R. Tolkien: Myth, Morality and Religion.* San Francisco CA: Ignatius Press, 2003.

The Quran. Oxford: Oxford University Press, 2004.

RADDATZ, Gregor. 'Ethik oder Ethiken Tolkiens?' *Hither Shore* 2 (2005): 225-242, 244-245 (English summary).

RATELIFF, John. ''And All the Days of Her Life Are Forgotten'. *The Lord of the Rings* as Mythic Prehistory.' *The Lord of the Rings, 1954-2004: Scholarship in Honour of Richard E. Blackwelder.* Eds. Wayne G. Hammond and Christina Scull. Milwaukee, WI: Marquette University Press, 2006. 67-100.

'Review of *Tolkien's Shorter Works'. Tolkien Studies* 6 (2009): 304.

'*She* revisited.' *Tolkien and the Study of His Sources.* Ed. Jason Fisher. Jefferson NC and London: McFarland, 2011. 145-161.

"That Seems to Me Fatal': Pagan and Christian in *The Fall of Arthur.*' *Tolkien Studies* 13 (2016): 45-70.

RATZINGER, Joseph. *Introduzione allo spirito della Liturgia.* Milano: San Paolo, 2001.

REALE, Giovanni. *Storia della Filosofia Antica.* Five volumes. Milan: Vita e Pensiero, 1987.

REILLY, R.J. *Romantic Religion.* Great Barrington MA: Lindisfarne Books, 2006.

REYNOLDS, Patricia (ed.). *Proceedings of the J.R.R. Centenary Conference.* Milton Keynes and Altadena CA: The Tolkien Society and the Mythopoeic Press, 1996.

'Death and Funerary Practices in Middle-earth.' 2008. http://www.tolkiensociety.org/ed/death.html (Accessed: 20/12/2013).

RIALTI, Edoardo. 'Come oro cadono le foglie. La caduta, la morte , la macchina ne Il Signore degli Anelli.' *Uno sguardo fino al mare*. Eds. Pietro Baroni, Caterina Isoldi, Edoardo Rialti and Mattia Lupo. Rimini: Il Cerchio, 2004. 15-18, 83-92.

RIES, Julien. *Incontro e dialogo*. Milan: Jaca Book, 2009.

ROSEBURY, Brian. *Tolkien: A Cultural Phenomenon*. Houndmills, Basingstoke: Palgrave Macmillan, 2003.

'Revenge and Moral Judgment in Tolkien.' *Tolkien Studies* 5 (2008): 1-20.

RUTLEDGE, Amelia. "'Justice is not healing': J.R.R. Tolkien's Pauline Constructs in 'Finwë and Míriel'." *Tolkien Studies* 9 (2012): 59-74.

RYAN, John S. *Tolkien's View: Windows into his World*. Zurich and Jena: Walking Tree Publishers, 2013.

SAXTON, Benjamin. 'Tolkien and Baktin on Authorship, Literary Freedom and Alterity.' *Tolkien Studies* 10 (2013): 167-183.

SCHLÜSSELBURG, Konrad Martin. *Theologiae Calvinistarum libri tres*. Frankfurt: 1594.

SCOVILLE, Chester N. 'Pastoralia and Perfectibility in William Morris and J.R.R. Tolkien.' *Tolkien's Modern Middle Ages*. Eds. Jane Chance and Alfred Siewers. New York: Palgrave Macmillan, 2005. 139-154.

SEAMAN, Gerald. 'Tolkien e la revisione della tradizione romantica.' *Endóre* 3 (2000): 4-15.

'Review of *Tolkien's The Lord of the Rings: Sources of Inspiration*. Eds. Stratford Caldecott and Thomas Honegger. Zurich and Bern: Walking Tree Publishers, 2008.' *Tolkien Studies* 6 (2009): 298.

SECOND VATICAN COUNCIL. http://www.vatican.va/archive/hist_councils/ ii_vatican_council/index.htm (Accessed 7/1/2017).

SEN, Amartya. *On Ethics and Economy*. Oxford: Oxford University Press, 1990.

SHIPPEY, Tom. 'Tolkien's Sources: The True Tradition.' *Readings on J.R.R. Tolkien*. Ed. Katie De Koster. San Diego CA: Greenhaven Press, 2000. 153-161.

J.R.R.Tolkien: Author of the Century. London: HarperCollins, 2000b.

'Foreword.' *A Tolkien Compass*. Ed. Jared Lobdell. Chicago IL: Open Court, 2003. i-xi.

The Road to Middle-earth. 3rd ed. London: HarperCollins, 2005.

Roots and Branches. Zurich and Jena: Walking Tree Publisher, 2007.

'Tolkien and the Appeal of the Pagan: *Edda* and *Kalevala*.' Tom Shippey. *Roots and Branches*. Zurich and Jena: Walking Tree Publisher, 2007b. 19-38.

'Heroes and Heroism.' Tom Shippey. *Roots and Branches*. Zurich and Jena: Walking Tree Publisher, 2007c. 267-284.

'Tolkien and Iceland: The Philology of Envy.' Tom Shippey. *Roots and Branches*. Zurich and Jena: Walking Tree Publisher, 2007d. 187-202.

'Tolkien and the *Beowulf* Poet.' Tom Shippey. *Roots and Branches*. Zurich and Jena: Walking Tree Publisher, 2007e. 1-18.

'Tolkien's Academic Reputation Now.' Tom Shippey. *Roots and Branches*. Zurich and Jena: Walking Tree Publisher, 2007f. 203-212.

'New Learning and New Ignorance: Magia, Goeteia and the Inklings.' *Myth and Magic*. Eds. Thomas Honegger and Eduardo Segura. Zurich and Jena: Walking Tree Publishers, 2007g. 21-46.

'Tolkien and the 'Homecoming of Beorhtnoth'.' Tom Shippey. *Roots and Branches*. Zurich and Jena: Walking Tree Publisher, 2007h. 323-340.

'Review of *Sigurd*.' *Tolkien Studies* 7 (2010): 291-324.

and Franco MANNI. 'Tolkien between Philosophy and Philology.' *Tolkien and Philosophy*. Eds. Roberto Arduini and Claudio A. Testi. Zurich and Jena: Walking Tree Publishers, 2014. 21-72.

SIEWERS, Alfred K. 'Tolkien's Cosmic-Christian Ecology: The Medieval Underpinnings.' *Tolkien's Modern Middle Ages*. Eds. Jane Chance and Alfred Siewers. New York: Palgrave Macmillan, 2005. 139-154.

SIMONSON, Martin. *The Lord of the Rings and the Western Narrative Tradition*. Zurich and Bern: Walking Tree Publishers, 2008.

Sir Gawain e il Cavaliere Verde (Sir Gawain and the Green Knight). Milan: Adelphi, 1986.

SMITH, Ross. *Inside Language, Linguistic and Aesthetic Theory in Tolkien*. Zurich and Berne: Walking Tree Publishers, 2007.

SOLOPOVA, Elizabeth. *Language, Myth and History*. Oxford and New York: North Landing Books, 2009.

SOMMAVILLA, Guido. *Peripezie dell'epica contemporanea*. Milan: Jaca Book, 1983.

SPIRITO, Guglielmo. *Tra San Francesco e Tolkien*. Rimini: Il Cerchio, 2003.

'Speaking with Animals.' *Tolkien's Shorter Works*. Eds. Margaret Hiley and Frank Weinreich. Zurich and Jena: Walking Tree Publishers, 2008. 17-36.

STEFANO, Giuliano. *J.R.R. Tolkien. Tradizione modernità nel Signore degli Anelli*. Milan: Bietti, 2013.

STEIMEL, Heidi and Friedhelm SCHNEIDEWIND (eds.). *Music in Middle-earth*. Zurich and Jena: Walking Tree Publishers, 2010.

STENSTRÖM, Anders. 'A Mythology? For England?' *Proceedings of the J.R.R. Centenary Conference*. Ed. Patricia Reynolds. Milton Keynes and Altadena CA: The Tolkien Society and the Mythopoeic Press, 1996. 310-314.

STEPHEN, Elizabeth. *Hobbit to Hero. The Making of Tolkien's King*. Gloucestershire: ADC Publications, 2012.

STERLING, Grant C. "The Gift of Death': Tolkien's Philosophy of Mortality.' *Mythlore* 21.4 (1997): 16-18.

STEVENS, Jen. 'From Catastrophe to Eucatastrophe. J.R.R. Tolkien's Transformation of Ovid's Mythic Pyramus and Thisbe into Beren and Lúthien.' *Tolkien and the Invention of Myth*. Ed. Jane Chance. Lexington KY: University Press of Kentucky, 2004. 119-132.

STURCH, Richard. *Four Christian Fantasists. A Study of the Fantastic Writings of George MacDonald, Charles Williams, C.S. Lewis & J.R.R. Tolkien*. Zurich and Bern: Walking Tree Publishers, 2007.

SUCHECKI, Zbigniew. *La cremazione nella legislatura del Diritto Canonico e Civile*. Rome: Libreria Editrice Vaticana, 1995.

SULLIVAN, Francis A. *Salvation Outside the Church?* Eugene: Wipf, 2002.

SULLIVAN III, C. W. 'Tolkien the Bard.' *J.R.R. Tolkien and his Literary Resonances*. Eds. George Clark and Daniel Timmons. Westport CT and London: Greenwood Press, 2000. 11-20.

TACITUS. *De Origine et situ Germanorum*. In *Opera Omnia*. Turin: Einaudi, 2003.

TAGLIAGAMBE, Silvano. *Florenskij*. Milan: Bompiani, 2006.

TERESA OF AVILA. *The Collected Works of St. Teresa of Avila*. Vol. 3. Washington D.C.: ICS Publication, 1985.

TESTI, Claudio A. 'Tolkien, Tommaso d'Aquino e l'analogia.' *Divus Thomas* 2 (2004): 73-99.

'Tolkien, l'analogia e la verità delle fiabe.' *Endóre* 10 (2007): 17-26.

'Tolkien's Legendarium as a *meditatio mortis*.' *The Broken Scythe. Death and Immortality in the Works of J.R.R. Tolkien*. Eds. Roberto Arduini and Claudio A. Testi. Zurich and Jena: Walking Tree Publishers, 2012. 39-68.

'Logic and Theology in Tolkien's Thanatology.' *The Broken Scythe. Death and Immortality in the Works of J.R.R. Tolkien*. Eds. Roberto Arduini and Claudio A. Testi. Zurich and Jena: Walking Tree Publishers, 2012b. 175-192.

'Tolkien's Work: Is It Pagan or Christian? A Synthetic Approach.' *Tolkien Studies* 10 (2013): 1-47.

'Quale teologia per la Terra di mezzo di J.R.R. Tolkien.' *Lateranum* 3 (2013b): 583-612.

'Tra letteratura e metafisica. Tolkien e Tommaso d'Aquino.' *Tolkien e i Classici.* Eds. Roberto Arduini, Cecilia Barella, Giampaolo Canzonieri, and Claudio A. Testi. Cantalupa: Effatà Editrice, 2014. 103-112.

'Analogy, Sub-Creation and Surrealism.' *Hither Shore* 12 (2016): 178-193.

TOLKIEN, Simon. 'Intervista a Simon Tolkien.' *Mallorn* 50 (2010): 42-45.

THOMAS AQUINAS. 'De Rationibus Fidei.' *Opuscula Theologica.* Turin: Marietti, 1954. 251-68.

'In Boethii De Trinitate Expositio.' *Opuscula Theologica.* Turin: Marietti, 1954b. 293-433.

De Veritate. Vol. 1 of *Quaestiones Disputatae.* Turin: Marietti, 1964.

De Malo. Vol. 2 of *Quaestiones Disputatae.* Turin: Marietti, 1965.

Summa contra gentiles. Turin: Marietti, 1967.

Somma Teologica. Bologna: Edizioni Studio Domenicano, 1985.

Commento al Vangelo di S. Giovanni I-VI. Rome: Città Nuova, 1990.

Commento alle Sentenze. Bologna: Edizioni Studio Domenicano, 2001.

TURNER, Allan. *The Silmarillion Thirty Years On.* Zurich and Bern: Walking Tree Publishers, 2007.

TURVILLE-PETRE, Edward O.G. *Myth and Religion of the North.* Westport CT: Greenwood Press, 1975.

TUZZI, Federica. *Athrabeth Finrod ah Andreth. Proposta di traduzione e commento.* Tesi di Laurea. Udine: Facoltà di Lingue e Letterature Straniere. Academic year 2008-2009.

TWORUSCHKA, Udo. 'Pagani.' *Dizionario comparato delle religioni monoteistiche.* Casale Monferrato: Piemme, 1998. 517-519.

USPENSKIJ, Boris. *La pala d'altare di Jan Van Eyck a Gand: composizione e opera.* Perugia: Lupetti, 2001.

VINK, Renée. 'The Wise Woman's Gospel.' *Lembas-Extra* 2004. 15-40.

'Immortality and the Death of Love: J.R.R. Tolkien and Simone de Beauvoir.' *The Ring Goes Ever On. Proceedings of the Tolkien 2005 Conference.* Two volumes. Ed. Sarah Wells. Coventry: The Tolkien Society, 2008. Vol. 2, 117-127.

Wagner and Tolkien. Zurich and Jena: Walking Tree Publishers, 2012.

'Fan Fiction as Criticism.' *Hither Shore* 10 (2013): 188-203.

'Human-stories or Human Stories?' *Hither Shore* 12 (2015): 22-35.

WALFORD, David. *Theoretical Philosophy, 1755-1770.* Cambridge: Cambridge University Press, 1992.

WALKER, Steve. *The Power of Tolkien Prose.* New York: Palgrave Macmillan, 2009.

WELLS, Sarah (ed.). *The Ring Goes Ever On. Proceedings of the Tolkien 2005 Conference.* Two volumes. Coventry: The Tolkien Society, 2008.

WEST Jr, John. *Celebrating Middle-earth.* Seattle WA: Inklings Books, 2002.

WEST, Richard. 'The Interlace and Professor Tolkien: Medieval Narrative Technique in *The Lord of the Rings.*' *Orcrist* 1 (1966-1967): 26-49. (Republished in *A Tolkien Compass.* Ed. Jared Lodbell. Chicago IL: Open Court, 2003. 75-92).

Tolkien Criticism. An Annotated Checklist. Revised Edition. Kent OH: Kent State University Press, 1981.

'Turin's Ofermod.' *Tolkien's Legendarium.* Eds. Verlyn Flieger and Carl Hostetter. Westport CT and London: Greenwood Press, 2000. 233-246.

"'And She Named Her Own Name': Being True to One's Word in Tolkien's Middle-earth.' *Tolkien Studies* 2 (2005): 1-10.

WHITTINGHAM, Elizabeth. *The Evolution of Tolkien's Mythology.* Jefferson NC: McFarland, 2007.

WILSON, Edmund. 'Oo Those Awful Orcs.' *The Nation* April 1956. (Republished in *The Tolkien Scrapbook.* Ed. Alida Becker. New York: Grosset&Dunlap, 1978. 50-55).

WOLF, Alexandra. 'Die 'Athrabeth Finrod ah Andreth' oder Das Menschenbild in Tolkiens Mythologie.' *Hither Shore* 1 (2005): 137-150.

WOOD, Ralph. *The Gospel According to Tolkien.* London: John Knox Press, 2003.

'Conflict and Convergences in Fundamental Matters.' *Renascence* 55.4 (2003b): 315-338.

'Tolkien's Augustinian Understanding of Good and Evil: Why *The Lord of the Rings* is not Manichaean.' *Tree of Tales: Tolkien, Literature and Theology.* Eds. Trevor Hart and Ivan Khovacs. Waco TX: Baylor University Press, 2007. 85-102.

'Tolkien e il Post-Modernismo.' *Endóre* 13 (2010). http://www.endore.it/endore13/ (Accessed 15/1/2014).

'J.R.R. Tolkien: His Sorrowful Vision of Joy.' *C.S. Lewis and Friends.* Eds. David Hein and Edward Henderson. London: SPCK, 2011. 117-134.

(ed.). *Tolkien Among the Moderns*. Notre Dame IN: University of Notre Dame Press, 2015.

WRIGLEY, Christopher. *The Return of the Hero: Rowling, Tolkien, Pullman*. Sussex: Book Guild Publishers, 2005.

WU, Ming 4. *L'Eroe Imperfetto*. Milan: Bompiani, 2010.

'Foreword.' to *J.R.R. Tolkien: Il Ritorno di Beorhtnoth figlio di Beorhthelm*. Milan: Bompiani, 2010b. 5-20.

Difendere la Terra di Mezzo. Bologna: Odoya, 2013.

and Andrea MONDA. 'Tolkien a Catholic Philosopher?' *Tolkien and Philosophy*. Eds. Roberto Arduini and Claudio A. Testi. Zurich and Jena: Walking Tree Publishers, 2014. 85-124.

WYNNE, Patrick H. 'Tom Shippey's *J.R.R. Tolkien: Author of the Century* and a Look Back at Tolkien Criticism since 1982.' *Envoi* 9.2 (2000): 101-167.

YESKOV, Kirill. *The Last Ringbearer*. 2010. (English translation: https://www.sendspace.com/file/90t0sc (accessed 17/7/17).

Zettersten, Arne. *J.R.R. Tolkien's Double Worlds and Creative Process*. New York: Palgrave Macmillan, 2011.

ZIMMER, Mary E. 'Creating and Recreating Words with Words. The Religion and Magic of Language in *The Lord of the Rings*.' *Tolkien and the Invention of Myth*. Ed. Jane Chance. Lexington KY: University Press of Kentucky, 2004. 49-60.

Analytical Index

A

Allegory
  definition 17-18
  and interpretation 17-21
Analogy 19, 63
Applicability 20-21
Assumption
  of the first Men 56
  of Mary 56 n. 55
Atheism 101
Athrabeth: see 'Debate between Finrod and Andreth'

B

Beowulf
  analysis 82-87
Betrothal
  among the Elves 102
Body: see *hröa*

C

Catholicism
  of Tolkien 8 n. 38
  definition 127 ff
Creator 27-28 (see also "Eru" "Ilúvatar", "One (the)" in the 'General Index and Index of Names')
Cremation 106
Cults: see "Rituals"

D

'Debate between Finrod and Andreth' (*Athrabeth Finrod ah Andrteth*): 48, 53 ff.
Dialectic
  and the *Legendarium* 57 ff.
  and contradiction-opposition 62-63

E

Ecology
  in Tolkien 27, 31
Eucharist: see "Lembas"
Evil 57-59
  and creation 24-25
Exemplification
  and symbolism 15-17, 38, 40

F

Fall 52, 107-109
Fate 86, 112 ff.
  elvish concepts (*Umbar/Amarth-Ambar/Amar*) 112-15
  in *LotR* 115-17
  and Providence 117-120
Fëa (rational soul): 35 n. 31; 52, 54-56; see also *hröa*
Finn and Hengest 96
Frodo
  as *alter Christus* 19, 41
  as tragic figure 19

G

Galadriel
   and Mary 22
Giants 25 n. 60

H

Harmony of nature and grace (and reason and faith)
   in Catholicism 127-133
   in Islam: 51 n. 43, 131 n.34
   in Orthodox Christianity 131 n. 35
   in Luther 131-133
Heathen 28, 69, 85, 104-106
   Tolkien as a converted h. 92
   in Catholicism 130-131
   in Luther 132
Hope
   for the Elves 56 (*Amdir*), 57 (*Estel*)
   for men 56 (Old Hope), 108 (h. and death)
Hröa (body)
   harmony between *hröa* and *fëa* 35 n. 31, 54-56 (see also *fëa*)
Hybris 89

I

Incarnation 123, 15, 17, 31, 34, 68, 79, 99-101

L

Lembas
   and Eucharist: 18, 23, 105

M

Magic: see "Power"
Marriage
   among Elves 102
   for Tolkien 8 n. 8
Mythopoeia 80-82

N

Natural Law 62 n. 64
Natural Theology 42, 57, 86, 98 ff. (in Tolkien's world);
Nature
   definition 68 n.1; *passim*; see also "Harmony of nature and grace"
Neoplatonism
   in Tolkien 33
   and Christianity 33
   in Aquinas 34, 130

O

Ofermod (overmastering pride) 88-90, 123-125
On Fairy Stories 75-78; *passim*

P

Pagan (see also "Heathen" and "Salvation of the pagans")
   definition 68-71
   historical paganism 36-38;
Pantheism 31-32; 38
Points of views (see also "Polyphony")
   in Tolkien 43-46
Polyphony (see also "Points of view")
   definition 43-47
   in Tolkien 47-50
Polytheism 29, 38, 69, 83, 100-101
Power 40, 108
   and magic 37
Praeparatio Evangelii
   definition 129
   analysis 72-73, 140
   in Luther 132
Providence 119-120; see also "Fate"

R

Reason (see also "Harmony of nature and grace")
   and Fantasy in Tolkien 76-77

Reincarnation 7, 34-35
Resurrection
    of Christ 15, 31, 68, 79
    of the body 25 n.59, 35, 52, 106, 110
Rituals (and Cults)101-105 (see also "Marriage", "Betrothal")
    funeral rituals 104-105, 144
    choice of the name as elvish ritual 102-103

S

Salvation of the pagans
    in *Beowulf* 86-87
    in the Catholic tradition 128-131
    in Luther 132
Secret Fire 38, 98
    and the Holy Spirit 101
Sir Gawain and the Green Knight 91, 92 ff.
Soul: see *fëa*
Sources
    and representation 21 ff
    for Tolkien 22-24, 84
Sub-creator 27-28, 77, 80-81
Supernatural (see also "Nature")
    dimension 68-69, 78 (in fairy-stories), 128-129

Symbolism
    as hidden meaning (rejected by Tolkien) 15-17
    as exemplification in Tolkien 17, 134-136
    and allegory 16 n. 17
    in Catholic readings 19ff
    symbolic reading of Tolkien 38-40

T

Tale of Adanel 52 n. 48; 103, 108
The Homecoming of Beorhtnoth Beorhthelm's Son 90 ff; 123
The Legend of Sigurd and Gudrun 96
The Lord of the Rings passim
The Silmarillion
    and Christopher Tolkien 44-46; *passim*
Tolkien's Razor 7, 14, 52, 57, 139

U

Ultimate Destiny
    of the world: 56-7, 110
    of Men 59, 109
    of the Elves 109

General Index and Index of Names

A

Abbagnano, Nicola 68, 99, 155
Abel 128
Abraham 17, 70, 123, 129
Adanel 52, 103, 108
Ælfwine 44, 45, 70, 164
Aeneas 130
Aesthetic 16, 174
Afterlife 59
Agamemnon 123
Agnoloni, Giovanni 109, 155
Agøy, Nils Ivar ix, 13, 15, 32, 52, 100, 155, 167
'Ainulindalë' 29, 45, 98, 169
Ainur 6, 20, 24, 28, 29, 33, 38, 45, 57, 59, 70, 75, 98, 99, 101, 107
'Akallabêth' 51
Albaqarah, Sura 51
Alcuin 85, 90, 97, 130, 143
Alessio, Giancarlo 155, 157, 159
Al-Ghazālī 131
Alighieri, Dante 155
Al-Kindi 131
Alqualondë 107
Aman 107, 109
Amar 113
Amarth 112, 113
Ambar 112, 113, 114, 115, 120
Ambrose, St 130
Amdir 56 (see also "Estel")
Anadûnê 51, 98, 103
Anawím 18
Anderson, Poul 4, 44, 123, 155
Andreini, Alessandro 133, 155

Andreth 48, 52, 53, 54, 55, 56, 57, 155, 176, 177
Angelic (Powers) 17, 29, 54, 107
Angels 8, 24, 25, 29, 79, 99, 100, 101, 144
Anglo-Saxon 16, 45, 69, 72, 82, 97, 119, 142, 161, 166
Anglo-Saxons 97
Antigone 132, 133
Aotrou 96 (see also "Itroun")
Apocalypse 52, 110, 112
Aragorn 18, 19, 27, 49, 50, 62, 99, 104, 116, 121, 124, 135, 163
Arda 14, 33, 38, 52, 53, 54, 55, 56, 99, 101, 103, 107, 108, 109, 110, 113, 155, 168
Arduini, Roberto i, 44, 82, 109, 145, 155, 156, 158, 169, 170, 174, 175, 176, 178
Areopagus 34, 129
Aristides 132
Aristotle 42, 68, 80, 99, 129, 130, 133, 156
Arnor 122
Ar-Pharazôn 101
Arrigoni, Adalberto ii
Arthurian iv, 7, 14, 22, 96 (see also "King Arthur")
Arwen 22, 27, 121, 122
Athrabeth 15, 35, 48, 52, 53, 56, 100, 110, 155, 176, 177
Atomists 119
Auden, Wynstan Hugh 114, 121, 156
Augustine of Hyppo 59, 117, 156, 157, 177

Averroes 131
Avicenna 131

B

Baggins 45, 46, 159, 163 (see also "Bilbo" and "Frodo")
Bakhtin, Michail 47, 48, 49, 156, 173
Balin 116
Balrog 89, 124
Baptism 132
Barahir 122
Barbarians 129
Barbiano, Paolo 7, 156
Bard 175
Barella, Cecilia i, 156, 176
Barnes, J. 156
Baroni, Pietro 156, 173
Barrow-downs 35
Barsotti, Divo 3, 129, 156
Barth, Karl 132, 133
Bassham, Gregory 156, 169
Battle of Maldon 87, 88, 89, 157
Becker, Alida 156, 177
Benassi, Luciano ii
Benedict XVI 133, 156 (see also "Ratzinger, Joseph")
Bëor 52
Beorhthelm 88, 90, 178
Beorhtnoth 88, 90, 123, 124, 166, 174, 178 (see also "Byrhtnoth")
Beorhtwold 90
Beowulf / Beowulf iv, 50, 69, 82, 83, 84, 85, 86, 87, 88, 91, 96, 105, 121, 123, 124, 142, 143, 158, 159, 162, 163, 165, 168, 174
Beregond 49
Beren 22, 52, 169, 175
Bernard of Chartres 84
Bernard of Clairvaux 59, 156
Bertani, Greta 13, 24, 156
Bertilak de Hautdesert 93, 95
Berto, Francesco 61, 157
Bible 18, 25, 128, 157

Bilbo 45, 46, 113, 114, 115, 118, 122, 135, 145 (see also "Baggins")
Billanovich, Giuseppe 127, 157
Birks, Annie 112, 157
Birzer, Bradley J. 6, 26, 52, 72, 129, 157, 171
Black Riders 116
Blackham, Robert 103, 157
Blackwelder, Richard E. 163, 165, 172
Bliss, Alan 96
Boethius 58, 59, 120, 130, 157, 162, 167, 176
Boffetti, Jason 21
Bologna, Tullio 41, 157, 172
Bonechi, Simone 37, 157
Bonvecchio, Claudio 41, 157, 161
Boromir 39, 104, 116, 122, 123, 124, 164
Bowman, Mary R. 89, 124, 157
Boyer, Régis 128, 157
Bratman, David 4, 26, 157
Bree 114
Brewer, D.S. 142
Bronson, Eric 156, 169
Bruner, Kurt 20, 157
Bultmann, Rudolf 133, 168
Burke, Jessica 86, 158
Burns, Marjorie 6, 22, 72, 158
Byrhtnoth 164 (see also "Beorhtnoth")

C

Cain 25
Caldecott, Stratford 13, 18, 22, 158, 163, 170, 173
Calvino, Italo 3, 158
Campanini, Massimo 51, 131, 158
Candler, Peter 72, 158
Cantoni, Pietro 35, 158
Canzonieri, Chiara i
Canzonieri, Giampaolo i, 103, 156, 158, 176
Caperan, Louis 129, 131, 132, 133, 158

Carbone, Giorgio O.P. ii
Cardini, Franco 158
Carpenter, Humphrey 29, 43, 44, 80, 158
Carruthers, Leo 72, 158
Carter, Susan 22, 159
Casseri, Gianluca 41, 159
Cato 17, 132, 133
Cavallo, Guglielmo 127, 159
Celeborn 23, 52, 144
Celtic Mythology 6, 158
Cerrigone, Mario Enrico ii
Chance, Jane 5, 6, 8, 20, 37, 73, 77, 85, 86, 101, 114, 115, 119, 122, 144, 158, 159, 161, 162, 163, 166, 169, 171, 173, 174, 175, 178
Chatman, Seymour 44, 159
Chesterton, Gilbert Keith 89, 159, 166, 170
Chiesa Isnardi, Gianna 111, 159
Children of Ilúvatar 99
Chivalry 89, 95
Christ 16, 18, 19, 23, 31, 41, 42, 59, 68, 79, 85, 89, 99, 105, 128, 129, 131, 132, 142 (see also "Jesus" and "Son of God")
Christensen, Bonniejean 121, 159
Christmas 128
Christopher, Joe R. 4, 44, 45, 51, 52, 78, 80, 92, 96, 159, 160, 165, 178
Cicero 117
Cilli, Oronzo 5, 159
Circe 22
Clark, George 4, 121, 123, 159, 170, 175
Clement of Alexandria 129, 159
Colebatch, Hal G. 121, 160
Coleridge, Samuel Taylor 77, 170
Colgrave, Bertram 142
Commandments 95
Communion 8, 23, 76
Communists 16
Conan 123 (see also "Howard, Robert E.")

Conscience 47, 62
Corbin, Henry 51, 131, 160
Cornelius, Centurion 132
Coulombe, Charles A. 18, 160
Crack of Doom 115, 135
Crawford, S.J. 142
Creator 27, 31, 42, 78, 100, 101, 118
Cristofari, Cécile 15, 160
Croft, Janet Brennan 4, 19, 160
Cucci, Giovanni 18, 160
Curry, Patrick 27, 30, 31, 34, 36, 38, 73, 160
Curtius, Ernst R. 17, 160
Cynewulf 23

D

D'Ancona, Cristina 51, 131, 160
Daeron 45
Damrod 99
Danes 69, 89, 96
Danielou, Jean 70, 127, 128, 129, 133, 160
Dawson, Christopher 78, 160
De Beauvoir, Simone 60, 176
De Koster, Katie 160, 173
De Lubac, Henri 129, 133, 160
De Turris, Gianfranco 5, 27, 36, 38, 39, 41, 159, 160, 165, 169, 172
Del Corso, Lucio 5, 161
Demiurge 99, 117, 120
Denethor 49, 69, 104, 106, 124
Denzinger, Heinrich 53, 161
Devaux, Michaël 35, 161
Dickerson, Matthew 31, 72, 120, 161
Dimond, Andy 110, 161
Divinization 105
Dodds, Eric R. 117, 161
Donovan, Leslie A. 4, 160
Dostoyevsky, Fyodor 47, 48, 156
Dragon
    in *Beowulf* 91
Dragons 77, 81, 167
Dronke, Peter 127, 161

Drout, Michael D.C. 4, 5, 6, 13, 22, 86, 88, 91, 110, 161, 164
Druids 167
Du Chaillu, Paul B. 36, 162
Dubs, Kathleen E. 112, 162
Dumézil, Georges 39
Dunharrow 69, 124
Duotheism 38
Dwarves 16, 17, 20, 62, 104, 111
Dyonisius 33
Dyson, Hugo 80

E

Eä 25, 38, 56, 113
Eagles 141
Eaglestone, Robert 161, 162
Eärendel 23, 44
Éarendel 16
Ecology 31, 174
Edda 174
Eden 53, 130
Edwards, Raymond 8, 26, 162
Egyptians 36, 53
Eimarméne 117
Elbereth 18, 22, 23, 107
Eldalië 14, 17
Eldar 14, 56, 99, 102, 113, 120
Eldarin 113, 115
Elder Days 46
Elendil 35
Eliade, Mircea 111, 128, 162
Elias 129 (see also "Elijah")
Elijah 130 (see also "Elias")
Elrond 40, 48, 49, 122
Elves *passim*
Endorë 5, 157, 173, 175, 177
Enlightenment 43
Enoch 130
Ents 77, 111, 160, 161
Entwives 171
Environment 68
Envy 89, 108, 110, 158, 174
Éomer 49, 62

Éowyn 124
Epicurus 119
Erasmus 132, 171
Erebor 114
Eregion 17, 40
Eressëa 19, 45
Eriador 160, 161
Eriol 45
Erkenwald, St 131, 142
Eru 24, 28, 29, 35, 38, 52, 53, 54, 56, 59, 98, 99, 100, 101, 102, 103, 107, 113, 114, 115, 119, 120, 121, 123, 170 (see also "Ilúvatar" and "(the) One")
Eru-Bēnī 98
Eru-Hîn 99
Essecarmë 102
Esseclimë 102
Estel 57, 122 (see also "Amdir")
Eternal Return 111
Ethics 42, 85, 88, 91, 94, 95, 123, 125, 173
Eucatastrophe 31, 44, 79, 141, 175
Eucharist 18, 22, 23, 32, 164
Euripides 129
Eurydice 22
Eusebius of Caesarea 129
Evans, Jonathan 31, 43, 161, 162
Evola, Julius 38, 39, 40, 162
Excalibur 121

F

Fabro, Cornelio 34, 162
Faërie 4, 76, 78, 163, 164
Fairies 76, 78, 162
Fairyland 78
Faramir 17, 49, 104, 105, 116, 135
Fascina, Vito 5, 162
Fëa 35, 52, 54, 55, 56, 99, 109
Fëanor 23, 48, 107, 109
Fehrenbacher, Richard W. 87, 124, 162
Fernandez, Irène 119, 162

Ferrari, Franco 80, 162
Filmer-Davies, Kath 18, 162
Fimi, Dimitra 4, 6, 162
Findegil 45
Finn 96, 97
Finrod 48, 52, 54, 55, 56, 57, 100, 155, 176, 177
Finwë 48, 173
First Age 108, 109
Fisher, Jason 120, 163, 166, 172
Fisher, Matthew 6, 21, 82, 163
Flieger, Verlyn i, v, ix, 4, 6, 8, 18, 19, 22, 35, 43, 44, 46, 50, 51, 52, 53, 57, 70, 73, 79, 96, 109, 112, 121, 157, 159, 163, 164, 167, 177
Florenskij, Pavel 131, 164, 175
Forest-Hill, Lynn 89, 91, 124, 158, 164
Fornet-Ponse, Thomas 7, 19, 23, 52, 77, 112, 120, 133, 164
Fourth Age 6, 75
Francesco, Pope 157, 164, 174
Freda 123
Frisians 96, 97
Froda 85
Frodo 17, 18, 19, 20, 41, 45, 49, 61, 85, 105, 113, 114, 116, 121, 122, 123, 124, 135, 141, 142, 144, 145, 157, 158, 159, 163 (see also "Baggins")
Fromm, Erich 122, 164
Fui 14 (see also "Nienna")
Fusco, Sebastiano 41, 165

G

Galadriel 18, 22, 23, 36, 52, 116, 159
Galahad 121
Gamgee, Sam: see "Sam Gamgee"
Gammarelli, Lorenzo i
Gandalf 17, 18, 19, 20, 36, 37, 49, 50, 69, 89, 98, 99, 106, 114, 115, 118, 122, 124, 141, 142, 145, 161
Gandhi 50
Garbowski, Christopher 48, 72, 73, 165
Garth, John 4, 6, 165
Gawain 91, 92, 93, 94, 95, 131, 142, 174
Gee, Henry 77, 165
Geiger, Louis Bertrand 34, 165
Genesis, Book of 20, 24, 25, 51, 53, 68, 112
Gift, of Men 28, 52, 108, 175
Gildor 115
Gilliver, Peter ix, 79, 165
Gilson, Robert Quilter 19, 163
Gimli 23, 49, 62, 100, 111
Giuliano, Stefano 39, 161, 165, 174
Glenn, Jonathan A. 121, 165
Glofcheskie, Tanya 48, 50, 165
Glorfindel 35
Goblins 81
God 13, 17, 19, 22, 25, 28, 29, 30, 31, 32, 33, 38, 40, 42, 46, 51, 58, 68, 71, 79, 80, 81, 85, 86, 87, 91, 98, 99, 100, 101, 105, 117, 118, 120, 122, 123, 128, 129, 130, 131, 132, 133, 135, 141, 143, 157
Gods v, 17, 29, 30, 70, 81, 83, 86, 89, 100, 111, 119, 120, 121, 141, 158
Goeteia 174
Gojim 68
Golden Age 110
Gollum 115, 116, 135
Gondor 104, 106, 116, 122, 124, 141
Gorbag 49
Gordon, E.V. 88, 90
Gospel 19, 25, 44, 51, 57, 68, 71, 76, 78, 79, 80, 85, 123, 130, 132, 144, 167, 176, 177
Grant, Edward 40, 48, 110, 131, 175
Graves, Robert 165
Gray, William 71, 111, 165
Great End 110
Green, Roger L. 80, 165
Green, William H. 6, 165

Grendel 91
Grishnákh 49, 116
Guardian Angels 8 (see also "Angelic" and "Angels")
Gudrún 96
Guénon, René 40
Guglielmi, Federico i (see also "Wu Ming 4")
Guinevere 22
Gulisano, Paolo 156
Guthláf 141

H
Halbarad 116
Halflings 19, 45, 46, 104
Hammond, Wayne G. 5, 23, 80, 106, 128, 135, 163, 165, 172
Hardon, John A. 129, 165
Hart, Trevor 165, 168, 177
Harvey, David 19, 166
Hastings, Peter 6, 34
Heathen 28, 69, 85, 89, 92, 104, 106, 124, 132, 166
Heaven 14, 25, 33, 56, 78, 82, 103, 132, 133, 141
Heidegger, Martin 62, 166
Hein, David 166, 177
Hein, Rolland 26, 166
Hell 14, 33, 78, 86, 87, 112, 128
Helm's Deep 124
Helms, Randall 77, 166
Henderson, Edward 166, 177
Hengest 96, 97
Heraclitus 129
Hercules 132, 133
Heresy 58
Heroes 90, 121, 122, 123, 142, 160, 167, 174
Heroism 89, 90, 92, 124, 174
Hesiod 53, 110, 166
Hiley, Margaret 164, 166, 174
Hinieldus 85, 90, 143

Hitler, Adolf 59
Hoban, Russell 30, 31
Hobbits *passim*
Holmes, John 30, 69, 72, 111, 124, 166
Holy Spirit 101, 130, 132
Honegger, Thomas ii, ix, 4, 5, 6, 22, 73, 90, 121, 124, 131, 140, 158, 163, 164, 166, 169, 170, 173, 174
Hooper, Walter 80, 165
Horstman, Carl 131, 167
Hostetter, Carl F. 4, 6, 157, 159, 164, 167, 177
Houghton, John 59, 156, 158, 163, 167
Houseless 109
Howard, Robert E. 71, 123 (see also "Conan")
Hrethel 86
Hrothgar 86
Husserl, Edmund 111
Hutton, Ronald 22, 27, 28, 30, 32, 33, 34, 36, 37, 38, 155, 167
Hybris 89

I
Ilúvatar 25, 56, 98, 99, 103, 108 (see also "Eru" and "(the) One")
Imbar 113
Immaculate Conception 36
Incarnate 34, 54, 120
Ingeld: see "Hinieldus"
Inklings 33, 44, 100, 158, 172, 174, 177
Iphigenia 123
Isaac 123
Isaacs, Neil 156, 163, 167
Isengard 49
Islam 131, 158, 160
Isoldi, Caterina 156, 173
Ithilien 141
Itroun, see also Aotrou 96

J

Jackson, Peter 6
Jaeger, Werner 89, 129, 167
Jaki, Stanley L. 131, 168
Jaspers, Karl 133, 168
Jeffrey, David Lyle 4, 168
Jesus 18, 20, 51, 59, 70, 99, 128, 131, 132 (see also "Christ" and "Son of God")
Jewish 68, 69
Jews 69, 70
Job, Book of 128
John of Salisbury 84, 130, 168
John of the Cross, St 33
John Paul II, St 133, 168
Johnson, Judith A. 6, 168
Jonah, Book of 128
Jonas, Hans 68, 168
Jones, Leslie E. 6, 168
Joyce, James 5
Judaism 25, 128
Judgement 35, 68, 112
Justin 129, 168

K

Kalevala 174
Kane, Douglas Charles 4
Kant, Immanuel 61
Keesee, Neal 167
Ker, W.P. 141
Kerry, Paul 7, 18, 155, 157, 158, 166, 167, 168, 170, 171
Khazad-Dûm 89, 98, 116, 124
Khovacs, Ivan 165, 168, 177
Kierkegaard, Søren 123, 168
Kilby, Clive S. 3, 4, 101, 168
King Arthur 91, 92, 121, 167 (see also "Arthurian")
Klinger, Judith 104, 168
Kloczko, Edouard J. 168
Knowles, Dom David 143
Koch, Ludovica 168

Kocher, Paul 4, 72, 121, 129, 161, 168
Kolediejchuk, Brian 33, 171
Kolpaktchy, Gregorio 110, 169
Kraemer, Hendrik 133
Kraus, Joe 73
Kreeft, Peter J. 13, 18, 19, 73, 169
Kullervo 96

L

Ladavas, Alberto i, 103, 169
Lancelot 22
Larsen, Kristine 77, 169
Laurelin 105, 108 (see also "Telperion" and "Two Trees")
Lawrence, D.H. 37
Legendarium *passim*
Legolas 49, 62, 100, 111
Lembas 18, 23, 105, 176
Lewis, C.L. 32, 49, 70, 80, 143, 145, 165, 166, 175, 177
Librán-Moreno, Miryam 22
Limbo 130
Lindo 45
Lingerers 109
Liturgy 68, 128
Lobdell, Jared 169, 173, 177
Lodigiani, Emilia 5, 169
Lombardo, Alberto 27, 29, 169
Long, Rebekah 19, 169
Lönnrot, Elias 163
Lórien 18, 116
Lucas, George 71
Lupo, Mattia 156, 173
Luther, Martin 131, 132, 169
Lúthien 22, 169, 175
Lynch, James 18, 169

M

MacDonald, George 22, 166, 175
Madsen, Catherine 27, 28, 31, 41, 169
Maiar 33, 99, 100
Maiettini, Giulio 13, 170

Maimonides 131
Malicidium 59
Mandos 14, 35, 109 (see also "Vefántur")
Manichaeism 58, 59, 177
Mankind 56, 76, 86, 140
Manni, Franco i, 5, 13, 72, 73, 111, 112, 129, 156, 170, 174
Manwë 45, 100, 102
Marach 52
Marchi, Carlo ii
Marshall, Jeremy 165
Mary 8, 18, 22, 23, 36, 56, 94
Maurier, Henri 69, 170
Mazzoleni, Sandra 129, 170
McIntosh, Jonathan S. 129, 169
Medea 22
Melancton 133
Melchizedec 128
Melian 25, 100
Melkor 24, 37, 49, 50, 54, 56, 59, 100, 101, 103, 107, 108 (see also "Morgoth")
Meneltarma 103
Merry 35, 49
Middle Ages 16, 33, 131, 159, 163, 166, 169, 171, 173, 174
Middle-earth *passim*
Miesel, Sandra 168
Milbank, Alison 89, 129, 170
Milburn, Michael 77, 170
Milton, John 144, 145
Minas Tirith 111, 171
Mindolluin 104
Mingardi, Alberto 5, 15, 170
Míriel 48, 109, 173
Miruvor 105
Misomythos 80
Mitchell, Philip I. 72, 170
Mitchison, Naomi 60
Modernity 39, 40, 73, 163, 164, 167
Möhler, Adam Johann 133, 170
Moira 117

Monda, Andrea i, 5, 7, 13, 18, 19, 20, 160, 170, 178
Mondin, Battista 68, 170
Monotheism 29, 31, 37, 86, 103, 135
Morali, Ilaria 129, 170
Morandi, Emmanuele ii
Mordor 21, 39, 40, 49, 50, 116
Morgana 93
Morganti, Adolfo 172
Morgoth 17, 104 (see also "Melkor")
Moria 17, 40
Morīah 16
Morillo, Stephen 27, 36, 171
Morini, Massimo 4, 171
Morrigan 22
Morris, William 111, 173
Mother Teresa of Calcutta, St 33
Mount Doom 19, 20, 39, 48, 115, 169
Muhammad 51
Müller, Michael 129, 171
Mûmakil 99
Murray, Robert 22, 134
Muslims 51, 69, 70, 131
Mythopoeia 14, 21, 31, 63, 78, 80, 81, 85

N
Nagel, Rainer 35, 171
Nagy, Gergely 4, 73, 80, 171
Najoivits, Simson 36, 171
Narnia 70, 143
Narsil 121, 122
Nazis 90
Necromancer 114
Neidorf, Leonard 142
Neopagan 29, 41, 69
Neoplatonism 33, 34
Nephilim 25
Newman, John Henry 133, 155, 164
Nienna 14 (see also "Fui")
Nimmo, Andrew 129, 171
Noah 68, 128
Novissimi 112

Númenor 28, 34, 46, 50, 51, 70, 98, 103, 104, 110, 115
Númenórean 17, 36, 37, 46, 52, 100, 103, 105, 106, 144

O

O'Rourke Boyle, Marjorie 132, 171
Obedience 49, 62, 90
Oedipus 50
Ofermod 88, 89, 90, 91, 92, 123, 124, 125, 177
One, the 28, 29, 38, 98, 100, 135, 143 (see also "Eru" and "Ilúvatar")
Orcrist 177
Orcs 14, 16, 17, 46, 49, 177
Oromë 99
Orpheus 22, 169
Orthodoxy 24, 25, 27, 29, 32, 36, 44, 58, 128, 131
Osiris 110
Otherworld 109

P

Paganism *passim*
Paggi, Marco 171
Palantir 116
Pantheism 30, 38
Paradise 18, 20, 59, 81, 82, 109, 112, 130, 145
Parenti, Sergio O.P. ii
Passaro, Enrico 7, 29, 110, 171
Patchen, Mortimes 73, 171
Patriarchs 18, 86, 132
Pearce, Joseph 6, 13, 18, 21, 24, 25, 26, 156, 158, 160, 171
Pecere, Paolo 5, 161
Pelennor Fields 116, 124
Penco, Gregorio 127, 172
Pengolod 44, 45
Petty, Anne C. 73, 84, 172
Phelpstead, Carl 6, 172
Philomythos 80

Piantanida, Donato 110, 169
Pippin 49
Plato 33, 48, 54, 73, 80, 99, 117, 129, 133, 167, 171, 172
Plotinus 99
Polia, Mario 41, 157, 160, 172
Polyphony 47, 48, 49, 50, 142, 145
Polytheism 29, 38, 69, 83, 100, 101
Poppi, Angelico 41, 51, 172
Postmodern 73, 163, 171, 177
Poupard, Paul Joseph 170, 172
Praeparatio Evangelii 72, 129, 132, 140
Prati, Marco ii
Prophets 30, 132
Protestantism 133
Protestants 131
Pseudo-Dyonisius 33
Pullman, Philip 71, 111, 178
Purgatory 14, 109, 112
Purtill, Richard 24, 73, 172
Pyramus 22, 175

Q

Queen of Sheba 128
Quenya 112, 113
Quest 18, 114, 121, 156
Quran 51, 131, 172

R

Radagast 36
Raddatz, Gregor 125, 172
Ragnarök 110, 157, 161
Ransom 145
Rateliff, John D. 13, 20, 22, 26, 82, 96, 167, 172
Ratzinger, Joseph 105, 172 (see also "Benedict XVI")
Reale, Giovanni 117, 119, 172
Reilly, R.J. 100, 172
Renaissance 110, 162
Respinti, Marco 7, 13, 110, 171

Resurrection 15, 25, 31, 35, 52, 68, 79, 106, 110
Rettig, John W. 144
Reynolds, Patricia 104, 105, 106, 167, 172, 175
Rialti, Edoardo 110, 156, 173
Riddermark 62
Rider Haggard, H. 22, 37
Ries, Julien 128, 173
Ripheus 130, 142
Rivendell 46, 122
Roddenberry, Gene 71
Rohan 49, 62, 116
Rohirrim 99, 124, 141, 166
Romanini, Angiola Maria 162
Rosebury, Brian 4, 6, 121, 155, 173
Rosenberg, Alexander 111
Rúmil 44, 45
Rutledge, Amelia 48, 173
Ryan, John S. 4, 173

S

Sacraments 101, 105
Sam Gamgee 18, 19, 23, 45, 116, 141, 142, 144
Sanctification 23, 91, 128
Santa Claus 128
Saruman 73
Satan 24, 59, 145
Sauron 37, 40, 49, 50, 59, 70, 101, 103, 104, 106, 108, 109, 113, 122, 142, 169
Saxo Grammaticus 85
Saxton, Benjamin 48, 50, 173
Sceaf 143
Sceafing 143
Schlüsselburg, Konrad Martin: see Schlusselburgii, Conradi
Schlusselburgii, Conradi 133, 173
Schneidewind, Friedhelm 169, 175
Scoville, Chester N. 111, 173
Scull, Christina 5, 23, 80, 106, 128, 135, 163, 165, 172

Scyld 143
Seaman, Gerald 22, 77, 173
Second Age 40
Secret Fire 38, 98, 101, 158
Segura, Eduardo 167, 169, 174
Sen, Amartya 7, 173
Shelob 49
Shippey, Tom i, ix, 3, 4, 5, 6, 36, 37, 49, 58, 59, 72, 79, 82, 83, 85, 90, 91, 92, 96, 100, 106, 112, 119, 120, 131, 143, 145, 162, 173, 174, 178
Shire 19, 23, 36, 60, 61, 121, 122, 142
Sibyls 130
Siegfried 96, 121 (see also "Sigurd")
Siewers, Alfred K. 31, 73, 159, 163, 166, 169, 171, 173, 174
Sigurd 96, 174 (see also "Siegfried")
Silmarils 107
Simonelli, Saverio 5, 170
Simonson, Martin 4, 48, 174
Sindarin 112, 113, 122
Skafloc 123
Smith, Adam 7
Smith, Arden R. 6, 167
Smith, Geoffrey Bache 19, 163
Smith, Ross 79, 174
Snowmane 99
Socrates 129, 132, 133
Solar System 113
Solopova, Elizabeth 79, 174
Sommavilla, Guido 13, 15, 174
Son of God 13, 19, 101 (see also "Christ" and "Jesus")
Sons of God 25
Sons of Ilúvatar 25
Spengler, Oswald Arnold Gottfried 111
Spina, Norbert i
Spirito, Guglielmo 18, 20, 172, 174
Stagnaro, Carlo 5, 15, 170
Stalin, Joseph 59
Star Trek 71

Star Wars 71
Steimel, Heidi 169, 175
Stenström, Anders 6, 175
Stephen, Elizabeth 121, 171, 175
Sterling, Grant C. 175
Stevens, Jen 22, 175
Stoa 117
Stoics 119, 129
Strider 52, 114
Strumia, Alberto ii
Sturch, Richard 26, 175
Sturluson, Snorri 85
Suchecki, Zbigniew 106, 175
Sullivan, C. III 4, 131, 175
Sullivan, Francis A. 129, 133, 175
Sun 16, 77, 105, 108
Surrealism 176

T

Tacitus 36, 175
Tagliagambe, Silvano 131, 175
Tal-Elmar 46
Teleri 23, 107
Telperion 105, 108 (see also "Laurelin" and "Two Trees")
Teresa of Avila, St 33, 122, 175
Testi, Claudio A. iii, v, 19, 35, 42, 53, 72, 109, 142, 145, 155, 156, 158, 169, 170, 174, 175, 176, 178
Théoden 104, 116, 124, 141
Thingol 25, 100
Third Age 14, 75, 105, 109, 161
Thomas Aquinas, St ii, 34, 36, 42, 53, 62, 69, 86, 99, 117, 120, 129, 131, 176
Thomism 170, 171
Thorin 104, 114, 115
Tídwald 90
Timmons, Daniel 4, 159, 175
Tolkien, J.R.R. *passim*
Tolkien, Priscilla 89
Tolkien, Simon 176
Tom Bombadil 46, 114, 115

Tombs 103, 104, 168
Torhthelm 90
Trajan 130, 131, 142
Tréowine 35 (see also "Voronwë")
Trinity 13, 99, 131
Troy 123
Túrin 124, 171, 177
Turner, Allan 4, 176
Turville-Petre, Edward O. 36, 111, 176
Tuzzi, Federica 176
Two Trees 105, 107, 108 (see also "Laurelin" and "Telperion")
Tworuschka, Udo 69, 176
Tyrn Gorthad 116

U

Uglúk 49
Umbar 112, 113, 114, 115, 117, 118, 119, 120
Uruk-Hai 49, 116
Uspenskij, Boris 47, 176
Uthred of Boldon 143

V

Valar 14, 20, 23, 29, 33, 34, 35, 38, 45, 48, 54, 56, 99, 100, 103, 105, 107, 109, 110, 135, 143
Valgard 123
Valinor 20, 109
Varda 100, 102
Vefántur 14 (see also "Mandos")
Vikings 36
Villa, Claudia 157
Vink, Renée 4, 50, 52, 176
Voronwë 35 (see also "Tréowine")

W

Waldman, Milton iv
Walford, David 168, 177
Walker, Steve 4, 177
War of the Ring 45, 50

Ware, Jim 20, 157
Weiner, Edmund 165
Weinreich, Frank 73, 163, 164, 166, 167, 174
Wells, Sarah 165, 176, 177
West, John Jr. 13, 172, 177
West, Richard 4, 6, 124, 140, 155, 177
Westron 46
White Tree 104
Whittingham, Elizabeth 4, 29, 110, 177
Wiccan 37
Wilson, Edmund 3, 177
Witch King 116
Wolf, Alexandra 52, 177
Wood, Ralph 13, 15, 52, 59, 62, 73, 80, 177
World War I 19
Wormtongue 116
Wrigley, Christopher 71, 178
Wu Ming 4 i, 7, 43, 57, 58, 59, 60, 61, 62, 63, 121, 170 (see also "Guglielmi, Federico")
Wynne, Patrick H. 4, 5, 6, 13, 22, 162, 178

Y

Yeats, William Butler 37
Yeskov, Kirill 50, 178
Yule 18, 128

Z

Zak, Lubomir ii, 132
Zettersten, Arne 79, 178
Zeus 117
Zimbardo, Rose 156, 163, 167
Zimmer, Mary E. 33, 178
Zwingli, Huldrych 132, 133

Walking Tree Publishers
Zurich and Jena

Walking Tree Publishers was founded in 1997 as a forum for publication of material related to Tolkien and Middle-earth studies.

http://www.walking-tree.org

Cormarë Series

The *Cormarë Series* collects papers and studies dedicated exclusively to the exploration of Tolkien's work. It comprises monographs, thematic collections of essays, conference volumes, and reprints of important yet no longer (easily) accessible papers by leading scholars in the field. Manuscripts and project proposals are evaluated by members of an independent board of advisors who support the series editors in their endeavour to provide the readers with qualitatively superior yet accessible studies on Tolkien and his work.

News from the Shire and Beyond. Studies on Tolkien
Peter Buchs and Thomas Honegger (eds.), Zurich and Berne 2004, Reprint, First edition 1997 (Cormarë Series 1), ISBN 978-3-9521424-5-5

Root and Branch. Approaches Towards Understanding Tolkien
Thomas Honegger (ed.), Zurich and Berne 2005, Reprint, First edition 1999 (Cormarë Series 2), ISBN 978-3-905703-01-6

Richard Sturch, *Four Christian Fantasists. A Study of the Fantastic Writings of George MacDonald, Charles Williams, C.S. Lewis and J.R.R. Tolkien*
Zurich and Berne 2007, Reprint, First edition 2001 (Cormarë Series 3), ISBN 978-3-905703-04-7

Tolkien in Translation
Thomas Honegger (ed.), Zurich and Jena 2011, Reprint, First edition 2003 (Cormarë Series 4), ISBN 978-3-905703-15-3

Mark T. Hooker, *Tolkien Through Russian Eyes*
Zurich and Berne 2003 (Cormarë Series 5), ISBN 978-3-9521424-7-9

Translating Tolkien: Text and Film
Thomas Honegger (ed.), Zurich and Jena 2011, Reprint, First edition 2004 (Cormarë Series 6), ISBN 978-3-905703-16-0

Christopher Garbowski, *Recovery and Transcendence for the Contemporary Mythmaker. The Spiritual Dimension in the Works of J.R.R. Tolkien*
Zurich and Berne 2004, Reprint, First Edition by Marie Curie Sklodowska, University Press, Lublin 2000, (Cormarë Series 7), ISBN 978-3-9521424-8-6

Reconsidering Tolkien
Thomas Honegger (ed.), Zurich and Berne 2005 (Cormarë Series 8), ISBN 978-3-905703-00-9

Tolkien and Modernity 1
Frank Weinreich and Thomas Honegger (eds.), Zurich and Berne 2006 (Cormarë Series 9), ISBN 978-3-905703-02-3

Tolkien and Modernity 2
Thomas Honegger and Frank Weinreich (eds.), Zurich and Berne 2006 (Cormarë Series 10), ISBN 978-3-905703-03-0

Tom Shippey, *Roots and Branches. Selected Papers on Tolkien by Tom Shippey*
Zurich and Berne 2007 (Cormarë Series 11), ISBN 978-3-905703-05-4

Ross Smith, *Inside Language. Linguistic and Aesthetic Theory in Tolkien*
Zurich and Jena 2011, Reprint, First edition 2007 (Cormarë Series 12),
ISBN 978-3-905703-20-7

How We Became Middle-earth. A Collection of Essays on The Lord of the Rings
Adam Lam and Nataliya Oryshchuk (eds.), Zurich and Berne 2007 (Cormarë
Series 13), ISBN 978-3-905703-07-8

Myth and Magic. Art According to the Inklings
Eduardo Segura and Thomas Honegger (eds.), Zurich and Berne 2007 (Cormarë
Series 14), ISBN 978-3-905703-08-5

The Silmarillion - Thirty Years On
Allan Turner (ed.), Zurich and Berne 2007 (Cormarë Series 15),
ISBN 978-3-905703-10-8

Martin Simonson, *The Lord of the Rings and the Western Narrative Tradition*
Zurich and Jena 2008 (Cormarë Series 16), ISBN 978-3-905703-09-2

*Tolkien's Shorter Works. Proceedings of the 4th Seminar of the Deutsche Tolkien Gesellschaft
& Walking Tree Publishers Decennial Conference*
Margaret Hiley and Frank Weinreich (eds.), Zurich and Jena 2008 (Cormarë Series
17), ISBN 978-3-905703-11-5

Tolkien's The Lord of the Rings: Sources of Inspiration
Stratford Caldecott and Thomas Honegger (eds.), Zurich and Jena 2008 (Cormarë
Series 18), ISBN 978-3-905703-12-2

J.S. Ryan, *Tolkien's View: Windows into his World*
Zurich and Jena 2009 (Cormarë Series 19), ISBN 978-3-905703-13-9

Music in Middle-earth
Heidi Steimel and Friedhelm Schneidewind (eds.), Zurich and Jena 2010 (Cormarë
Series 20), ISBN 978-3-905703-14-6

Liam Campbell, *The Ecological Augury in the Works of JRR Tolkien*
Zurich and Jena 2011 (Cormarë Series 21), ISBN 978-3-905703-18-4

Margaret Hiley, *The Loss and the Silence. Aspects of Modernism in the Works of
C.S. Lewis, J.R.R. Tolkien and Charles Williams*
Zurich and Jena 2011 (Cormarë Series 22), ISBN 978-3-905703-19-1

Rainer Nagel, *Hobbit Place-names. A Linguistic Excursion through the Shire*
Zurich and Jena 2012 (Cormarë Series 23), ISBN 978-3-905703-22-1

Christopher MacLachlan, *Tolkien and Wagner: The Ring and Der Ring*
Zurich and Jena 2012 (Cormarë Series 24), ISBN 978-3-905703-21-4

Renée Vink, *Wagner and Tolkien: Mythmakers*
Zurich and Jena 2012 (Cormarë Series 25), ISBN 978-3-905703-25-2

The Broken Scythe. Death and Immortality in the Works of J.R.R. Tolkien
Roberto Arduini and Claudio Antonio Testi (eds.), Zurich and Jena 2012 (Cormarë
Series 26), ISBN 978-3-905703-26-9

Sub-creating Middle-earth: Constructions of Authorship and the Works of J.R.R. Tolkien
Judith Klinger (ed.), Zurich and Jena 2012 (Cormarë Series 27),
ISBN 978-3-905703-27-6

Tolkien's Poetry
Julian Eilmann and Allan Turner (eds.), Zurich and Jena 2013
(Cormarë Series 28), ISBN 978-3-905703-28-3

O, What a Tangled Web. Tolkien and Medieval Literature. A View from Poland
Barbara Kowalik (ed.), Zurich and Jena 2013 (Cormarë Series 29),
ISBN 978-3-905703-29-0

J.S. Ryan, *In the Nameless Wood*
Zurich and Jena 2013 (Cormarë Series 30), ISBN 978-3-905703-30-6

From Peterborough to Faëry; The Poetics and Mechanics of Secondary Worlds
Thomas Honegger & Dirk Vanderbeke (eds.), Zurich and Jena 2014
(Cormarë Series 31), ISBN 978-3-905703-31-3

Tolkien and Philosophy
Roberto Arduini and Claudio R. Testi (eds.), Zurich and Jena 2014
(Cormarë Series 32), ISBN 978-3-905703-32-0

Patrick Curry, *Deep Roots in a Time of Frost. Essays on Tolkien,*
Zurich and Jena 2014 (Cormarë Series 33), ISBN 978-3-905703-33-7

Representations of Nature in Middle-earth
Martin Simonson (ed.), Zurich and Jena 2015, (Cormarë Series 34),
ISBN 978-3-905703-34-4

Laughter in Middle-earth
Thomas Honegger and Maureen F. Mann (eds.), Zurich and Jena 2016
(Cormarë Series 35), ISBN 978-3-905703-35-1

Julian Eilmann, *J.R.R. Tolkien – Romanticist and Poet,*
Zurich and Jena 2017 (Cormarë Series 36), ISBN 978-3-905703-36-8

Binding Them All Interdisciplinary Perspectives on J.R.R. Tolkien and His Works.
Monika Kirner-Ludwig, Stephan Köser, Sebastian Streitberger (Cormarë Series 37),
ISBN 978-3-905703-37-5

Claudio Testi, *Pagan Saints in Middle-earth*
Zurich and Jena 2017 (Cormarë Series 38), ISBN 978-3-905703-38-2

Tolkien and Literary Worldbuilding
Dimitra Fimi and Thomas Honegger (eds.), forthcoming

Music in Tolkien's Work and Beyond
Julian Eilmann and Friedhelm Schneidewind (eds.), forthcoming

Middle-earth, or There and Back Again
Łukasz Neubauer (ed.), forthcoming

"Something has gone crack": New Perspectives on J.R.R. Tolkien and the Great War
Janet Brennan Croft and Annika Röttinger (eds.), forthcoming

Beowulf and the Dragon

The original Old English text of the 'Dragon Episode' of Beowulf is set in an authentic font and bound in hardback as a high quality art book. Illustrated by Anke Eissmann and accompanied by John Porter's translation. Introduction by Tom Shippey. Limited first edition of 500 copies. 84 pages. Selected pages can be previewed on: http://www.walking-tree.org/beowulf

Beowulf and the Dragon
Zurich and Jena 2009, ISBN 978-3-905703-17-7

Tales of Yore Series

The *Tales of Yore Series* provides a platform for qualitatively superior fiction that will appeal to readers familiar with Tolkien's world:

The Monster Specialist

Sir Severus le Brewse, among the least known of King Arthur's Round Table knights, is preferred by nature, disposition, and training to fight against monsters rather than other knights. After youthful adventures of errantry with dragons, trolls, vampires, and assorted beasts, Severus joins the brilliant sorceress Lilava to face the Chimaera in The Greatest Monster Battle of All Time to free her folk from an age-old curse. But their adventures don't end there; together they meet elves and magicians, friends and foes; they join in the fight to save Camelot and even walk the Grey Paths of the Dead. With a mix of Malory, a touch of Tolkien, and a hint of humor, The Monster Specialist chronicles a tale of courage, tenacity, honor, and love.

The Monster Specialist is illustrated by Anke Eissmann.

Edward S. Louis, *The Monster Specialist*
Zurich and Jena 2014 (Tales of Yore Series No. 3), ISBN 978-3-905703-23-8

Tales of Yore Series (earlier books)

Kay Woollard, *The Terror of Tatty Walk. A Frightener*
CD and Booklet, Zurich and Berne 2000, ISBN 978-3-9521424-2-4

Kay Woollard, *Wilmot's Very Strange Stone or What came of building "snobbits"*
CD and booklet, Zurich and Berne 2001, ISBN 978-3-9521424-4-8

Information for authors

Authors interested in contributing to our publications can learn more about the services we offer on the "services for authors" section of our web pages.

http://www.walking-tree.org/authors

Manuscripts and project proposals can be submitted to the board of editors (please include an SAE):

Walking Tree Publishers
CH-3052 Zollikofen
Switzerland

e-mail: info@walking-tree.org

Walking Tree Publishers, Zurich and Jena, 2018

www.ingramcontent.com/pod-product-compliance
Lightning Source LLC
Chambersburg PA
CBHW070739160426
43192CB00009B/1501